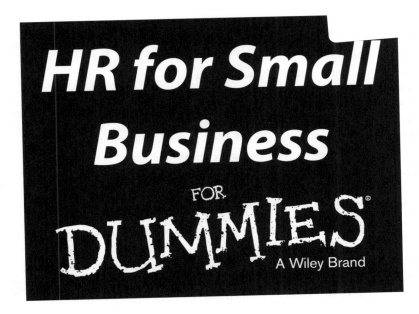

HR for Small Business

FOR

DUMMIES®

A Wiley Brand

by Marc Bishop and Sharon Crooks

FOR

DUMMIES®

A Wiley Brand

HR for Small Business **For Dummies**®

Published by: **John Wiley & Sons, Ltd., The Atrium, Southern Gate, Chichester,** www.wiley.com

This edition first published 2016

© 2016 by John Wiley & Sons, Ltd., Chichester, West Sussex

Registered Office

John Wiley & Sons, Ltd., The Atrium, Southern Gate, Chichester, West Sussex, PO19 8SQ, United Kingdom

For details of our global editorial offices, for customer services and for information about how to apply for permission to reuse the copyright material in this book, please see our website at www.wiley.com.

For general information on our other products and services, please contact our Customer Care Department within the U.S. at 877-762-2974, outside the U.S. at 317-572-3993, or fax 317-572-4002. For technical support, please visit www.wiley.com/techsupport.

Wiley publishes in a variety of print and electronic formats and by print-on-demand. Some material included with standard print versions of this book may not be included in e-books or in print-on-demand. If this book refers to media such as a CD or DVD that is not included in the version you purchased, you may download this material at http://booksupport.wiley.com. For more information about Wiley products, visit www.wiley.com.

Library of Congress Control Number: 2015954401

ISBN 978-1-119-11132-0 (pbk); ISBN 978-1-119-11133-7 (ebk); ISBN 978-1-119-11134-4 (ebk)

Printed and Bound in Great Britain by TJ International, Padstow, Cornwall.

10 9 8 7 6 5 4 3 2 1

Contents at a Glance

Table of Contents

Introduction

Welcome to the world of Human Resources, or HR for short. From the peaks of strategy to the foothills of statistics, you will travel through the law of the land, with a peek at European regulation, and some diversions into amateur psychology along the way, but don't be daunted! Armed with this basic guide and a good dose of common sense, you can avoid most of the pitfalls and may even enjoy the ride.

About This Book

We wrote this book for people running small businesses who have ambitious plans and don't want to spend all their time sorting out people problems. Whether you are dealing with a tricky employee issue right now, or you can see opportunity or trouble coming down the road, grab this book and you will find some practical tips about how to handle it.

In its broadest sense, *HR* covers every aspect of people at work, so we offer advice about how to attract the right people to work for your business, and how to manage them so that they add value. We show you some of the ways you can create a positive relationship with your employees, using the employment contract, the working environment, pay and benefits, and creative career development. We also share some ideas about how your leadership and management can make a big difference to people's performance.

To make it easier for you to find what you need, *HR for Small Business For Dummies* follows certain rules. When we introduce an important new term, we put it in *italics,* and if one item on a list is really important, we write it in **bold**. You will find some content in shaded grey boxes, and this is material that we think you might find interesting, but it's not critical to your knowledge of HR. There are lots of inter-related topics in HR so throughout the book as you read about one area, we will point you to other relevant chapters. Sometimes you will want to go straight there, but you can also save it for later.

Foolish Assumptions

Whilst we like to think we're experts, and we give you lots of golden rules to follow, it would be foolhardy to think we know everything, so treat these pages as a guidebook rather than a Bible.

We're not lawyers, but we've based our advice on the laws of England and Wales, assuming we are still in the EU, so if you are using this book somewhere else, bear that in mind.

Lord Denning is quoted as saying 'the law is an ass' and it may well be, but who wants to be kicked by an ass? We've provided lots of signposts to online legal and government advice, so if in doubt, follow these signs rather than taking a shortcut.

We've tried to anticipate many of the people issues you might face, but as the Yorkshire saying goes, 'there's nowt as queer as folk' so there are bound to be situations we haven't covered. If you're not sure what to do, our advice is to establish the facts, assess the risk and then make a decision in good faith that's right for the business and fair to the person.

Icons Used In This Book

To help you pinpoint vital information, we place icons throughout the text to highlight nuggets of knowledge.

This icon tells you we're using a real example to illustrate a point - of course all the characters are suitably disguised!

This icon offers you practical advice about how to apply some of the principles of good HR.

The Remember icon prompts you to pause and take note of something that could backfire if you don't pay attention.

Proceed with caution when you see this icon - usually we're letting you know that if you take a wrong step, you'll face a fine, or something worse!

This icon points you to other places online where you can find information and guidance. It is particularly useful for recent legal and government updates, because lots of HR and legal stuff changes at least twice a year.

This icon tells you that the paragraph goes into technical detail you may not need, so you could skip it, but reading it could give you more credibility and confidence.

Beyond The Book

As you scale the heights of HR knowledge, you can pick up extra tips and tools online. Check out the Cheat Sheet at www.dummies.com/cheatsheet/hrforsmallbusiness and some short bonus articles at www.dummies.com/extras/hrforsmallbusiness.

Where To Go From Here

This is a reference book, so you can read it from cover to cover, to improve your general understanding of HR, or you can just dive straight into the page that deals with your challenge. The best place to start is Chapter 1, which gives you the highlights of the whole book, and tells you where to find more detail on each topic.

We've been reasonably logical by organising the material to reflect your journey with employees, from finding them to working with them through rewarding and managing them to sometimes losing them.

HR is full of highs and lows so we hope that you use this book to climb to some of the heights of great HR as well as to plumb the depths of people problems!

Part I
Getting Started with HR

For Dummies can help you get started with lots of subjects. Visit www.dummies.com to learn more and do more with *For Dummies*.

In this part . . .

✔ Get off to a good start as an employer

✔ Find the right people for your business

✔ Get to grips with pay and benefits

✔ Find out how to fire people fairly

Chapter 1

Getting into the Business of People

A small business owner is more likely to groan than smile at the mention of HR because the term 'Human Resources' conjures up fear in many forms. You can't afford the time or money it costs to get it wrong. You're afraid to make a mistake that you'll have to defend at an Employment Tribunal. You worry about how to keep control, get in the right people and get rid of the wrong people as your business grows.

Human Resources is all about balancing people, time and money. If you apply common sense, common decency and a basic knowledge of your employees' rights, which you can read about in Chapter 7, you will avoid most of the pitfalls. But to turn to a sporting analogy for one moment, Formula One Racing drivers don't focus on avoiding the potholes — they focus on winning. Their sponsors pay for the best car and the best pit stop team so they can win races and make money. If you apply the knowledge in this book to how you do HR in your business, your employees will deliver great results, and your business will win.

Becoming an Employer

As soon as you become an employer, you acquire legal, tax and moral obligations.

Just because you pay someone to work for you does not automatically make you his or her employer. Following are three fundamental factors that determine whether someone is your employee:

✔ **Control:** You have control over someone if you or someone in your business has a contractual right to decide when, where and how the person does his or her work for you.

✔ **Personal service:** Personal service is a service provided by the person themselves, precluding the option of sending a substitute to do the work for you.

✔ **Mutuality of obligation:** Mutuality of obligation exists between you and another person if you have promised that person a minimum amount of work, and that person is obliged to do any work that you ask him or her to do.

Where someone is providing a personal service to your business under your control and you are contractually obliged to give them work and they are obliged to undertake the work, there is probably an employment relationship, so they are an *employee*.

If you want to avoid becoming an employer, you need to avoid taking control and creating a mutual obligation. In Chapter 2 you can read about the pros and cons of employing people or using other kinds of workers.

A *worker* is any individual who undertakes to do or perform personally any work or service for another party, whether under a contract of employment, or any other contract. They are protected by some of the employment legislation.

If you use *self-employed* people in your business, your relationship depends on the contract you have with them, often called a *Contract for Service*. They are protected by contract law and some discrimination law but not employment law.

Workers is an umbrella term, and all employees are also workers.

Employment status

You need to be clear about the status of the people doing work for you, so that you know which laws and regulations to follow.

Irrespective of the person's status, you have to follow Health and Safety and Data Protection regulations to protect anyone who is doing work for you. You can read more about these regulations in Chapter 6. If you want to know how to handle Whistleblowing, you can find out in Chapter 15.

Employees have the most protection, arising from European Regulations and UK law. Within the UK there are sometimes different rules for Scotland and Northern Ireland.

The following table gives you a snapshot of which rules you need to follow, depending on the status of the person doing work for you.

Employment status	Control	Personal Service	Mutuality of Obligation	Regulations you must follow
Employee	√	√	√	All employment law, based on length of service Disciplinary and Grievance rules Working Time Regulations including rests and holiday Pay, notice and pension rules Flexible working rules Paid and unpaid time off for certain reasons Transfer of Undertakings Regulations Redundancy provisions Employee Representation
Self employed	x	x	Only as a service provider	Some workplace discrimination laws Contract law
Worker	?	√	√	Some employment law Disciplinary and Grievance rules Working Time Regulations including rests and holiday Some pay and pension rules

Before you employ someone you must check that they have permission to work in the UK, either because they are a UK or EU citizen, or because they have a work visa. If you break the law you will be fined. Check out the rules in Chapter 14.

Employers' Liability Insurance

As soon as you take on your first employee, by law you must have Employer's Liability Insurance from an authorised insurance company to cover you for up to £5m liability, just in case your employee is injured or becomes ill because of the work they do for you. You have to display the insurance certificate where your employees can see it.

You can be fined £2,500 per day for every day that you are not properly insured.

Health and safety

By law you must display a health and safety poster or give each employee a leaflet, explaining their health and safety rights. Additionally, you can't allow employees to smoke in enclosed spaces, and you could be fined if you don't stop them.

You can download the health and safety poster for free from the Health and Safety Executive website: www.hse.gov.uk

Taxing work

Like it or not, as an employer you have tax obligations.

If you employ somebody and they earn above certain thresholds, you must

- ✔ Register with Her Majesty's Revenue and Customs (HMRC) as an employer and set up a payroll or get someone else to run one for you
- ✔ Deduct income tax, national insurance contributions and if applicable, pension or other deductions from your employees' pay before you pay them
- ✔ Send a return, called 'Real Time Information', to HMRC outlining payments and deductions you have made to employees after each pay date. Annually, send a return of taxable employee benefits you have provided
- ✔ Pay your Employer's National Insurance contributions to HMRC either monthly or quarterly depending on your size

You must provide a written or electronic pay slip for employees, giving them details of their pay and deductions.

For more information on your responsibilities as an employer when it comes to tax, plus plenty of helpful advice, check out: https://www.gov.uk/register-employer

Navigating the moral maze

There is a legal concept called *mutual trust and confidence,* which underlies the employment relationship. It is the assumption that neither party, the employer nor the employee, will do anything deliberately detrimental to the other party. This means that you could reasonably assume that your employees will not deliberately bring your company into disrepute through their actions, steal from the company or reveal confidential information to outsiders. Similarly, the employees should reasonably assume that you will not defame them, subject them to harassment or undue stress or expect them to break the law on your behalf.

Although none of these assumptions are explicit in the employment contract, each party is obliged to fulfil them. Many cases that are heard at Employment Tribunals arise because of a 'breakdown of mutual trust and confidence', which amounts to a breach of contract.

Whilst you can never presume to know what your employees are thinking, if you respect your employees' rights, stick to the rules and behave reasonably, you will minimise the risk of causing such a breach.

Getting the right people into your business

Chapter 2 provides some ideas for attracting and selecting the right people to work for you, and in Chapter 14 there's advice on how to avoid the common recruitment pitfalls and make a legally compliant job offer.

HR: Balancing people, time and money

You wake up one morning and decide to recruit an Apprentice. You've only got a tiny budget so you think that's all you can afford. Think again.

Q: Will the Apprentice fill a skill or knowledge gap in your business?

A: Not immediately, of course. But they probably will in time.

Q: Are you prepared to invest your time, or someone else's time, to teach the Apprentice what he or she needs to know, and supervise the Apprentice until he or she learns the ropes?

A1: If you are, calculate the actual cost of that time to the business and count it as part of the cost of employing the Apprentice.

A2: If you're not, don't recruit an Apprentice. It's not fair to them, and it will ultimately cost you time and stress to manage a failing apprenticeship

Q: What are your personal beliefs about apprentices? Cheap labour or potential stars?

A: If you commit time and energy to developing an Apprentice, your short-term investment will probably pay off in the medium to long term.

Q: Does this fit with your strategic plan for the business?

A1: Your Apprentice is unlikely to stay with the business after his or her training, unless you can offer some new opportunities and more money. If you are planning for growth, those opportunities may arise.

A2: If you can't offer progression, expect a successful Apprentice to move on. Start again with a new one. It's an equally valid strategy, and you give another Apprentice an opportunity to learn.

Before you start looking, be clear about what you're trying to find. Consider the following:

- Your medium and long term plans for the business
- The skills and knowledge you've already got in the business - your own or other people's
- The gaps in skills and knowledge that you want to fill in the short and medium term
- Your values and how you do business
- How much money you've got to spend

Then write a *job description,* which is what you want the person in the job to do, and a *person specification,* which is a description of the kind of person you are looking for. Read more about these in Chapter 2.

Managing People, Pay and Rations

With just one employee you can limit your HR knowledge to the basics of employment contracts and employment rights, which are covered in Chapter 7. Once you grow beyond the first two or three employees, you need to broaden your understanding to include equal pay, which you can read about in Chapter 4, and HR policies, which are introduced in Chapter 6.

Working together: The psychological contract

You might think that the employment contract embodies your entire relationship with your employees, but in addition to the written words, and the implicit assumptions of mutual trust and confidence outlined earlier in this chapter, there is another dimension to the relationship, called the *psychological contract.*

The psychological contract is a combination of unwritten mutual obligations and expectations between the employee and employer, which can be specific to individual employees, and can change over time. You can read more about it in Chapter 15, and it can sometimes explain why employees behave in an apparently irrational way and take you by surprise.

Whilst you can't hope to control the intangible constituents of the psychological contract, you can build trust, which is a key component, by treating people fairly and consistently, being open, dealing with issues when they arise, keeping your promises and recognising people's hard work.

Paying fairly

Following are some fundamental facts about pay you need to know:

- ✓ **You must pay all employees and workers at least the National Minimum Wage.** This is set each year based on the age of the person doing the work. You can read more about this in Chapter 4.

- ✓ **From 2016 at the latest, depending on your size, you must provide a pension scheme and automatically enroll all your employees and workers in it.** You can find all the details in Chapter 16.

- ✓ **You must pay at least Statutory Sick Pay to qualifying employees who are off sick.** There are rules about how people qualify and how much you must pay. The rates are updated every year in April. You can be more generous by paying company sick pay. Find out more in Chapter 4.

- ✓ **You must pay at least the statutory pay to qualifying employees while they are on maternity, adoption or shared parental leave.** There are lots of rules about dates and payments. You can read more in Chapter 7.

   You can reclaim 92% of the costs of paying statutory maternity, adoption or shared parental pay to your employees. You may even be refunded with 103% if you qualify for Small Employers' Relief.

- ✓ **You must pay men and women equal pay for work of equal value.** Read about the basics in Chapter 4, and learn how to do an equal pay audit in Chapter 16.

- ✓ **You must pay people their contractual salary or wages, and any contractual commission or bonus payments if the employee has fulfilled the criteria for payment.** Otherwise you will be in breach of contract.

- ✓ **You can't deduct money from an employee's wages without permission, even if you're trying to recoup an accidental overpayment.** The employee could make a claim to an Employment Tribunal for unfair deduction of wages.

- ✓ **If an employee leaves without taking all his or her holiday entitlement, you must pay the employee for the outstanding balance.** Find out how to calculate holiday entitlement in Chapter 6.

- ✓ **If you dismiss someone and give notice, you must pay the employee for the statutory notice, which is 1 week for every year of service up to a maximum of 12 weeks, or the employee's contractual notice, whichever is longer.**

- ✓ **If you make someone redundant and he or she has worked for you for more than two years, you have to pay at least the statutory redundancy amount, based on the employee's age and length of service.** Read more about this in Chapter 17.

Setting the rules for your business

Having said you can't control every aspect of your relationship with employees, this wouldn't be an HR book without a bunch of juicy rules to control the important things at work. In Chapter 6 you can discover the signs that your business needs some rules and policies, and once you see the signs, it's worth taking action to put some in place.

There are some minimum legal requirements, and if you don't create your own policies, you have to follow the statutory rules. These are

- ✔ Disciplinary policy and procedure to manage misconduct or poor performance
- ✔ Grievance procedure to allow employees to raise grievances
- ✔ Health and Safety policy and procedure
- ✔ Equal Opportunities policy
- ✔ Sickness absence policy
- ✔ Flexible working
- ✔ Time off work for certain activities or reasons
- ✔ Maternity, paternity, shared parental leave

Your business may have particular requirements and obligations. Find out more about setting the ground rules for your business in Chapter 6.

Handling people who don't follow the rules

HR is often perceived as a policing function in a business because of the focus on enforcing the rule book. At its heart, good HR practice provides the same foundation to your business as the police provide to society. The rules are for the protection of law-abiding citizens as much as for the punishment of the rule breakers.

Most of the time, the rule book is not required, but for the good of the business, and the good opinion and continued motivation of the majority of employees, when someone breaks the rules, you must be prepared to use the disciplinary policy and procedure. Using it consistently and correctly will protect you from claims of unfair treatment, discrimination or unfair dismissal.

Find out how to write a disciplinary policy in Chapter 6 and how to follow the procedure properly, especially if you might end up dismissing an employee (covered in Chapter 5).

If one of your employees has a complaint or *grievance* against you, the business or another employee, you need to have a process for them to raise it. You need to show that you are taking the matter seriously, with the aim of resolving it. Read more about this in Chapter 6.

If an employee makes a claim to an *Employment Tribunal*, which is an independent body that hears claims by employees against their employer, the Advisory, Conciliation and Arbitration Service (Acas) will get involved and ask if you and the employee have tried to resolve the problem. You will be in a much stronger position if you've followed the right disciplinary or grievance procedure.

You could lose your case at a Tribunal hearing just because you didn't follow the right procedure.

Staying on the right side of employment law

Your employees' and workers' rights come from UK common law, UK employment law and European regulations, and broadly fall into the following categories:

- ✔ Equality of opportunity and treatment
- ✔ Terms and conditions including pay and working hours
- ✔ Time off work
- ✔ Parents' and carers' rights
- ✔ Representation
- ✔ Redundancy, retirement or transfer

In Chapter 7 you can get to grips with the fundamentals of employee rights.

Acas provides excellent resources for employers, and some useful checklists especially written for small businesses; check these out at www.acas.org.uk. If you read the online guidance and you still have questions, they offer a free helpline: 0300 123 1100 (8am–8pm Monday to Friday and 9am–1pm Saturday)

Equality of treatment

If you discriminate against an employee, potential employee or worker because of a *protected characteristic,* they can take you to an Employment Tribunal, and if they win, you will have to pay them compensation.

Unlike other compensation, which is capped, there is no limit on the size of compensation payment for unlawful discrimination.

Protected characteristics include age, being or becoming a transsexual person, being married or in a civil partnership, being pregnant or having a child, disability, race including colour, nationality, ethnic or national origin, religion, belief or lack of religion/belief, gender and sexual orientation.

Direct discrimination is where you treat someone with a protected characteristic less favourably than other people, by reason of the protected characteristic. For example: Not offering someone a job because he is 75 years old would be direct age discrimination.

Following are a couple tricky aspects of discrimination:

✔ **You indirectly discriminate against someone if you create a condition that a person with a protected characteristic would be less likely to be able to meet.** For example, you select people for redundancy based on their flexibility to work shifts, which is a condition that fewer women with caring responsibilities are likely to be able to fulfill.

✔ **You are not allowed to discriminate against someone because they are associated with someone who has a protected characteristic.** For example, you don't offer someone a job because their partner is just about to have a baby and you don't want to offer shared parental leave.

Read all about avoiding discrimination in your recruitment process in Chapter 14 and how to avoid discrimination in your pay practices in Chapter 4.

Contract of employment

The contract of employment may be made up of a number of documents, including an offer letter, a *Statement of Employment Particulars* and a handbook.

The Statement of Employment Particulars is often referred to as the contract, because it has all the terms you must specify in writing, within eight weeks of an employee starting work with you. Some of the terms may be detailed elsewhere, but you must refer to them in this document.

When you offer someone a job, make it a *conditional offer,* which means the employee must meet certain criteria for the offer to remain valid. Most importantly, include the condition that they have permission to work in the UK. You could also require satisfactory references, evidence of qualifications, and a Disclosure Barring Service certificate if that is relevant. Give them a time limit to accept the offer.

Read about all these conditions, and what to include in the contract, in Chapter 14.

Statutory entitlements

If you don't give employees at least their statutory entitlements to pay and time off you may

- ✔ Incur fines from HMRC of up to £3,000 for some offences.

- ✔ Have to pay compensation and legal costs if your employee takes you to an Employment Tribunal and wins

Read more about employee rights and the consequences of breaching them in Chapter 7.

Following procedures

Just like the disciplinary and grievance procedure, there are statutory procedures you must follow to ensure that you stay on the right side of the law for

- ✔ Managing sickness absence

- ✔ Responding to flexible working requests

- ✔ Enrolling and administering opting out for workers in your company pension scheme

- ✔ Handling the notice, time off and return to work arrangements for employees on maternity, paternity or shared parental leave

- ✔ Handling retirement

If in doubt, visit the government website www.gov.uk, which gives you a step by step guide to statutory entitlements and procedures.

Representation

Employees have a legal right to be informed and consulted about how things that are happening in your business may impact their jobs and working conditions.

It is good practice to have an employee representative group, which can take various forms, including a Trade Union. Read more about how to elect and work with employee representative groups in Chapter 15.

Managing redundancy, retirement or transfers

Most employment law was written to protect employees from being exploited by unscrupulous employers, and one of the fundamental principles behind many of the rules is to protect the employee's job from being taken away unfairly.

If you are considering making employees redundant, read Chapter 17 to understand your obligations about consulting employees, notifying the right authorities, and following a fair redundancy selection process. The penalties for getting it wrong can be very high.

Because of age discrimination legislation, you can't force people to retire at a certain age.

A *Transfer of Undertakings* takes place when a business, part of a business or the provision of a service moves from one organisation to another. There are regulations to protect employees' jobs and terms and conditions in these circumstances. Just like with redundancy situations, you have a number of obligations, whether you are transferring employees in or out of your business. Read all about it in Chapter 12.

Growing People as Your Business Grows

In the juggling act that is HR, with the people, time and money balls constantly rotating between your hands, it is the people ball that offers the most potential for you to make a difference. The time and money balls are tangible and quantifiable. When you have them under control, it feels good. Good but dull. The people, on the other hand, are unpredictable. They go off in different directions, change size, demand your attention, and steal your time.

Let's assume that you have all the controllable aspects of the people ball under control: you have clear employment contracts, good HR policies, and tight HR processes (or that you're working them!). That's great, but none of these aspects of HR will add value to your business.

Growing the value of your business

Throughout this book we refer to growth, and the HR demands that come with it, not because we assume that every small business owner is constantly striving to have a bigger, more profitable business, but because standing still in business isn't an option.

Growth comes in many forms, and the only right and wrong kinds of growth are the ones that work or don't work for your business. Nature provides some useful analogies.

> Oak trees grow taller, lay down another ring of bark, and spread their branches a little bit wider by year. The growth is slow, incremental and invisible in the moment. They can live for hundreds of years. If the oak tree wasn't growing it would be dying.

> Stagnant water hosts algae that multiply so often they block the sunlight from other organisms in the water and kill them off. Happy algae, dead fish.

> Magnificent stag beetles with their emblematic 'horns' and shiny black carapaces spend six years in the larval stage feeding off a low-nutrient dead woodpile and emerge for only a few weeks to mate and then die.

Whether your business is based on making things, serving things, inventing things or delivering things, you need people. As in the rest of nature, people thrive when they are in the right environment, and have the opportunity to grow. The thriving might look different depending on who they are!

Creating the environment for growth

Some of the HR fundamentals outlined earlier are important in creating the right environment for growth, but there are some other important ingredients to add.

Providing leadership

Your personal values will shape how you do business, and how you treat your employees. Understanding what makes you tick is a good place to start, and you can find some tips about how to use your values to shape the culture of your business in Chapter 3. Because you're not the exception to the rule, your personal growth will have a significant impact on how the business grows. Understanding the role you play in the team and the management style you tend to adopt will help you to influence others. Chapter 9 unpacks some theories about team roles. Read more about how you can manage your transition from entrepreneur to business leader in Chapter 11.

Encouraging flexibility

Encourage people to work flexibly, and recognise and reward them when they do. Give people the tools to work in different ways. Get some ideas about how to create a culture of flexibility in Chapter 12. Read about factoring in flexibility to your pay and incentives in Chapter 8.

Growing skills and knowledge

Invest in training people not only for the job they are doing now, but the job you might want them to do next. Don't worry about wasting money on training people who will just leave. Focus on the value they will add while they are in your business, and factor that in to your thinking about the costs. In Chapter 13 you find some useful tips about how to access 'cheap and cheerful' training if money is still a barrier.

Structuring your business to allow for growth

The time and money dynamics are inescapable in a small business. You need to optimise the time and effort people are putting in to get maximum value out.

Build in some flexibility to your structure by using contracts creatively, and thinking about different ways to get the work done. You find some good ideas in Chapter 12.

Think about who is 'doing' your HR now. At its simplest level it is very transactional, but as you employ more people, and build an organisational structure with more layers, HR will become more complex. Chapter 10 takes you through the pros and cons of keeping HR in house or contracting it out to others and gives you some tips about protecting your employees' confidential data.

Growing through improved performance

Like the oak tree you may want your business to grow steadily and healthily without too much visible fuss. Alternatively you may want to gear everyone up for fast growth to kill off the competition.

Your strategic plan is the description of your growth ambitions. You should express your shorter term targets in the annual business plan. The strategic plan gives you the headlines to tell employees where you are hoping to take the business in financial terms, and often includes target numbers of customers and employees. Your annual business plan brings the horizon a bit closer, and should help people to focus on the immediate priorities. Chapter 11 has more detail about getting everyone in the business aligned and pointing in the same direction.

The key to achieving growth through improved performance is to

- ✔ Be clear with employees about the big picture as well as the short term priorities.
- ✔ Help everyone to see where their job and their targets fit in.
- ✔ Keep track of progress against the targets, and share it with employees as you go along.
- ✔ Be prepared to take action if people are not performing well.
- ✔ Reward and recognise the people who are performing well.

- ✔ Train managers to pro-actively manage the people in their teams to perform well.

Read Chapter 8 to find out how to link your business goals with employee goals, and discover some good principles for setting objectives.

Get some guidance on mentoring and coaching your managers in Chapter13.

Rewarding and motivating people

People are not just working for the pleasure of growing in your metaphorical field or pond. A fundamental principle of the employment relationship is that people expect to be paid for their efforts, and rewarded fairly for their discretionary efforts.

A fundamental principle of good business is that it's not worth doing, if it's going to lose money. The time and money balls come back into play when you juggle people's expectations about pay and reward with what the business can afford. You need to have a good grip on the financial numbers before making any promises.

Reward has become the popular collective term to encompass all the elements of pay, incentives and benefits that you provide to your employees.

Base pay

Base pay is effectively the wages or salary that someone can expect to receive every week or month. These are the costs you need to build into your business plan, and ensure that you can meet them every month, even when cash flow is tight.

When you are deciding the base pay for a job, you will need to consider

- ✔ Your legal obligations about National Minimum Wage
- ✔ What the business can afford
- ✔ What similar jobs are being paid in the external market
- ✔ The skills and experience required of the person doing the job
- ✔ The base pay of similar jobs in your business
- ✔ What incentives or other benefits you plan to provide
- ✔ The relative size and scope of the role compared to other jobs in the business

You find out about *benchmarking pay*, which is comparing pay between jobs and organisations in Chapter 16.

Incentives

Incentives or bonuses are incremental payments you make when an employee has achieved a goal. Usually, incentives are paid for discretionary effort on the part of the employee, based on adding value to the business.

Creating good incentive schemes is both an art and a science. It requires an understanding of what makes people tick, as well as the law of unintended consequences. A well designed incentive scheme will be based on sound financial analysis and sensible assumptions about the business.

A poorly designed incentive scheme can

- ✔ Reward the wrong behaviours, causing employees to compete with each other without creating an overall benefit to the business
- ✔ Cost more than planned because the targets and measures were unrealistic

✔ Demotivate people if they work really hard but don't feel fairly rewarded

✔ Inadvertently create inequalities in pay between people doing the same work

Find out how to avoid the pitfalls in Chapter 16.

Benefits

This is the term for extras you provide, on top of pay.

Employees often don't fully appreciate that the benefits they receive are costing your business money, so you should take the opportunity when you are offering a job, or taking the employee through induction, to explain the value of any benefits that you provide.

Examples of 'invisible' benefits an employee might take for granted are Life Assurance plans, Pension contributions and Employee Assistance Programmes.

Some people count holiday as a benefit, and if you are offering more than the statutory minimum holiday entitlement, that is a legitimate description.

Although from 2016 you are legally obliged to offer a pension plan, your employer contributions are a benefit, and you should tell employees how much you are paying into their pension pot.

Child care vouchers and canteen meals are examples of benefits that are not taxable and can have a high perceived value to employees while incurring a relatively low cost to the business.

If money is tight, think creatively about how to spend it on benefits that will have a high perceived value to employees.

Telling employees the value of a benefit is particularly important when they will have to pay tax on it, because they may want to opt out of the benefit if they don't think it's worth paying the tax. Read more about this in Chapter 16.

If you provide a company vehicle or a mobile phone and allow the employee to have it for personal use, the employee should pay tax on the personal element of the benefit.

HMRC provide guidance on which benefits and expenses should be taxed on their website: https://www.gov.uk/expenses-and-benefits-a-to-z

Engaging and motivating your employees

Employee engagement is a frequently-used phrase in the world of HR and has a range of meanings and definitions. What the descriptors all have in common is a recognition that when employees are highly engaged, they are more productive, customer satisfaction ratings are higher, and typically the business will perform better than competitors in the same sector.

The factors that indicate employee engagement include employees' stated intention of being in the organisation in a year's time, employees' level of satisfaction with the leadership and communication in the business, and the employees' view of the quality of their working relationships, especially with their managers.

What surprises some people is that whilst money and benefits are important, many employees, especially those in their 20s, are much more interested in getting the personal and career development they want, and fast, than they are in money.

Many of the factors affecting employee engagement are in your control, and with some focus and follow through, your actions can significantly impact on the level of employee engagement, and therefore on the performance of the business. Read about how to manage communication, consultation and employee engagement surveys in Chapter 15.

Losing People without Losing Business, Money or Face

People leave their jobs for lots of different reasons, some positive and some negative, some in your control and some outside of your control. From an HR perspective, your focus should be on protecting the interests of the business, whilst ensuring that you respect people's legal rights and fulfill your contractual and moral obligations as an employer.

Dismissing employees fairly

There are only five fair reasons for dismissal:

- ✔ Capability or qualifications
- ✔ Conduct
- ✔ Illegality or contravention of a statutory duty

✔ Redundancy

✔ Some other substantial reason

All other reasons are automatically unfair.

If you dismiss someone unfairly, he or she can take you to an Employment Tribunal. If that person wins, you will have to pay compensation, legal costs and possibly reinstate the employee to his or her job.

The best way to avoid this situation is to have a fair reason, follow a fair process, and show a reasonable response.

A fair reason for dismissal has more to it than meets the eye. The catch-all phrase 'some other substantial reason' does offer some opportunity for creative interpretation, but read about some of the potential pitfalls and how to build a good case for dismissal in Chapter 17.

It is incredibly important to follow a fair process, and that is not just your idea of a fair process, but one that has a statutory minimum number of steps. Chapter 5 takes you through all the steps in the process. Chapter 6 gives you some principles around which to design your own processes. For redundancy there are extra steps you should follow, which you find in Chapter 17.

A *reasonable response* is a subjective idea that your dismissal of the employee was a reasonable response, based on consideration of all the facts, any mitigating circumstances and any precedents.

If you are ever in doubt about whether your response is reasonable, imagine yourself in the 'dock' at an Employment Tribunal defending your actions. It can sometimes be a sobering and moderating process!

Protecting your business and your reputation with a Settlement Agreement

Sometimes it proves impossible to manage a dismissal smoothly because of mistakes you've made along the way, or politics or emotions complicating matters. If it is really important to reach a positive outcome, to protect the business or to recognise when you have been at fault, you may be able to negotiate a *Settlement Agreement,* which is a confidential contract between the employee and employer in which the employee waives his or her right to make a claim at an Employment Tribunal in exchange for a payment. There are rules about what it should contain, and you must pay for the employee to obtain independent advice on the agreement before signing it. Read more in Chapter 17.

Chapter 2

Recruiting Your First People

- -

In This Chapter

▶ Knowing when you need more people and where to find them

▶ Selecting the best people for the job

▶ Making a successful job offer

- -

*W*hen you've set up your own business, and done things your own way for a while, the idea of taking on an employee can be daunting. It's a bit like sharing your flat with a stranger, or finding a partner who will put up with all your quirky habits (go on, you do have some, don't you?). The longer you sit on the sofa and think about it, the more intimidating it seems. But just like a flatmate or a partner, employees can bring quite a lot to the party. The secret is first to know when the time is right, and then to figure out who will fit the bill.

Knowing Your Business Model and Business Plan

Your business model is the fundamental building block on which everything else rests. If you've grown your business this far by just working your socks off night and day, making quick wardrobe changes between unpacking your stock and pitching at sales meetings, you may not have had time to describe your business model to yourself, never mind anybody else.

It's worth pressing the pause button before jumping to the conclusion that if only you had another pair of hands, everything would be ok. If your business is in hospitality, health or personal services, it is likely to be quite people intensive, and you will quickly reach the limit of your personal capacity to deliver the services yourself. If however, you are providing a remote service, or one that can be easily automated, or you are providing an intermediate service, such as insurance brokering, or importing coffee from Guatemala, you may be less dependent on other people to support your business growth.

Have a close look at your margins, and whether you have enough of a difference between the price you are charging, and the costs you are incurring.

Often, people who run small businesses undervalue, or don't put any value, on their own time. This creates a risk that you might be running a business that is not financially viable in the long run, because you haven't built in enough margin to pay other people to do things for you.

The business plan doesn't need to be very complex, but you should have some idea of how big you want to grow the business, and how quickly. If you're first to market with a unique proposition, and want to grow quickly before the competition catches up, get some sales people out there working for you.

You may prefer to grow organically and have a strong pipeline of potential customers before you take on anybody else to work for you.

Before you even think about taking on any employees, do a quick break-even analysis, to tell you how many sales you would need to cover all your costs, and a cash flow forecast, to tell you when the pinch points might come.

Recognising that your business is ready to take on people

A few tell-tale pointers will quickly highlight whether you need to start recruiting for your first employees.

If you can check all of the boxes on the following list, start recruiting right now! If you can check several of them, start thinking about bringing in your first employees in the near future:

❏ You have enough margin built in to your pricing to pay other people to do some of the work.

❏ You have a good pipeline of future customers.

❏ You recognise that while you are a good all-rounder, you don't know everything.

❏ You are close to winning a big contract, and can't sleep at night because you don't know how you will deliver it.

❏ You can't keep up with the orders because the business has grown faster than you expected.

❏ You've spotted a gap in the market and you need some help to exploit it.

❏ Your flatmate or partner never sees you and you laugh out loud when people talk about work-life balance.

Analysing the costs and benefits of employing people

Getting that spare pair of hands you need can be achieved in several ways. You might not need to employ anybody yet, or indeed, ever: before taking on employees, think about your longer term future, as once you have employees, you take on various legal responsibilities for them. Read more about employee rights in Chapter 7.

A person is classed as an *employee* if they work under a 'contract of employment' which can be created in writing or verbally or by a mixture of both. A *worker* is any individual who undertakes to do, or perform personally, any work or service for another party, under a contract of employment, or any other contract. They may be an employee, an independent contractor, or an agency worker.

Employees (as opposed to workers) come with bells, whistles and strings attached, the main points of which are outlined in Table 2-1.

Table 2-1	Pros and Cons of Employing People
Pros	**Cons**
Depending on the job they are doing, it may be cheaper to employ people than to use independent contractors or agency workers.	You have to run a payroll, deduct tax and National Insurance and report to HMRC every month.
	You have to pay Employer's National Insurance.
	You have to have Employer's Liability Insurance.
They are more likely to stick around, buy into your values and provide continuity for your customers and clients.	You have less flexibility to increase or decrease your workforce at short notice because they have employment rights.
	They can claim unfair dismissal, and you may have to pay redundancy pay.

(continued)

Table 2-1 *(continued)*

Pros	Cons
If you give people feedback, training and opportunities to develop, they will often deliver better value to your business over time than a contractor or agency worker.	If they're not doing a great job, and not listening when you give them feedback, you have to go through a formal process to get them to improve or leave.
You can decide what kind of employment contract to offer, to meet the needs of the business, and you have control over their work and when they can take holiday.	You have to pay them for maternity and paternity leave if they meet the criteria, and they can ask for parental leave and flexible working.
	If someone buys your business, or you take over another business, they have transfer rights.
	If your business goes bust, they have rights as preferential creditors.
	You are vicariously responsible for their actions when they are acting on your behalf, including breaches of Health and Safety legislation.

Employing people or using contractors

If you've looked at all the pros and cons of taking on employees and decided that you're not ready for all the strings, you may decide to take on a contractor.

There are lots of rules about employing contractors, so you need to make sure that you don't inadvertently make someone an employee. The two main tests that are used to decide if someone is an employee – therefore making you an employer, with all the strings attached – are *control* and *mutuality of obligation*.

The essence of control and mutuality of obligation is how much control you have over the person, and whether you are obliged to give them work, or they are obliged to do it, how and when you ask them.

Even if they are invoicing you rather than being paid on your payroll, you are probably someone's employer if

✔ You or one of your team are in control of how, when, where and with whom they do their work.

✔ You provide their equipment and work space.

> ✔ They can't say no, or send someone else when you ask them to do some work.
>
> ✔ They are not doing much work for anybody else.
>
> ✔ You have made a commitment to provide them with a certain amount of work and pay.

Assessing What Skills and Experience Your Business Needs

Before you take anybody on and start handing over some of your hard earned money, make sure that you know what you're looking for so you don't just offer a job to the first person you get chatting to in the pub. Think about what the business needs, and what you've got already, so you can focus on filling the gaps. This section helps you to focus on what you might need.

Assessing what you've got in the business already

Starting with yourself, write down a list of your skills that are useful for your business.

Think of skills as stuff you can do, rather than making it too high level or abstract; for example, these are the sort of skills we mean:

✔ Web design

✔ Negotiating with suppliers

✔ Speaking Spanish

✔ Driving a forklift truck

✔ Creating Excel spreadsheets

Experience and knowledge are harder to define, so think about relevant things you know, that are required in your particular business. For example:

✔ Specialist product knowledge, such as chemical formulae or packaging regulations

✔ Specialist service knowledge, such as service level agreements or data protection

✔ Statutory requirements, such as VAT rules or Health and Safety regulations

Then think about what general business knowledge you have in areas like marketing, balance sheets and lease agreements, which are needed in many businesses. Add them all to the list.

After you've listed your own skills and knowledge, if you already have some people working for you, make a list for them, too.

Identifying the gaps

Once you have a list of skills within the business (see the preceding section), go back to your business model and your business plan. Focus on where you want to take the business in the next six months to a year. Identify if there are any gaps in your skills and knowledge that might stop you getting there.

These are the most important gaps to fill. And this could be the beginning of a job description for your first employee.

Sometimes the gaps might be very varied, and one person is unlikely to fill them. If you said in your business plan that you would take on five new customers per month for the next year, and closing deals with new customers isn't one of your own strengths, that's an obvious gap.

But if you also need help with the book keeping, it's unlikely you'll find someone who is good at both.

Be realistic, and prioritise the skills gaps that will make the biggest difference to your business in the short term. Resist the temptation to create a job that will be impossible to fill.

As a small business owner or manager, with a little bit of knowledge about a lot of things, you are relatively unusual. You won't find another you as your first employee. If they are out there, they are probably running their own business. So don't look for your mirror image in your first employees.

Anticipating what skills you will need in the short and medium term

You might think that job descriptions and person specifications are a bit corporate or best suited to a job in the local council. You may even think that if someone needs a job description, they won't be flexible: you want them to turn their hand to whatever is needed on the day, and you dread to hear them say that classic line, 'but that's not in my job description.' Luckily for you, as you're the person writing your job descriptions, it needn't be like this at all. A *job description* is really just a list of the things you want done by your employee.

Spend fifteen minutes writing a job description before you start recruiting and save yourself many hours of grief.

Write a list of the things you want the person in the job to do. During the process of writing the list, focus your own mind on what the business needs. If the list is getting very long, you may have unreasonable expectations, which means you can then prioritise the tasks that will make the biggest difference to your business.

Sometimes it is easier to give the job a title after you've written the list of tasks. If you start off with the idea that you need a Finance Manager, you will write a job description for a Finance Manager, rather than for the things you need doing. Once you get going, and write the list, you might find you actually need a Customer Service Manager and a part time Book Keeper.

The job description becomes the foundation of a job advert, a set of interview questions, and a tool you can use to tell the person in the job what you expect. It is well worth fifteen minutes of your time. Check out the sidebar 'Writing a job description' to help you get started.

Writing a job description

Writing a useful job description needn't be a chore, or even take up too much of your time:

1. Give the job a title that makes sense to the outside world

2. Make a heading called 'Key responsibilities'

3. Use verbs like '*Maintain* customer database', '*Update* stock list', and '*Serve* customers'

4. Include measures like 'Update stock list *daily*'

5. State standards like 'and are maintained *in line with* Data Protection Regulations'

6. Keep it to a maximum of ten key responsibilities

7. When you've written the list, create a summary 'Purpose of the role' sentence and put it at the top

Always include a catch-all phrase at the end of the list, like 'Undertake any other similar responsibilities as requested from time to time'

Recruiting the people to create your business culture

'Person specification' sounds even more corporate than the job description, but it is simply a list of your requirements. Having written the job description, it is reasonably straightforward to work out what skills and experience someone must have to do the job, and this forms the basis of your person spec. Check out the sidebar 'Writing a person specification' for a quick guide to creating one.

Skills and experience

Depending on how fussy you are, you can specify whether certain skills and experience are essential or desirable. Thinking about this also focuses your mind, and helps you to avoid snapping up the first candidate who comes through the door, because you click with them.

If you are running a funky software development business, you will need some very technically able developers, but they might not be your best sales people. When you write the person specification, include the job specific skills and experience the person needs.

Attitude and aptitude

It is not just skills and experience you need in your business. Some people say you should recruit for attitude and train for skills. This is particularly true in service businesses, where the customer is always king, and your employees need to be their willing subjects.

When you are writing the person specification, think about what kind of people you want to work with every day. Ask yourself what kind of people you want your customers to meet when they do business with you.

The way people work is sometimes described as their *soft skills*. These skills include how a person communicates, whether they are a team player, whether they are adaptable, and how they build relationships. In some jobs, the soft skills can be just as important as the task skills. A Receptionist may not necessarily have a complex set of tasks, but the person doing that job is often the most important ambassador for your business – ignore that at your peril!

You may also want all your employees to have some other attribute, like the ability to think outside the box, a passion for pastrami, or an affinity with android technology. If it's important to the job, add it to the person specification.

Armed with the job description and person specification, you are ready to go out there and find the perfect person for the job.

Writing a person specification

We recommend following this numbered list to quickly create a useful person spec:

1. Look at the job description

2. Identify what skills are needed for each task

3. Decide if they are essential or desirable

4. Identify what knowledge the person needs, to do this job

5. Decide if they need it now, or could learn it

6. Describe the soft skills for this job

7. Describe any attributes you want everyone in your business to have

Make sure your criteria are not discriminatory, and might exclude people with protected characteristics.

Attracting the Right People

In the days of weekly newspaper adverts and notices in the local newsagent's window, attracting the right people to work for your business could be protracted and a bit hit and miss. The pendulum has swung almost entirely the other way now, as the people you are trying to attract are bombarded with constant adverts, Facebook and LinkedIn updates and job board alerts.

Using your network

Even in the old days, the best place to start recruiting was in your own network. Family businesses often employ cousins, neighbours and friends. People tend to recruit in their own image, from a pool of people who are more likely to share their background, values and work ethic. That principle applies equally to 'old boy networks', connections on LinkedIn, other mums at the school gate, graduates from the same university, and friends who have tried your new recipe.

Start with your own network, whatever that looks like.

Remember the old adage about friends and money not mixing . . . if you feel uncomfortable about paying a friend to work for you, don't go there!

Advertising

A job advert is a great way to promote your business as well as attract people to work for you. Always have a few lines of introduction about the business, then briefly describe the job, and finish with a few lines about the kind of person you are looking to recruit.

Be clear about the closing date, your contact details, and what you want to see from them. It's a good idea to ask for a covering email or letter as well as a CV because you can get more of a feel for them as a person, and a better idea of their written communication skills.

Application forms have gone out of fashion a bit, but you might want to use one if you have very particular requirements they need to meet. Charities and public sector organisations tend to use them as it is easier to directly compare candidates and they are usually very careful to avoid discrimination.

Advertising in the broadsheet newspapers and specialist magazines now usually includes an online advert. Depending on the nature of your business, this may also be a good way to build awareness of your brand and your credibility in the market as well as attracting the kinds of people you want to employ. However it is one of the most expensive ways to get the word out.

Using your own website

If you have a website already you can advertise the job there. It gives a good impression of your business, and if you do advertise elsewhere, you can provide a link to your website on the job advert, to raise your business profile.

Job boards

Job boards is a collective term for various kinds of online recruitment advertising, some of which is managed or hosted by recruitment agencies.

General job boards such as CV Library (www.cvlibrary.co.uk) or Jobsite (www.jobsite.co.uk) are good places to advertise roles that do not require specialist skills; specialist job boards do exist for certain sectors, such as www.charityjob.co.uk, and for specific jobs such as www.simplysalesjobs.co.uk.

Many of the general job boards offer sub-sections for certain types of jobs. If you enter the job title you are recruiting into a search engine, you will be offered a plethora of options!

On any job board there is a section for employers or recruiters, and a section for candidates. Some of them are more transparent than others about their costs to advertise so you might have to call their sales number.

Advertising a job on www.indeed.co.uk is free. This is an umbrella job board that claims one search covers all jobs. As with most free services, there is an opportunity to 'upgrade' by paying to post targeted and featured adverts, and to search their CV database.

Recruitment agencies

If you place a job with a recruitment agency they will charge you a placement fee, typically between 15 per cent and 25 per cent of the first year's remuneration. I use that word advisedly, because some of them include bonuses, car allowances and lots of other things in the total remuneration package, to bump up their fees. Just ask for their terms and conditions and you'll find it in the small print. Typically the placement fee is due when you offer the person the job.

Some specialist agencies may charge the fee split into three, the first tranche due when they take the brief and start looking for people, the second on presentation of a shortlist of candidates, and the final one when you offer someone the job. Typically this arrangement is used for *head hunting*, or pro-active searching for your candidates, rather than 'just' having them registered on their database.

Most agencies have a guarantee period, within which they will pay back some of the fee if the employee leaves. Read the small print because lots of strings are often attached.

Jobcentre Plus and local employment schemes

As with most things now, the job centre has gone online. Universal jobmatch (https://jobsearch.direct.gov.uk) is the portal where you can post jobs, and people looking for jobs can post their CVs or look at the jobs that are available in their area.

You need to log on and create an account, but once you've done that, you can post jobs, search CVs and get basic advice about employing people, as well as accessing any special employment schemes that may be operating in your area.

Some Local Authorities run wage subsidy or other schemes to support certain categories of people into work and this might be a cost effective way for you to employ someone.

You can find out more about using the Job Centre to aid recruitment here: www.gov.uk/jobcentre-plus-help-for-recruiters

Word of mouth

Word of mouth is just as powerful in the job hunting market as it is anywhere else. If people who apply for work with you have a good experience they will probably talk about it, even if they are unsuccessful.

Over time, your reputation develops, and people will pro-actively come to you. If you follow the same principle of keeping an open mind, and keeping in touch, you can significantly reduce your recruitment costs and have a warm pipeline of people ready for your next vacancy or growth spurt.

Dealing with the Candidates

Make it easy for yourself by putting a closing date on the advert, and unless you are in a real hurry, wait until then to review all the applicants at one time. You are more likely to be objective if you look at them in one batch, you can concentrate, and you can get all the responses out of the way.

Put all the applications in a folder, either a physical one or an email one. There is a very slim chance someone might come back and complain that you didn't select them, and it's a lot easier to deal with those kinds of complaints if you know where you put everything.

Try to respond to everyone who has applied for the job. They might be potential customers, or you might want to go back to them in a few months when you are recruiting again. In the world of online recruitment, people have gotten used to sending off applications that are never acknowledged, so you will stand out from the crowd for showing this simple courtesy.

Several birds with one stone

You know the old saying, 'Kill two birds with one stone'? Well, let's not get hasty with the killing, but a shrewd employer will use the interviews for one job to identify high quality candidates for other roles too. And again, go easy on the killing. A fast growing social enterprise in south London filled four different jobs in a few months from one online advert for a project manager role.

Keep an open mind when you talk to candidates, especially if you are expanding. They might not be exactly right for this job, right now, but you can save a lot of money and time by spotting people who might be right in the future, and keeping in touch with them.

Selecting the Right People

Once you have your applications in, and the closing date has passed, you can start to evaluate your candidates. Be ruthless when you are reviewing the CVs and keep referring back to the person specification to remind yourself what you are looking for. It is really easy to get distracted and shortlist people who don't fit the bill.

If any of the skills you need is absolutely essential, make that really clear in the advert to reduce the number of time wasters.

If you have placed an advert on a job board, some of them offer filtering questions you can use to weed people out early on in the process.

Using the right selection tools

Interviewing is the obvious selection tool, because we all assume that it's the best way of finding the right people. They have a high face validity, meaning we believe that they are effective, but in fact they can be seriously flawed, unless you follow a few simple rules.

Even before investing time in interviewing people there are a number of other methods you can use to really hone down your shortlist.

Telephone interview

Consider using a brief telephone interview of 15–20 minutes. Send an email to invite the person to the telephone interview at a time that suits you, and ask them to confirm they will be available, and the best number on which you should call them.

It's a two line email, and how they respond gives you a really simple early indication of a few things, like attention to detail, simple grammar, tone and speed of response.

In the telephone interview you can reiterate the main points of the job description, and ask a few key questions. If the job involves them using the phone, you can hear how they sound.

If you think you might be paying slightly below the market rate for the job, find out their earnings expectations on the call. If you can't be flexible on the pay, be honest at this stage, and it can save you a lot of time.

Case study or presentation

If you are short of time and want to find out as much as possible about the candidate with just one meeting, prepare a case study or a presentation topic, and ask the candidates to come to the first interview, prepared for a discussion or presentation. You can test their specialist knowledge, presentation skills, communication skills and organisational skills in a very practical way.

Verbal references

Depending on the job, if references are important to you, ask for the details of at least one referee before the interview, and have a phone call with them if possible. Give the referee an idea of the job, so they can comment on the candidate's suitability. Ask a few key questions about how the person works. Listen for the silences, hesitations and non-committal comments that people use when they don't want to tell a lie but know that you might not want to hear the truth!

Group exercises

These can be challenging to organise if you haven't done them before but they can also save you a lot of time. If you have been inundated with applicants and can't really tell between them on paper, invite them to come to a session where you give them a challenge, and watch how they interact. You can manage the process a bit like a casting director running auditions.

For a bunch of fresh graduates competing to join you as in intern you could give them some sample products and ask them to come up with ideas about how to promote them on social media. For a sales job you can ask them to role play selling to each other. Just be clear about what you're looking for, and create a simple grid with marks out of 3 or 5. Every time a candidate demonstrates one of the behaviours you are looking for, give them a score.

Following the group exercise, you can let some of them know they are not through to the next stage, and just interview the ones who've hit your minimum standard. If it's practical, have someone else there with you, just to keep everything on track and to offer a second opinion.

Some candidates will be in their element and really shine in a group situation, but that doesn't necessarily mean they are the best person for the job. Keep an eye on everyone, even the quiet ones.

Testing technical skills

A typing test is the most common, and is useful for data entry and customer service jobs as well as secretarial positions. If you want someone to fill in invoices or complete VAT returns on your behalf, it is always worth giving candidates a little practical challenge, to test whether they can do it. People regularly claim on their CVs that they have intermediate Excel skills, but if you ask them to add a column of numbers, they still get the calculator out. Put them to the test!

Creating great interviews

Most of us can't resist using an interview as a key part of the selection process. We're human and we need to feel a connection with people and like the conversation to flow, but there are a few good reasons for making the interview quite structured:

- ✔ You can avoid any subconscious prejudices you might have by using objective criteria, and asking broadly the same questions, based on what the job needs.

- ✔ It's a lot easier to make a decision if you give each candidate a score straight after the interview.

- ✔ If someone is not happy with your decision and complains, you have good evidence of your objectivity and can avoid a discrimination claim.

Preparing

Look at the job description and person specification. Think about what you need to find out from all the candidates, and create a set of eight to ten standard questions you will ask everybody. Have a look at Chapter 20 for ten great interview ideas that you can use when selecting for any job.

Review the candidate CVs and add two or three questions specifically for each person. You might have spotted a gap in their employment history, or they might have had a particularly interesting gap year, or not worked for a while.

TIP

Create a one page note taking template, with the questions numbered and a gap between each one for you to make notes of the candidate's answer.

At the bottom, create a table with the selection criteria from your person specification and a column for the scores against each.

Make it easy for yourself by having the maximum score adding up to something easy, like 50 or 100, so you don't have to do major calculations to work out the scores. Table 2-2 shows a sample scoring sheet.

Table 2-2	Sample Scoring Sheet	
Candidate Name	**Score/10**	**Comments**
Business Development experience Breadth and depth – inc SME	8	Has done a lot of cold calling, and meetings etc and really understands the challenges of small businesses. Not sure how much actual success she has had at last role – she blames the model – high cost to employer and charity not using a sustainable model
Understanding of sales cycle and own selling style	6	Understands need for cold calling, meetings, investment of time and energy and persistence. (Not sure if she is a 'closer')
Experience of working with young people with poor employment records	7	Set up enterprise scheme for young people, currently mentoring young people, and works at another charity

Candidate Name	Score/10	Comments
Experience of creating guidelines / protocols	6	Helped marketing team to do it. Has good understanding and good writing skills - something she could do
Telephone style and communication throughout the process including presentation of CV and covering letter	8	CV and covering letter strong. Nice telephone manner, very warm, builds instant rapport. Emails professional and timely.
Evidence of collaborative working style and joined up working	7	Gave good examples of how it should work. Was trying to improve it at last job - should she have made more of a difference? Not sure in such a short time
Understanding of third sector – impact reporting, outcomes, target groups	6	Passionate about giving young people a chance. Knows about importance of targets, and real outcomes rather than statistics – not deep understanding of impact reporting as a concept
Apparent fit with our company ethos	8	Ethical, talked about not over promising, managing expectations, being patient, building relationships, understands small business challenges
Direct line management experience or experience / knowledge of working in a small business	5	Doesn't enjoy line management, prefers to have colleagues than people reporting in to her. Has not directly managed young people or a small business herself although she has worked in them
Fit with logistics of job requirements – availability for fixed term contract period	8	Would ideally like to start before Christmas. Looking at a few other opportunities
Total	69/100	Minimum score of 75 for 2nd interview

Doing the interview

Try to do the interview somewhere you won't be interrupted. It doesn't need to be silent; you might have it in a coffee shop, but you do need to be focussed.

Start on time if you can, as this will give the candidate less time to get nervous and sets the right professional tone.

Put the candidate at ease with a bit of small talk and start by taking them through the steps in the process you are going to use, and when you are hoping the make the appointment, so they can settle down.

Explain that although you have a set of standard questions, you'll try not to make it too stilted, and offer them the opportunity to ask questions as you go along.

You can explain that the standard questions are there to ensure that everyone has an equal chance, and that you will be taking notes.

Aim to complete the interview within 45 minutes to an hour, depending on the job. After that, you and they will be getting tired.

If you are doing lots of interviews in one day, allow about 15 minutes between each one for you to score the candidates straight after their interview, and to have a quick comfort break and stretch before the next one.

Always give the candidate an opportunity to ask questions at the end if they haven't raised them during the interview.

Finish by reminding them what the next steps will be, and when they will find out if they are through to the next stage.

Have a look at the sidebar 'Interview etiquette' for a reminder of polishing your Ps and Qs.

Interview etiquette

Having a few pointers to bear in mind is usually helpful; these tips will help you to make the most of your interviews:

✔ Keep an open mind. Appearances can be deceptive.

✔ Avoid questions with a yes/no answer, unless that is the answer you need!

✔ Avoid asking people about personal circumstances or background that could be perceived as discriminatory.

✔ Where possible, ask everyone the same questions with just a few relevant additional ones.

✔ Don't interrupt, answer the question yourself, or start with 'I presume, 'or' I suppose'.

✔ Listen to the answers.

✔ Really listen to the answers – and read the body language and pauses as well as hearing the words.

✔ Score the candidate straight away against your selection criteria, before you meet the next one.

Using psychometric profiling tools

You may have heard people talking about Myers Briggs, or OPQ, or PPA. These are all *psychometric profiling tools*, designed to give you an insight into the working styles, or behavioural preferences, of your candidates. Some also give pointers about how people may react under pressure.

These tools can provide useful insights, but they are sometimes overused, and should only be interpreted by a trained practitioner. It's not best practice to use them in isolation as a tool to eliminate people during a selection process.

If you want to use a psychometric profile as part of your selection process, ask a qualified practitioner to do the assessment and provide you with a report. Based on this, you can develop some probing interview questions, and use the answers to decide if the person is right for the job. These reports are also useful as a prompt to thinking about how you might need to manage the successful candidate, so that you will press all the right buttons and get the best out of them!

The sidebar 'Psychometric profiling tools' lists some useful online resources should you wish to roll your sleeves up and find out more about using these tools to find your ideal candidate.

Psychometric profiling tools

These and other popular tools have been validated by various bodies, as providing statistically valid indicators of how people are likely to, or prefer to, behave at work:

Myers Briggs: `www.myersbriggs.org`

OPQ: `ceb.shl.com/assets/resources/opq-uk.pdf`

PPA: `www.thomasinternational.net/en-gb/Candidate/howtodoassessments/PPA.aspx`

16PF: `www.opp.com/tools/16pf/`

Taking up references and doing background checks

Once you've narrowed down your list of candidates to one or even a handful of possibilities, trust not only in your own judgement but seek the advice of those people who have already worked with that candidate. Doing this formally is known as *taking up a reference*.

We recommend taking up two references, where possible from former employers. Character referees can be useful for fresh graduates or people early in their careers, but they are often a family friend or relation who is unlikely to be objective.

Employers are obliged to give factually accurate references, but also not to give a reference that even if it is factually true, may be misleading. This means that some employers will only provide the bare facts, of job title, dates of employment, salary and reason for leaving.

Even these basics are useful to validate a candidate's CV and to make sure that they haven't misled you about how much they were earning or how senior they were in their previous role.

If you have time, it is useful to take up at least one reference verbally, because you get a better feel for what the person was like at work.

Start by giving the former employer some idea of what your business is like, and the job you are looking to fill.

You can ask questions like 'How should I manage this person, to get the best out of them?' or 'How can I best support them to cope with a busy workload?' This often unleashes a torrent of advice, giving you some really good insights into how the candidate manages their time, or how much direction they need. People are usually more honest on the phone than they would be in writing, on their company headed paper.

It is also a good idea to ask about how much time off work the candidate has had in the last 12 months or if they are generally punctual. Finish with a general question like, 'Any more tips?'

In addition to references, a growing number of companies carry out background checks, including residential and job history, credit history and county court judgements, as well as Disclosure Barring Service checks for certain jobs that require them.

Considering how time consuming all this research is, you may decide only to carry out some or all of these checks because your business is in financial services, or in the education or health care sectors. It is well worth forking out the fee for someone else to do it. They will also check that the candidate has permission to work in the UK, which you are legally obliged to establish before employing anyone.

Making a Job Offer

Congratulations! You've made your excellent job description and person spec, advertised like a twenty-first century employment guru, and have selected your dream candidate. So now you need to offer them a job.

When you make a job offer, even verbally, it's a contract, and when someone accepts, it is legally binding. If you change your mind and withdraw it, the person can sue you for breach of contract. If they think you've withdrawn it for discriminatory reasons, they can claim wrongful dismissal. In both cases, if they were successful you would have to pay compensation.

Making a legally binding offer

When you verbally offer someone a job, make sure that you add some caveats at this stage, so you have a get-out clause if you need it.

Always say that the job offer is conditional, subject to satisfactory references, background checks if you use them, and permission to work in the UK.

Follow up promptly with an offer in writing. Although legally you have two months before you have to provide a written statement of particulars, it is best to do it as soon as you can. Then if there has been any misunderstanding, or you've forgotten to mention something important, you can resolve it quickly and it doesn't colour the working relationship.

An employment contract can be a mix of verbal and written terms, and over time, custom and practice can also shape the nature of the entire contract.

It's a good idea to put a time limit by which the person has to confirm their acceptance of the offer. If they have a few irons in the fire, they might keep you waiting while they decide between a few different options. Two weeks is a reasonable period, so you can say that the offer expires if they haven't accepted by a certain date.

Including the right things in the job offer

You need to tell people certain things about the job you are offering. Some employers have a simple, less formal covering letter with the headlines, and then attach a more detailed statement of particulars which has all the legal stuff in more formal terms.

It's pretty much what you would expect: the names of the parties to the contract, effective date, where they will work, how much and when they will be paid, hours of work, holiday entitlement, notice period, reporting relationship, sick pay, any collective agreements, any requirement to work outside the UK, pension arrangements and how you will handle disciplinary, grievance and dismissal. You can read more about this in Chapter 14.

The Arbitration, Conciliation and Advisory Service provides a template statement of employment particulars on their website: www.acas.org.uk

Chapter 3

Working Together

In the early days of running a business, the boundaries between work and the rest of life can be blurred. You make calls from the breakfast table, check emails on the sofa late at night and get up at 4am to buy the freshest produce from the market (or the non-foodstuff equivalent of this!). *You* are your business. But as soon as you employ your first person, that all changes. This chapter guides you through the best way to operate as you at first gain and then increase your number of employees.

Getting The Practicalities Right

Being successful in business isn't just about how you work, how you market your ideas, or the calibre of your employees: you need your own Bat Cave from which to operate, and it needs to have the right feel and the right functionality. Not only that, but the vibe of your business is also important: employees want to feel well-managed and valued. Get this right from the beginning, and everything else will feel that little bit more achievable (and you will hopefully avoid teeth-grindingly embarrassing situations such as that described in the sidebar 'Appearances matter!').

Choosing the location, facilities and business tools

Provide your employees with a safe and convenient work environment, and you'll be at least part way towards having a happy workforce. This section looks at some of the issues and challenges – big and small – that will help to promote your business as a place worth working in.

Appearances matter!

An environmental consultant was taking on lots of new clients and advertised for a graduate trainee to join the business. There wasn't enough money to rent an office so he ran the business from the loft room of his house. Although there were two desks with swivel chairs, an Internet connection, phone lines, computers, printers, wall planners and a respectable bookshelf full of environmental text books, the only thing his first candidate noticed was the king-sized bed, since the loft also served as his guest room!

The candidate was fantastic; she had a 2:1 degree in Geography, a passion for the environment, and a real talent for analysis. He offered her the job the next day, on the salary she had asked for, and even offered to pay her travel expenses. He was surprised to receive a polite email turning down the job, and called her to find out why. After some probing she admitted that her Dad had told her she shouldn't take a job working with some middle aged guy who had a double bed in his office!

Location

The acclaimed business strategist Michael Porter and several TV producers have well-aired views on the importance of location, location, location for your customers and for your ideal home. It is equally important for your employees. The workplace sets the tone for the company culture and ways of working. Think about accessibility and nearby facilities when you select your work location.

You have a legal obligation to tell your employees

✔ The location of their place of work

✔ Any requirement for them to work at other locations

✔ Whether the employee may be required to work outside the UK for more than a month in any year, and if so, what arrangements you will put in place

Mobility clause

If you think you might need to change an employee's work location in the future, use a *mobility clause* in the employment contract. This is a clause that allows you to change the employee's work location within reason, without triggering a potential redundancy situation.

Without a mobility clause in the employment contract, if you change an employee's work location from one place that is quite easy for them to reach from home, to somewhere farther away or more difficult to reach, the employee can claim that the job at the current location is redundant and refuse to move.

Even with a mobility clause in the employment contract, you should give your employees reasonable notice of a proposed change of workplace.

Redundancy arises when there has been, or is going to be either:

- ✔ The closure of the business
- ✔ The closure of the workplace
- ✔ A diminution in the need for employees

With regard to the focus of this chapter, if you close one work location and move to another you may have to pay employees a redundancy payment, if they meet certain criteria. Read more about this in Chapter 5. You don't have to pay compensation to your employees for relocation, unless it is specified in the employment contract. You can read more about this in Chapter 14.

Travel expenses

If an employee's place of work is home, and you are expecting them to occasionally or regularly come to the office, tell them what travel expenses they can claim, and how to make a claim.

Create a simple form, ask them to provide receipts and pay them out of the petty cash, or add it to their pay, but don't deduct the tax.

If your employee is based at your office or workspace and needs to travel to meetings, clients or sales calls, you should be clear about what travel expenses you will pay. If your employee will be using public transport, be specific about what class of travel expenses you will reimburse.

HMRC provides guidelines about the mileage rates people can claim for using their own cars for work travel. Use these guidelines to avoid any tax liability for paying more generous rates. Find out more here: `https://www.gov.uk/government/publications/rates-and-allowances-travel-mileage-and-fuel-allowances`

Facilities

Whether you're running the business in a shared building, a renovated hangar or the garden shed, your employees have some basic needs.

Toilets

Giving your employees access to toilets is non-negotiable, according to the The Workplace (Health, Safety and Welfare) Regulations 1992, and the standard and cleanliness of the toilets in your workplace can be a real bugbear for some employees. Even if you only have one female employee you must make arrangements for sanitary waste disposal. If you're not employing a cleaner, either clean the toilets yourself or create a rota for everyone to share the burden. Provide clean towels and soap and keep an eye on the supply of toilet rolls!

Heat and smoke

There are no legal limits on work temperatures, but the Health and Safety Executive recommends that the workplace should be at a minimum temperature of 13 degrees Celsius where a lot of physical work is being done, and a minimum of 16 degrees Celsius for other work environments. Most people are comfortable in an office temperature of 18 to 20 degrees Celsius.

You may read the Health and Safety Executive guidelines on workplace temperatures at `http://www.hse.gov.uk/temperature/faq.htm#minimum-maximum-temperature`

If their work involves hot or cold processes, you should provide your employees with somewhere cool or warm to have their breaks.

And, of course, you can't have smoking on the premises but think about whether you are able to offer an outdoor space to employees who feel the need for a fag. Clearly define such areas to prevent 'smoker's creep'.

Kitchen or kettle?

Most people like to have a cuppa at some point during their working day, and if you can afford it, provide the teabags and coffee, even if you make the employees buy their own milk and sugar. Employees may even ask for a toaster, microwave or other kitchen tools so they can bring their own food to work.

You can avoid the messiness of multiple boxes and jars, and most people won't nick extra teabags. If the teabags do disappear very quickly, mention in conversation that you'll have to stop buying the teabags if they keep disappearing at such a rate, and rely on peer pressure to do the rest. And it's not only your bottom line that could suffer if you don't address the all-important British question about supplying tea: check out the sidebar 'Motivating factors and hygiene factors' for some scientific thinking, too.

Motivating factors and hygiene factors

In the 1960s Frederick Herzberg, an American psychologist, developed a theory that people at work were motivated or satisfied by certain factors, and dissatisfied by others. The two sets of factors were independent of each other.

What he labelled *motivating factors* include recognition, challenging work and responsibility, and are usually intrinsic, or built into, the job. *Hygiene factors*, he claimed, include working conditions, pay, and job security. His theory was that people just want the hygiene factors to be sorted out, as a given, or they will be dissatisfied. The question of whether pay falls into the hygiene factor category is a matter for on-going debate, but most people in the UK would expect reasonable physical working conditions and some common sense people policies in their workplace, even if the idea of job security is a thing of the past.

Business tools and equipment

As soon as you have more than one person in a business, and you are sharing tools, documents and contacts, you need to develop systems for managing it all.

If your employees are provided with a company phone or laptop, a van, or indeed any tools or equipment to do their job, you should have a clear statement in their contract of employment that states you are:

- ✔ Providing the tools and equipment as a condition of the employment
- ✔ Expecting the employee to return them at the end of the contract
- ✔ Expecting the employee to promptly report any loss or damage to company assets

Remote workers

If your employees are *working remotely,* that is, not under the supervision of your beady eye, give them clear guidelines about:

- ✔ How they are permitted to use any company computers, tablets or phones
- ✔ Personal use of company tools, equipment and vehicles

If you expect home working employees to have access to broadband, or to be able to make and receive mobile calls on their own phones, you should be clear about this, and decide if you will pay some or all of the costs.

Depending on the nature of your business, you may need to have some rules about how to manage data, information and customer details to ensure that you are compliant with the Data Protection Act. You can read more about this in Chapter 6.

Personal Protective Equipment

You can ask chefs to bring their own knives, hairdressers to bring their own scissors, and painters to bring their own brushes to work, but if your employees are working in hazardous conditions, and there is a risk of personal injury, you have to provide the appropriate *Personal Protective Equipment* (PPE) free of charge.

The Health and Safety Executive provides guidance on the necessary equipment and when it should be used: `http://www.hse.gov.uk/pubns/indg174.pdf`

Managing the workload

No matter what their job descriptions say, you always need to be prepared to adjust the responsibilities of your employees to meet the needs of the business (and sometimes their job descriptions, too!).

As your business grows, new tasks and responsibilities will come up and you will need to allocate them to people. There will be times when everyone in the business is working very hard because there is so much to do, but you haven't got enough money to take on another pair of hands.

When new work comes up, don't just give it to the first person who passes your desk. Before you allocate it, think about:

- People's existing workload, especially any looming deadlines
- Who has the best skills and experience to do the work
- Who has expressed an interest in taking on new things
- How much you are paying people
- If there is other work you could move around, so that the right person is freed up to take on this work
- If there are any customer or supplier relationships to take into account
- The costs and benefits of paying for overtime to get the work done
- Your longer term plans to train and develop people, and where this work fits in
- Whether asking someone to do it would be completely unreasonable
- Whether you would need to make any adjustments so that an employee with a disability could do the work
- Whether allocating the work to someone would significantly change their job, and possibly their job title

Always have a clause in your employment contracts which requires people to work additional hours if necessary to meet the needs of the business, even if you don't pay overtime. Read more about this in Chapter 7.

Setting the Culture and Values of Your Business

At its simplest level the *culture* of your business is 'the way we do things around here'. It evolves over time, as the business grows and more people join the company. If you set up the business, it starts with you. Even if you don't own the business, if you are 'the boss', you will shape the culture of the organisation by the way that you work and how you manage others.

What are your values?

Your values are the things that you believe are important in how you live and work.

When you are living or working in a way that is aligned with your values, you are likely to be satisfied and happy, and more likely to be successful.

Knowing your values enables you to make better decisions every day and to make big life decisions when they come along.

If you have set up your own business, your values will determine how you run it. If the business is a partnership, your values will determine how you behave in that relationship. If you employ people, your values will influence how you treat your employees.

Mindtools provide a step by step guide to identifying your top personal values. Check it out here:

`http://www.mindtools.com/pages/`
`article/newTED_85.htm`

Figure out what drives you, and what matters to you. This will help you when you are managing other people in your business.

Setting the tone with your own behaviour

Larry Page, one of the founders of Google, is quoted during his early days as CEO as saying to his managers:

> 'Don't delegate, do everything yourself to make things go faster,' and 'Don't get in the way if you're not adding value. Let the people actually doing the work talk to each other while you go do something else.'

Fifteen years later, with over 55,000 employees, Google describes their culture on the company website as follows:

> 'We strive to maintain the open culture often associated with start-ups, in which everyone is a hands-on contributor and feels comfortable sharing ideas and opinions.'

You will set the tone and culture by your actions as well as your words. Think about the signals you are giving to employees with your

- ✔ **Working hours:** When do you arrive and leave? Do you take a lunch break or stop for coffee?
- ✔ **Email and phone habits:** Do you email and call people at all hours? Do you expect them to reply immediately?
- ✔ **Meetings:** Do you set regular meetings? Do you turn up on time? Do you cancel at short notice? Do you make the coffee? Do you take notes or remember what was agreed? Do you keep to the time that was put aside in the diary? Are you mostly talking or mostly listening?

✔ **To do lists:** Do you deliver on your promises? Do you hold people accountable when you've asked them to do something? Do you meet deadlines? Do you delegate?

✔ **Mistakes:** Do you own up to your own mistakes? Do you blame other people when things go wrong? Do you say sorry? Do you learn from your mistakes? Do you give people feedback when they make a mistake?

✔ **Ideas:** Are you the only one who has them? Are you encouraging people to come up with ideas and to try things, even if they fail?

✔ **Dress:** How do you dress? Does it matter?

Seeing your business through other people's eyes

You may have a website, a shop front, an office or a market stall. These are obvious 'windows' into your business for outsiders to peer through. Like any window, they can be dressed to give a good impression. But how you do business with your customers and how you treat your employees day to day will be the key to your success.

So long as you are single-handedly running the show, you decide how many times the phone will ring before you pick it up, and how quickly you respond to customer complaints.

But as soon as you take on your first employee, it's not so straightforward.

Think about all the ways in which your business is interacting with customers or potential customers, shareholders, suppliers and regulatory bodies. These are the signals your business gives to the outside world that are in your control. Decide which interactions have the biggest impact on your reputation, your revenue, your profit and your cash flow. Decide which tasks you are prepared to delegate to employees. Make some rules so that your employees are clear about your expectations. For example:

✔ If you have more than one phone, make sure they are all answered promptly and have a consistent greeting and voicemail message.

✔ Monitor voicemail and respond to queries promptly.

✔ Monitor links from your website to any general or 'info' email addresses and respond promptly.

✔ Check your 'hold' music by phoning in from outside to hear what your customers hear, and test any automated emails sent from your business accounts.

✔ Keep the newsfeed and blogs on your website up to date, or don't have them at all.

✔ Issue invoices promptly, follow them up, and chase for payment politely and professionally.

✔ Decide how promptly you want to pay suppliers, and be consistent.

✔ Make it easy for customers to complain if they are not happy, and be attentive to what they are saying.

✔ Make sure that your business record in Companies House is accurate and up to date.

✔ Promptly complete VAT returns, payroll returns and annual returns to the Charity Commission or Companies House.

✔ Greet and treat company visitors with respect.

Give your employees feedback if they are not meeting your expectations, and keep reminding them of the standards you want to maintain for the business. Be prepared to take disciplinary action if employees don't make the grade. Read about how to do this, and how to create other business rules, in Chapter 6.

Using your values to shape the way you do business

Your values shape your behaviour and your behaviour shapes the way you do business.

Start by asking what you are prepared to do to achieve success, and its corollary question, what are you not prepared to do?

Essentially, running a business boils down to people and money. Let's look at each in turn.

People

Whether you're providing a service or manufacturing a product, there will always be other people involved in your business. Two main values affect your dealings with other human beings (and, for that matter, little green men should they ever land): relationships and recognition

Relationships

If you value relationships highly, this shapes how you work with suppliers, partners, customers and employees. You may:

✔ Show flexibility on contractual terms

✔ 'Go the extra mile' to service a customer

✔ Sacrifice short term profit goals to build long term relationships

✔ Consult employees rather than instruct them

This approach usually means things take longer to achieve (but hopefully builds stronger relationships with your customers and clients)!

Recognition

If you value personal recognition, but you're the boss so there's no-one in the business who will pat you on the back, you can seek external validation in various ways. You can:

- ✔ Join a local Chamber of Commerce (`http://www.britishchambers.org.uk`)
- ✔ Become a member of the Federation of Small Businesses (`http://www.fsb.org.uk`)
- ✔ Try to win an award (see the sidebar 'Rewarding awards' for ideas).

Money

'The best things in life are free'; so sang The Beatles but you may disagree. If you measure your personal and business success financially, here are the key factors to watch out for: growth and profit

Growth

Constant upward movement is of course a Good Thing, but if you are aiming to achieve a certain market share you might sacrifice some profit margin to win big deals.

Even if you are growing fast, don't take shortcuts when you are employing new people! Take the time to select the right people for the long term.

Rewarding awards

The EY Entrepreneur of the Year Award judges look for people with 'the passion, vision and the drive to succeed.' So if you feel that you might be a 'compelling leader who embodies entrepreneurial spirit and who isn't afraid to take risks to drive their business forward', take a look at their webite:

`http://www.ey.com/UK/en/About-us/Entrepreneurship/Entrepreneur-Of-The-Year`

But if you want to be in the Sunday Times 100 Best Small Companies to work for, according to

Dominic O' Connell, the *Sunday Times* Business Editor, you will need to show that you are one of the 'enlightened and forward-looking leaders investing in the wellbeing and motivation of their most valuable assets: their employees.' Find out more here:

`http://features.thesundaytimes.co.uk/public/best100companies/live/template`

Profit

If the bottom line is your main focus, concentrate on keeping costs down. In the long run, if employees are underpaid, they may not hang around. Even Ryanair had to admit that making employees pay for plugging in their phone chargers at work wasn't worth it!

If you focus on money at the cost of the people, your business may grow more quickly and be more profitable, but you will probably have a higher turnover of customers, employees and suppliers.

Managing People

The culture of your business starts at the top, and how you choose to manage people has a significant impact on their performance. And how your employees perform ultimately determines how your business performs.

Deciding what kind of manager you want to be

Theories about leadership and management abound, and each carefully constructed management model has its own appeal. However they also have their flaws, because as the pithy Yorkshire phrase has it, 'There's nowt as queer as folk.'

Your values and personality will determine to some extent how you want to manage people. Your preferred style of management will work with some people and not with others.

Sometimes you will need to consciously adopt a management style that doesn't come naturally, to get the best results. Use a management style that brings the best out in people: they know you're the boss, and most people don't need to be reminded.

Factors that affect the most useful style to adopt include:

- ✔ The experience and skills of the person you are managing
- ✔ The complexity of the task or work
- ✔ The potential impact of getting the task or work wrong
- ✔ How much time you and the employee have to complete the work
- ✔ What potential reward is at stake

✔ How much input or creativity you want from the employee

✔ Whether you know what you are doing!

Your management style evolves with experience, but making a conscious decision from the start about what kind of manager you are aiming to be will make life easier for you and for your employees. The following sections look at common management styles.

Firm but fair

At interviews I often ask the question, 'What kind of manager are you?' and the most common answer is 'firm but fair.' Superficially this seems to be a good answer, reflecting someone who is definitely in charge, but treats everyone the same. This would work well for a bunch of baristas, but maybe not so well for a den of designers.

Freedom to succeed

When I ask people at interview how they like to be managed, they are most likely to say, 'I don't like being micro-managed but I like to know my boss is there if I need them.'

At Diageo, the multi-national drinks business, one of the values is 'freedom to succeed.' People are encouraged to be entrepreneurial, to take some risks and trust each other to do a good job. This has enabled generations of bright sparks to discover crazy flavours, design innovative packaging, and find new ways of working. It has been one of the secrets of Diageo's business success.

Deciding how much control to take

Various labels are pinned to management styles, but essentially they are describing the degree of control that a manager is exerting over his or her subordinates:

✔ **Low control**, labelled *laissez-faire* or 'let them get on with it', allows employees to work as they will. Use this for motivated employees and people who know what they are doing. Avoid it for lazy or incompetent employees – they are likely to under-perform and cost your business money.

✔ **High control**, or *autocratic,* styles involve laying down the law and making sure employees work in a certain way. Use this when it is critical to maintain high quality standards, work at a fast pace, or the employees are unskilled or inexperienced. Avoid it for experienced, competent employees. It will demotivate them and stifle their creativity.

Deciding whether to direct or consult

Whilst you probably have a personal preference for directing or consulting, you can consciously choose which to do, depending on the people and the circumstances.

When you need someone else to do some work, pause before you ask them. Think about the task, the person, and which approach is going to get the best result:

- ✔ **Directive management** assumes that the manager knows best. The manager specifies what the work is, how it will be done, by whom, and when it should be completed. This approach works well when you are faced with:

  - A critical deadline

  - Limited resources

  - Inexperienced or unskilled employees

  - A statutory requirement

  - Defined quality standard

  - A specific customer requirement

- ✔ **Consultative management** assumes that the people doing the work know best. The manager describes the end result and asks the employees to decide how best to achieve it. This approach works well when you have:

  - An experienced individual or team

  - A specialist task relying on the expertise of the individual or team

  - A need for creative ideas

  - Time to consider and experiment with alternatives

  - A manager who knows less about the work than the employees

  - An incentive or reward for the individual or team to deliver a great result

Keeping everyone in the loop

People do a better job when they know what's going on. Give them the information they need to anticipate problems, make good decisions and represent your business well. The two most effective ways to do so are via meetings and informative emails or business summaries.

Situational leadership

Ken Blanchard, a leading US business consultant, developed a model of leadership to match the nature of the person being managed and the task at hand. He called it *situational leadership*, and used the analogy of a parent teaching a child to ride a bike.

✔ When the child is first placed on a bike, they have no experience and little confidence, and don't know what to expect. The parent holds the bicycle, gives them plenty of reassurance, lots of instructions and runs alongside shouting encouragement. This is a *directing style* for a novice, someone completely new to a task.

✔ Once the child has wobbled off on the bike, had a taste of the sensation of rolling on wheels, and fallen off because they forgot how to use the brakes, they may lose their nerve. The parent encourages them to try again, reminds them about the brakes, and still holds the back of the saddle. This is a *supportive style* for someone who has the basic skills but lacks confidence.

✔ After a few successful straight line rides, the child wants to circumnavigate a tree, or take one hand off the handlebars to wave for a photo. The parent stands nervously on the sidelines, shouting reminders about the brakes, asking the child if they feel ok, and encouraging them to take a few more risks. This is a *coaching style* for a competent performer.

✔ Finally, when the child is flying over ramps on the BMX track, the parent can cheer, clap and celebrate their success. They discuss the next challenge and talk about getting a new BMX bike. This is a *delegating style* for a strong performer.

Team meetings

Make time to get everyone together regularly. Team meetings have two purposes. One is to reinforce relationships. The other is to share information. In the early days of a business, make them weekly.

✔ Have team meetings at the same time every week so people can plan for them

✔ If people don't work in the same place, use conference calls or video calls to include everybody

✔ Have a time allotted and an agenda and stick to them

✔ Share headline information about the business

✔ Ask people to share updates about their work

✔ Share issues or challenges and give people the opportunity to suggest solutions either at the meeting or afterwards

✔ Allow time for people to chat over a cup of coffee or lunch

✔ As your business grows, decide when to split the full team meetings into smaller ones

✔ Make one full team meeting a month or a quarter mandatory for everyone to attend

Emails or newsletters

Use emails or newsletter updates to keep people informed between team meetings, especially if your business is growing and the teams are dispersed.

Don't use emails to make big announcements: these are better done in person whether it's good news or bad news.

If your employees are already bombarded with emails in their day job, don't assume they will always read yours!

Letting people know how well they are doing, or not!

Irrespective of which management style you are using with people, you need to let them know how well they are doing at the job. You can do this informally in conversation, or in a one to one meeting. Keep this checklist at hand when preparing for such a meeting:

✔ First, be clear about what you expect.

✔ Tell even the confident, competent employees when they are doing well.

✔ Tell the less competent employees how they need to improve.

✔ Keep notes, even if they are brief.

✔ Always follow up: acknowledge the improvement if there is one, or set another goal if there hasn't been any improvement.

✔ If an employee is consistently under-performing, try to find out why.

You may wish to flick through to Chapter 8 to find out more about monitoring employees' performance.

As well as giving informal feedback as you go along, be sure to have regular one to one meetings with your employees to give formal feedback (whether good or bad):

✔ If you work in an open plan area, giving employees negative feedback can be difficult as other people might overhear.

✔ If something goes wrong you don't want to make a big deal of taking an employee to one side to talk to them about it: unless its urgent, just put it on your list of things to talk about in the next scheduled one to one meeting.

This tactic only works if the one to one meetings are already scheduled. If you have to set up a one to one meeting just to talk about an issue, the mole-hill will start growing into a mountain.

Create a culture of one to one meetings so that when the business grows and you take on team leaders or managers they follow the habit too.

In the meeting, which can be quite short, run through the following (and remember to listen as well as speak!):

1. **Ask the employee how their work is going.**

2. **Check if the employee needs anything from you to do the job better.**

3. **Give specific feedback about things they have done well or not so well.**

4. **Agree on any actions for both of you to take before the next meeting.**

5. **Keep notes!**

Asking people how well you are doing, or not!

It's good to know how well or badly you are doing in the job, but when you're the boss, not many people will be willing to tell you.

When your employees tell you something you don't like, take it on the chin, don't make excuses, and go away to think about it before you respond.

Create opportunities for employees to give you feedback by:

✔ Asking people to give you feedback in their one to one meetings.

✔ Using phrases like 'What could I do differently to make your job easier?'

✔ Making a physical or virtual space where employees can post comments.

✔ Being honest when you make mistakes, and asking for feedback about what you could do differently next time.

✔ Creating a simple survey and asking employees once a year what they think about your leadership and management. Use survey monkey (https://www.surveymonkey.com) to create a survey and find out what your employees think of work, anonymously. Chapter 15 provides more details about employee surveys.

Chapter 4

Managing Your Pay and Benefits

In This Chapter

▶ Rewarding staff in an effective way

▶ Understanding benefits your staff are entitled to

▶ Receiving assistance with making statutory payments

▶ Working out pay fairly and competitively

*T*his chapter shows the basics of reward management, specifically looking at how having the right reward approach is critical to your business success going forward. In addition, you'll start to understand benefits you have to provide legally and how to deal with the inevitable pay issues that arise. Lastly, you will establish how to use rewards to motivate those who work for you!

Understanding Reward Management

Reward is a key factor affecting relationships, motivation and engagement at work. The level and distribution of reward (pay and benefits) can have a considerable effect on the morale and productivity of your employees. Organisations must, therefore, develop pay systems that are appropriate for them, that provide value for money, and that reward workers fairly for the work they perform.

You can motivate people with rewards and incentives, but you need to recognise that not every person is motivated in this way. Therefore, your challenge is to establish how rewards might be used to underpin your business goals, whilst ensuring that everyone feels equally motivated through the use of appropriate goals and rewards.

Your legal responsibilities

All employers have legal responsibilities when establishing the reward arrangements of their employees.

You must ensure that you don't directly or indirectly discriminate against employees, and you are required by law to pay minimum wage. From 2016 onward all employers will be required to provide pension arrangements. As an employer you are also legally required to provide minimum levels of pay when employees are sick or absent on maternity leave.

Avoiding discrimination

As an employer you must give men and women equal treatment in the terms and conditions of their employment contract, if they are employed to do the following:

- ✔ 'Like work': work that is the same or broadly similar
- ✔ Work rated as equivalent under a job evaluation study
- ✔ Work found to be of equal value in terms of effort, skill or decision making.

Be aware that your employees can compare any terms in the contract of employment with the equivalent terms in a comparators contract. A *comparator* is an employee of the opposite sex working for the same employer, doing like work of equal value.

The Equality Act 2010 makes it unlawful to prevent employees from having discussions to establish if there are differences in pay. However, an employer can require their employees to keep pay rates confidential from people outside of the workplace.

The equal terms can cover all aspects of pay and benefits, including:

- ✔ Basic pay
- ✔ Overtime rates
- ✔ Performance related benefits
- ✔ Hours of work
- ✔ Nonmonetary terms
- ✔ Annual leave entitlements

An employee who thinks he or she is not receiving equal pay can write to you asking for information that will help him or her establish whether there is a pay difference, and if so, the reasons for the difference.

Working with the Minimum Wage

As an employer in the UK you have to adhere to the legal requirements to provide the National Minimum Wage to your employees.

It doesn't matter how small an employer is, all have to pay the minimum wage, and the level of pay depends on a worker's age and if he or she is an apprentice.

The National Minimum Wage is enforceable by HMRC or by an employee making a contractual claim through wrongful deduction of pay. In October 2013, new rules were introduced to "name and shame" employers who fail to comply with the law.

Every October the rate is reviewed and increased. Details of existing minimum rates can be found at www.gov.uk/national-minimum-wage-rates.

Living with the Living Wage

The idea behind a living wage is very simple: a person should be paid enough to live decently and to adequately provide for his or her family. At its heart is an ethical argument for preventing in-work poverty and ensuring that workers are not exploited through low wages. A basic outline of the components of living wage are:

- ✔ An hourly rate set independently and updated annually
- ✔ The current UK Living Wage is £7.85 an hour
- ✔ The current London Living Wage is £9.15 an hour

The Living Wage is calculated according to the basic cost of living in the UK, and employers choose to pay the Living Wage on a voluntary basis. It is not mandatory.

From April 2016, the UK government will introduce a new mandatory National Living Wage (NLW) for workers aged 25 and above, initially set at £7.20 – a rise of 70p relative to the current National Minimum Wage (NMW) rate, and 50p above the increase coming into force in October. That's a £1,200 per annum increase in earnings for a full-time worker or the current NMW. You should not confuse the new Government backed National Living Wage (NLW) with the previously described UK Living Wage as they are two different wage levels, validated by 2 different sources. The new National Living Wage will continue to rise incrementally to reach £9.00 an hour by 2020 at a rate to be determined by the Low Pay Commission.

At present most UK employers that tend to employ low paid employees don't pay living wage as it is seen to be cost prohibitive. However, the new legislation will change this, and employers will be required to comply from April 2016 onwards.

Accounting for Pension Provision

In October 2012, the UK government introduced new rules to encourage more people to save for retirement. This new process is called *auto-enrollment*.

Automatic enrolment is being phased in, starting with the largest UK employers. So if you're eligible (see below) and haven't yet created your workplace scheme, you should complete this by October 2018, at the latest.

All employees who are between ages 22 and state pension age and earn above a certain amount (£10,000 a year in 2014/15) are automatically enrolled into a pension scheme. If they work for a large employer, this will have happened in October 2012. For those working for medium and small companies, all staff must be enrolled into a pension by 2018.

Employees can 'opt out' and leave the scheme, but only after they have been automatically made a member. (See Chapter 16 for more details.)

Coughing Up SSP and Other Medical Payments

As an employer you are legally required to pay *Statutory Sick Pay* (SSP) if an employee is too ill to work. It's paid by the employer for up to 28 weeks.

The employee will be paid SSP if they have been off work sick for four or more days in a row (including nonworking days).

You can't pay less than the statutory amount. You can provide more if you decide to implement a company sick pay scheme (or 'occupational scheme').

For an employee to qualify for Statutory Sick Pay (SSP), they must meet the following criteria:

- Be classed as an employee and have done some work for their employer
- Have been ill for at least four days in a row (including nonworking days)
- Earn at least £112 (before tax) per week

✔ Tell you that they are sick before the daily deadline (usually before the working day commences), or within seven days if you don't have a deadline

The employee must give evidence of his or her incapacity. Employees can self-certify their absence for the first consecutive seven days; thereafter, form Med3 (Fit Note) is required from their general practitioner.

It is possible to opt out of the scheme but only if an employer's occupational sick pay scheme is equal to or more than SSP. (The rate of SSP paid changes every year; currently the rate for the 2015/16 tax year is £88.45.) There would still be a requirement to keep appropriate records to demonstrate compliance.

Statutory Maternity Pay and Leave

When a female employee takes time off to have a baby, you must provide both Statutory Maternity Leave and Statutory Maternity Pay.

When employees are on maternity leave they are protected while on Statutory Maternity Leave. This includes their right to:

✔ Receive pay rises

✔ Build up (accrue) holiday

✔ Return to work

Statutory Maternity Pay (SMP) is paid for up to 39 weeks. You must provide the following:

✔ 90% of the employee's average weekly earnings (before tax) for the first six weeks

✔ £139.58 or 90% of your employees average weekly earnings (whichever is lower) for the next 33 weeks

Please note SMP is paid in the same way as you pay an employee's salary.

SMP is payable provided the employee has met the following criteria:

✔ Started her maternity leave

✔ Given 28 days' notice of her maternity leave (unless with good reason)

✔ Provided medical evidence with a form (MATB1)

✔ Been employed continuously for 26 weeks up to and including her qualifying week

✔ Had *average weekly earnings* (AWE) above the Lower Earnings Limit in the relevant period

It is important to note that mothers have a legal entitlement to take up to 52 weeks off around the time of the birth of their baby, whether or not they qualify for SMP. This means that mothers can choose to take up to one year off in total.

Ordinary Statutory Paternity Pay (OSPP)

OSPP is paid to partners who take time off to care for the baby or support the mother in the first few weeks after the birth. OSPP was previously known as Statutory Paternity Pay.

It is available to:

- A biological father
- A partner/husband or civil partner who is not the baby's biological father
- A mother's female partner in a same-sex couple

The partner must meet the following criteria:

- Give 28 days' notice of the upcoming paternity leave (unless with good reason)
- Provide a declaration of family commitment on form SC3
- Has been employed continuously for 26 weeks up to and including their qualifying week
- Has had average weekly earnings above the Lower Earnings Limit in the relevant period

OSPP is payable for a maximum of 2 weeks. It must be taken as a block either one week or a complete fortnight, but not two separate single weeks. OSSP rates are set as follows (whichever is lower):

- 90% of AWE
- £139.58 for 2015/16 (£138.18 for 2014/15)

OSPP is treated as normal pay.

The calculation of average weekly earnings and the recovery of OSPP are subject to the same rules as for SMP. With effect from 1st October 2014, fathers have the right to take unpaid leave to attend up to two antenatal appointments.

Statutory Adoption Pay (SAP)

To qualify for *Statutory Adoption Pay* (SAP) an employee must meet the same earnings and service criteria as an employee seeking to qualify for SMP. An employee must provide his or her employer with evidence of the adoption and a declaration that he or she has elected to receive SAP. HMRC form SC4 provides a declaration form that can be used. A matching certificate from the adoption agency must be produced to the employer. SAP is paid at the same rates as SMP and follows the same rules with regard to recovery.

Shared Parental Leave (SPL)

New rights to Shared Parental Leave (SPL) are available to parents whose babies are due on or after 5 April 2015. In the case of adoptions, SPL will apply in relation to children matched with a person or placed for adoption on or after 5 April 2015.

Employed mothers are still entitled to 52 weeks of maternity leave. The mother can curtail her right to SMP and leave, and opt to take ShPL and Shared Parental Pay (ShPP). SPL and ShPP will be available provided the parents satisfy the eligibility requirements.

An employee can share SPL and ShPP with his or her partner if they are both eligible.

The nearby sidebar 'Working out parental leave' gives an example of how SPL works.

Working out parental leave

A mother and her partner are both eligible for SPL and ShPP. The mother ends her maternity leave and pay after 10 weeks, leaving 42 weeks available for SPL and 27 weeks available for ShPP. The parents can choose how to split this between the two separate employers.

SPL and ShPP must be taken between the baby's birth and first birthday (or within one year of adoption).

Note: Shared Parental Leave is a complex piece of legislation; therefore, you are advised to gain expert guidance or to review the UK Government's overview, which can be found at `https://www.gov.uk/shared-parental-leave-and-pay/overview`.

Claiming Financial Help with Statutory Payments

As an employer, you can usually reclaim 92% of employees' Statutory Maternity (SMP), Paternity (OSPP), Adoption and Shared Parental Pay.

You can reclaim 103% if your business qualifies for Small Employers' Relief. You get this if you paid £45,000 or less in Class 1 National Insurance in the last complete tax year before

- The 'qualifying week': the 15th week (Sunday to Saturday) before the week of the due date

- The 'matching week': the week (Sunday to Saturday) your employee was told they'd been matched with a child by the adoption agency

- The date on which your employee is adopting a child from another country

Calculate how much you'll get back using your payroll software or speak to your accountant and send the calculation to HM Revenue and Customs (HMRC).

You can contact the PAYE Employer Office to ask for a repayment if you can't set off the payments against the current year's liabilities. Use this link to contact the PAYE Employer office: `https://www.gov.uk/government/organisations/hm-revenue-customs/contact/employer-enquiries`

Exploring Different Approaches to Pay

Pay structures provide structure for managing the base pay arrangements of your employees. Many different approaches can be used, and in reality there isn't always an obvious answer with regard to what approach you should use.

You must make a judgement with regard to what is likely to work best for you and your business. More details of the type of schemes can be found in Chapter 16.

Market-based pay

Market-based pay attempts to link salary levels to those available in the market. It is often used in conjunction with an assessment of individual employee performance, which typically allows for higher salary increases for those who are high performers but are underpaid in comparison to the market or their internal peer group. Salary increases then reduce as employees start to earn above the market rate for their job or their peer group.

Service-related pay

Service-related pay is the most prevalent approach towards managing pay adjustments for employees. Simply, a pay adjustment is made annually, either on the anniversary of the date joined or at another agreed date. The adjustment might take account of the increase of cost of living (RPI/CPI) or may just be a simple percentage increase applied to everyone.

What you need to consider when reviewing your approach to reward:

- ✔ Accept that there will inevitably be a cost involved.
- ✔ Avoid most potential problems with a systematic, well-timed and carefully planned approach.
- ✔ Involve the workforce, or its representatives, as much as possible, perhaps through a joint working party.
- ✔ Gain expert help if needed.
- ✔ Don't just discard the existing system – discuss internally what works and could be changed.
- ✔ Look at the possible new systems and consider which might best suit the particular organisation, with or without alteration.
- ✔ Changes to pay make people anxious, and so the new system should be kept simple and should agree with the workforce and their representatives.
- ✔ Prepare the way carefully with briefings to the workforce and management. Look out for any changes to differentials and relativities. Document the system and if possible run it for a trial period.
- ✔ Make arrangements for maintenance, monitoring and evaluation.

Understanding Benefits

The first part of this chapter covers what benefits you are required to provide on a statutory basis. This part of the chapter looks at the general issues of benefits that you may *choose* to provide to your employees.

Common benefits include the following:

- ✔ Buying and selling holidays
- ✔ Childcare vouchers
- ✔ Advances and loans
- ✔ Company cars
- ✔ Company shares

- ✔ Private health schemes
- ✔ Medical insurance

Employee benefits are typically provided in order to increase the commitment and engagement of employees. In addition, in order to remain competitive in the external employment market, benefits often have to be provided.

Other intrinsic motivational reasons are often quoted as to why employers provide benefits. For example, they meet an actual or perceived personal need of employees concerning security or financial assistance.

Once employees can identify all the benefits they get at work, they may have the opportunity to exchange different parts of their reward. For example, childcare vouchers can be issued as an alternative to an element of pay.

The success of a particular element is often influenced by how the benefit will be treated for tax purposes. If the benefit is more tax efficient than the equivalent salary, there is an incentive to opt for the benefit rather than the salary. Company cars have proved to be less popular since the taxation rules have become more stringent.

The domestic circumstances of the employee are also important. For instance, someone with young children may be interested in purchasing additional holidays or exchanging pay for childcare vouchers. Someone who is simply interested in earning as much money as possible may prefer to trade in some holidays in exchange for pay.

Using share incentive schemes

Companies are usually owned by their founders or by shareholders who ultimately are financial investors. The common link is that they have key employees who are fundamental to the day to day successful running of these businesses.

Many owners want their key employees to be both loyal and help grow the company and be rewarded if the business is sold.

Employee share schemes have the potential to motivate staff by providing long-term tax-efficient incentives. In some cases, existing shareholders may not want to give them actual shares in the company, or they may not want them to leave still owning shares in the company, so flexibility is crucial.

Share incentive schemes involve the provision of shares to employees, either by giving them direct or allowing them to be bought. The aim is to encourage staff involvement in the company's performance and, therefore, improve motivation and commitment.

The type of employee share plans you implement are one of two choices:

✔ The Share Incentive Plan (previously the All-Employee Share Ownership Plan, or AESOP).

✔ The share incentive plan ("SIP"), which was introduced by the government as part of the 2000 Finance Act.

SIPs can include four types of shares:

- **Free shares:** Companies can give up to £3,000 worth of shares a year to each employee.

- **Partnership shares:** Employees can buy up to £1,500 worth of shares a year.

- **Matching shares:** Companies can reward this commitment by giving up to two matching shares for each partnership share an employee buys.

- **Dividend shares:** Companies can provide for dividends paid on free shares, partnership shares and matching shares to be reinvested in further shares.

Companies can award some or all of their free shares on the basis of performance, so long as they satisfy certain criteria laid down by HM Revenue & Customs. For more information visit www.hmrc.gov.uk/shareschemes.

Motivating employees

People can be motivated by rewards and incentives, but recognising that not every person is motivated in this way is important. Therefore, your challenge is to establish how reward might be used to underpin your business goals, whilst ensuring that everyone feels equally motivated through the use of appropriates goals and rewards.

In today's business world, linking targets with variable, performance-related reward has become a central and widely established leadership tool. The rest of this chapter looks in a little more detail at how you might use reward, specifically incentives, and your approach to base pay in order to motivate and engage your employees. We also look at how you stay legally compliant when making pay decisions, as well as what types of benefits you might wish to provide.

Providing incentive schemes

Incentive schemes may be short- or long-term. Schemes based on individual performance, such as weekly or monthly production bonuses or commission on sales, generally offer a short-term incentive. Longer-term schemes such as profit sharing and share option schemes may not provide as much incentive to individual workers as schemes based on personal performance.

In Chapter 16 you find lots more detail with regard to how to design incentive schemes and the issues you are likely to face.

Saying Thank You Goes a Long Way

Recognition doesn't always need to be financial. To help motivate employees you need to show genuine appreciation for good work and recognise the improvements they make.

Here are some steps you can take to make your employees feel that they're making a valuable contribution to your company:

- ✓ Say thank you - it is a powerful way of recognising someone's contribution and motivating them to keep performing

- ✓ Use internal publications, a note round the team or a poster to celebrate an individual's success and to show employees that their commitment and effort are appreciated.

- ✓ If you have an intranet, create a bulletin board or forum so employees can thank colleagues for their efforts and help with key issues.

- ✓ Give spot rewards for specific contributions or tasks where employees have exceeded all expectations. For example, this could be a personal reward relevant to their interests outside work.

- ✓ Establish an award scheme so employees can nominate colleagues for their work and the way they have helped drive the business forward.

- ✓ Host social events when you achieve key milestones or targets to thank your team or teams for their work.

- ✓ Hold celebrations for employees' personal milestones or significant life events.

Prioritise employee recognition, and you can ensure a positive, productive, innovative organisational climate. Provide employee recognition to say thank you and to encourage more of the actions and thinking that you believe will make your organisation successful.

Measuring the direct impact on profitability is difficult because it is only one of many factors influencing employees in every workplace. However, case studies make a persuasive case that bottom line benefits have been achieved through recognition schemes. The Walt Disney World Resort established an employee recognition program that resulted in a 15% increase in staff satisfaction with their day-to-day recognition by their immediate supervisors. These results correlated highly with high guest-satisfaction scores, which showed a strong intent to return, and therefore directly flowed to increased profitability.

Chapter 5

Parting Company

We have as many euphemisms for firing someone from their job as we have for saying that someone has died. The reasons are probably similar: we don't like it when good things come to an end. A business is an organic entity that needs to change to survive. Sometimes that change means 'letting people go'.

And not always on good terms.

This chapter guides you through good practice, making suggestions about how to hang onto your best assets and how to lose others overboard (in the nicest possible ways); it also covers the legal aspects of firing people fairly, specifically so you will not throw employees overboard into shark-infested waters.

Keeping the Right People in Your Business

You are not always in control of when employees decide to leave the business, but if you are aware of the main reasons why people move on, you have a fighting chance of keeping the good people for a bit longer.

Keeping people for the right reasons

As a business grows, it is likely to change. This suits some employees, but others will hate the change. The time will come when you have to handle your first resignation.

Common reasons for people leaving their jobs

A common phrase among HR people tells us that 'People don't leave their job, they leave their boss.'

This makes sense. A manager controls a lot of the factors that matter to people at work every day. People leave a job when they don't know

✔ What's going on in the business

✔ Where their job fits in to the big picture

✔ If the quality of their work is good enough

✔ What difference it would make if they did an amazing or a terrible job

✔ What training and career opportunities are on offer

✔ Whether you care if they turn up every day

✔ Whether you care about them at all

It's so simple – all you have to do is tell them!

Always ask people who resign why they are leaving. You can use this intelligence to

✔ Plan ahead and anticipate other resignations

✔ Avoid repeating any mistakes that might have caused them to leave

✔ Shape the recruitment for their replacement

✔ Consider any measures you might want to take to try to keep them

Nobody is indispensable! Think before you respond to a resignation. Your instant reaction might be to try to keep them at any cost, and to offer a pay increase or some other inducement that you later regret. If the business can survive that particular employee leaving, accept his or her resignation, agree on a leaving date and discuss how the employee will hand over the work to someone else.

Before you start recruiting for that employee's replacement, stop and think about whether you should recruit a direct replacement or use the resignation as an opportunity to make some tweaks. For example, you might opt for one of the following alternatives:

✔ Recruit someone who will bring new skills into the business.

✔ Give the job to someone who is already in the business.

✔ Split the job between other members of the team.

✔ Save money and not replace the person at all.

Avoiding the best staff members leaving

Take a few minutes and jot down the impact of losing a person who has handed in her resignation, and consider the reasons why you might want to try to keep her on board.

Table 5-1 lists some examples of what you might take into consideration when assessing the impact of losing a member of staff.

Table 5-1	Reasons for Retaining Staff
Business reasons to keep someone who has resigned	**Other reasons to keep someone who has resigned**
Important customer relationships	Loyalty: they've been in the business since the beginning.
Critical supplier relationships	They seem to know how everything works.
Specialist skills that are difficult to find	You'll have to pay more to a new person.
Leadership or management skills that are lacking in the rest of the team	They help you to keep your finger on the pulse by telling you what other employees are thinking.
The person has long term potential for your business.	You feel guilty because you want everyone in the business to be happy.

The points made in Table 5-1 may all be good reasons to keep a particular employee, but you can mitigate the risk of any individual becoming indispensable to your business by doing the following:

- Training other employees
- Ensuring that customers and suppliers have multiple contacts
- Building good relationships with all your employees so you don't need one person to act as a conduit
- Promoting your future managers and leaders from within the existing team
- Paying the market rate for specialist skills

If the business really can't do without the person who has resigned, consider what factors might persuade that person to stay. He or she might be looking for reduced working hours, increased pay, different working relationships, a promotion and new job title, or even a change to the job.

Offer the employee who has resigned only what your business can afford, and what is reasonable, but don't offer something you can't deliver. If the employee is looking for more money, don't get into a prolonged bargaining situation. Make one definitive 'take it or leave it' offer.

Think about the impact on the rest of the team before you offer something to an employee, just to stop him or her leaving the business; keep it fair.

Firing People Fairly

The law, mainly encompassed in the Employment Rights Act 1996, is quite particular about the definition of fairness when an employer dismisses an employee.

A *fair dismissal* must be for one of these five reasons:

- ✔ Capability or qualifications
- ✔ Conduct
- ✔ Illegality or contravention of a statutory duty
- ✔ Redundancy
- ✔ Some other substantial reason

Any other reasons for dismissal are unfair! The five fair reasons are discussed in this section (as are examples of unfair reasons).

As an employer, you *dismiss* an employee when you

- ✔ Terminate the employment contract, either with or without giving notice
- ✔ Don't renew a fixed-term contract when it ends
- ✔ Breach a fundamental clause of the employment contract and cause the employee to leave, with or without giving notice

An employee has the right to not be *unfairly dismissed* by their employer. Agency staff, contractors and casual workers do not have this right.

If you dismiss an employee, to protect yourself from an accusation of unfair dismissal, you need to show you had

- ✔ A fair reason
- ✔ A reasonable response
- ✔ A fair process

If you dismiss an employee without a fair reason, or without following a reasonable or fair process, the person can make a claim of unfair dismissal at an Employment Tribunal. (An *Employment Tribunal* is a legal forum where disputes between employers and employees are heard and settled.)

Some reasons for dismissal are automatically unfair, meaning that an employee doesn't need a qualifying length of service with you to make a claim of unfair dismissal. Read more later in this chapter: see the section 'Being automatically unfair'.

The Act states that 'capability in relation to an employee means his capability assessed by reference to his skill, aptitude, health or any other physical or mental quality.' If an employee does not have a qualification that is required to do a job, you can dismiss them, but you must be able to justify why the qualification is necessary, and you must follow a fair process before dismissing them.

If an employee claims you dismissed him or her unfairly, you have a stronger defense of your reasonable behaviour if you can show that dismissing the employee was a last resort.

If you lose your case at an Employment Tribunal, you may have to pay legal costs, a compensatory award, or even reinstate the employee you have dismissed. Read more details in the section 'Calculating the Cost of Getting It Wrong', later in this chapter.

Dismissal and the law

Wrongful Dismissal is when the employer terminates an employment contract without giving the contractual notice.

Constructive Dismissal occurs when an employee resigns because the employer has committed a fundamental breach of the contract. The most common breach is of the implied term of 'mutual trust and confidence' between the employer and the employee.

Unfair Dismissal occurs when an employer terminates the contract for an unfair reason or does not follow a fair process when dismissing an employee.

The law on unfair dismissal is principally contained in the Employment Rights Act 1996, with various additions and changes arising from other more recent statutes.

You can find as much detail as you can digest on the government website here:

```
http://www.legislation.gov.uk/
ukpga/1996/18/contents
```

Not doing things right: Capability

The Employment Rights Act 1996 defines the 'capability' of an employee as referring to

- ✔ Skill
- ✔ Aptitude
- ✔ Health or any other physical or mental quality

You may fairly dismiss an employee because he or she doesn't meet the requirements of the job, as defined by the following:

- ✔ **Qualifications:** Defined as 'any degree, diploma or other academic, technical or professional qualification relevant to the position'
- ✔ **Incompetence or poor performance:** Where an employee is simply incapable of delivering work to the required standard.
- ✔ **Illness:** Which prevents the employee from performing his or her duties

People with disabilities are protected from discrimination based on their disability. Don't dismiss an employee on the grounds of capability without following the correct procedure. Read more about this later in the chapter, in the section 'Following the Correct Procedure'.

Establishing the facts

Before dismissing an employee based on their lack of capability you have to show that you reasonably believed the employee was not capable of performing the job, following an investigation of the facts and circumstances.

Behaving reasonably

You have to tell the employee how they are not meeting the requirements of the job and give them the chance to improve before you can dismiss them fairly.

If an employee has an illness that prevents him or her from doing the job, you need to consider whether the illness could be a disability.

Under the Equality Act 2010, a person is classified as disabled if they have a physical or mental impairment that has a substantial and long-term effect on their ability to carry out normal day-to-day activities. *Long-term* is considered to be twelve months or more. Day-to-day activities include things such as using a telephone, reading a book or using public transport.

If an employee has a disability, you must consult him about any *reasonable adjustments* you could make to the work or the workplace, which would enable him to do the job. Reasonable adjustments include things like changes in lighting, access to the workplace or a variation of working hours. You should then make those adjustments and give the employee a chance to improve his performance before considering dismissal.

You can read more about reasonable adjustments in Chapter 7.

Following the correct procedure

Even if you can show that the employee is not capable of doing the job and you behave reasonably throughout the process, you must follow a *fair process*, or the dismissal will be considered unfair.

Helpful guidelines on fair process are provided by the Advisory, Conciliation and Arbitration Service (Acas). `http://www.acas.org.uk/media/pdf/f/m/Acas-Code-of-Practice-1-on-disciplinary-and-grievance-procedures.pdf`

Doing the wrong things: Conduct

This is more commonly expressed in the negative, as *misconduct*. Two levels of misconduct may justify your dismissal of an employee: misconduct and gross misconduct.

Differentiating between misconduct and gross misconduct

Misconduct at work is behaviour that the employer finds unacceptable. It could include, for example, an employee being repeatedly late for work, being absent from work without authorisation or being rude to customers or colleagues. You can include a list of examples in your disciplinary policy, but be clear that it may not be an exhaustive list.

Before dismissing an employee for this kind of misconduct, you need to follow the steps in your disciplinary procedure. Read more in Chapter 6.

So, if an employee is constantly, irritatingly late and you 'tell them off', but you don't take any formal action or give the employee any warnings, you can't suddenly fire them and expect to get away with it! Your actions would be considered unreasonable.

Follow your company disciplinary procedure, or use the statutory guidelines provided by Acas: `www.acas.org.uk/media/pdf/a/4/Discipline-and-grievances-Acas-guide.pdf`.

Gross misconduct is more serious, either because it has a significant negative impact on the business or on other people. Gross misconduct typically includes acts of theft, violence and using illegal drugs at work, for example. It could include employee refusal to follow a reasonable management instruction, if the consequences of the employee 'not following orders' was serious enough.

You may have a reason to dismiss an employee after one incident of gross misconduct.

You should tell your employees what constitutes gross misconduct in your business. You can write a list, as part of your Disciplinary Policy and Procedures (read more about this in Chapter 6).

Establishing the facts

Before dismissing an employee for misconduct you must establish a genuine belief that the employee has committed the act(s) of misconduct in question. Your belief must be based on reasonable grounds.

You have to carry out a full and thorough investigation into the circumstances of the misconduct, and consider any mitigating circumstances that might excuse the misconduct.

Behaving reasonably

A dismissal for misconduct will only be fair if it was

- ✔ A reasonable response by the employer
- ✔ Based on the facts known to the person making the decision to dismiss at the time of the dismissal.

If you dismiss the employee and she makes a claim to an Employment Tribunal for unfair dismissal, you will have to justify your decision.

The Employment Tribunal will consider whether dismissal was a reasonable response to the particular misconduct that caused you to fire the employee.

You can't dig out any of the employee's previous misconduct to justify your decision if you didn't consider it or refer to it at the time of the dismissal.

Following the right procedure

Even if you are justified in dismissing the employee for misconduct, you must follow a fair procedure.

Follow your own Disciplinary Policy or the statutory guidance provided by the Arbitration, Conciliation and Advisory Service (Acas): www.acas.org.uk/media/pdf/a/4/Discipline-and-grievances-Acas-guide.pdf.

Breaking the law: Contravention of a statutory duty

You can dismiss an employee if you or the employee would be breaking the law or if you would be in breach of statutory duties by continuing to employ that person.

A *statutory duty* is a duty imposed on you by law, for example in your capacity as an employer, or as a business or charity.

If you are dismissing an employee for breaking the law, you must still follow a fair process. Follow your own process or use the statutory guidance provided by Acas: www.acas.org.uk/media/pdf/a/4/Discipline-and-grievances-Acas-guide.pdf.

The following sections look at some common examples of breaching statutory duty in a business environment.

Health and safety

If you have a reasonable belief that an employee has put himself or others at work in danger by his actions, and following an investigation you find it to be true, you could dismiss the employee for breach of the Health and Safety Act.

The Health and Safety at Work Act 1974 places a statutory duty on employees to

- ✔ Take reasonable care for the health and safety of himself and of other persons who may be affected by his acts or omissions at work
- ✔ Co-operate with his employer, in fulfilling the employer's obligations under the Act

Driving

If you employ a sales person or driver who needs to drive a vehicle as part of her work and she loses her driving licence, you could dismiss her.

Investigate the reason for the loss of the license and ask for the evidence before deciding to dismiss an employee for losing her driving licence. If the employee has a suggestion, for example having a family member or friend driving her to appointments during the period of a driving ban, you may want to consider it. You can refuse if the cost of insurance or other factors mean it is not a viable option for the business.

Safeguarding of children and vulnerable adults

If your business is providing services to children and vulnerable adults and an employee's job requires him to have clearance from the Disclosure

Barring Service, you could dismiss the employee if he does not meet the requirements.

Information about the Disclosure Barring Service is provided at this government website:

```
www.isa.homeoffice.gov.uk/PDF/DBS%20Summer%202012%
20English%20leaflet%20web%20ready.pdf
```

Permission to work in the United Kingdom

All your employees must have permission to work in the UK, and you must collect the evidence when they join, even if they are British or European Union (EU) citizens.

If the employee comes from outside the EU, he must have a work visa.

If an employee has a visa to work in the UK, which then expires and is not renewed, you should dismiss this person as it would be illegal to continue to employ him.

You could be fined up to £20,000 for each illegal worker you employ and you could receive a prison sentence of up to two years. Read more about the penalties on the government website: www.gov.uk/penalties-for-employing-illegal-workers.

Your business no longer needs the employee's job: Redundancy

You can fairly dismiss an employee due to redundancy if there is a

- Reduced requirement for the work of a particular kind being carried out by the employee
- Cessation of business at the place where the employee is working
- Closure of the business as a whole

You could have a reduced requirement for the 'work of a particular kind' being carried out by an employee because, for example:

- Your business has lost a contract.
- You plan to stop offering a service that is provided by the employee.
- The sales are declining, and there is less work for the employee to do.

You could have a 'cessation of business' at the place where an employee is working if, for example:

- ✔ You are relocating all or some of the business to a new workplace.
- ✔ You are shrinking the business and closing a particular office, shop or other workplace.

If you have a mobility clause in an employee's contract, you may be able to move his or her job to a new location. If the employee refuses to work at the new location, you may not have to make a redundancy payment. Read about mobility clauses in Chapter 12.

If you are closing the whole business, there will be no job for the employee to do, so the job is redundant. If the business is insolvent you must still pay redundancy compensation to employees.

Establishing the facts

Write the *business case* for the potential redundancy. This is a description of the circumstances the business is facing and why you are considering redundancies. Include financial details, if possible, to support the business case. For example:

- ✔ A target annual cost saving that must be achieved
- ✔ The anticipated costs and savings from a proposed relocation
- ✔ The impact on sales of a proposed change of service level

Identify which job or jobs have a reduced requirement for 'work of a particular kind' because of the business circumstances.

Identify any other jobs that could be *affected by* a redundancy. An affected job is one that may change if the redundancies go ahead.

Always refer to the *job* being redundant, not the employee.

Behaving reasonably

In addition to the general principle of behaving reasonably, which applies in all dismissal situations, you must consult employees whose jobs are at risk of redundancy.

Consultation is a formal process when you ask the employee for ideas and suggestions about how to avoid redundancies, and you share the selection criteria you plan to use if redundancies are unavoidable.

You may also have to consult employees whose jobs are affected by the redundancy because of a knock-on effect on their jobs.

The consultation must be 'reasonable,' that is, for a reasonable length of time, and 'meaningful,' that is, with an open mind and the intention of mitigating the risk of redundancies.

If you have more than one job of a certain kind, you have to create a *selection pool* of the employees in those jobs. This is a formal process, and you must tell the employees whose jobs are in the pool that you will be selecting some of them for redundancy. Then you must go through a fair process to select which employee/s will be dismissed due to redundancy.

If you may make more than 20 jobs redundant in a 90-day period, you have to consult employees collectively as well as individually. For 20 or more redundancies, you must notify the Department of Business, Innovation and Skills (BIS).

Collective consultation is when you talk to employee representatives about your proposals and listen to their suggestions and answer their questions. There are rules about who can act as employee representatives. Read more about collective consultation, notification to BIS and employee representatives in Chapter 17.

You have to show that you have genuinely considered all other options and taken every reasonable measure to avoid redundancies before making a job redundant.

Redundancy pay

You have to pay employees who have more than two years' service at least the statutory redundancy payment if you dismiss them due to redundancy. The payment is calculated based on their age, weekly pay and length of service. The amount is revised by the government in April each year.

Go to the statutory redundancy calculator to find out what your employees are owed: www.gov.uk/calculate-employee-redundancy-pay

You can pay employees more than the statutory minimum. Any redundancy compensation you pay up to a maximum of £30,000 is tax-free to the employee.

If you have a redundancy payment policy you must treat all employees the same under the policy.

Following the right procedure

If you are dismissing an employee due to redundancy you must follow a fair process.

Follow your own process or use the statutory guidance for small scale redundancies found on the Acas website: www.acas.org.uk/index. aspx?articleid=4547

Dismissal for some other substantial reason

Some other substantial reason is one that allows employers to give a fair and substantial business reason why they need to dismiss an employee, which doesn't fall under the other four headings.

Examples of 'some other substantial reason' might include the following:

- An employee's unreasonable refusal to accept a change to pay or other terms of employment after a restructure in the business

- Pressure from a dissatisfied client or customer

- Conflict of interest, or a risk the employee may leak confidential information to a partner who works for a competitor

- An employee's failure to disclose his or her medical history, if it was requested at interview.

If you want to dismiss an employee for some other substantial reason, make sure you have all the facts, including:

- What the employee has allegedly done wrong

- The law that might have been broken

- The rules that apply in the circumstances

Once you have compiled these facts, consider if it would be reasonable for you to dismiss the employee in the circumstances.

Being automatically unfair

There are five fair reasons (shown earlier in this chapter) and a lot of _automatically unfair_ reasons for dismissal. An employee does not need a qualifying length of service with you to claim unfair dismissal if you fire them for any of these automatically unfair reasons:

- Time an employee takes off to care for dependents

- Employee request for flexible working

- Employee asking to be accompanied at a disciplinary or grievance hearing or acting as another worker's companion at a disciplinary or grievance hearing

- An employee's spent conviction (they've served their sentence and the relevant time limit to be allowed to take the conviction into account has expired)

✔ The transfer of an undertaking or a reason connected with it, unless for an economic, technical or organisational reason entailing changes in the workforce

✔ Trade union membership or non-membership or union activities, or participation in industrial action for a period of up to 12 weeks

✔ The employee's performance of duties as an occupational pension scheme trustee, as an employee representative, juror or reservist

✔ The employee taking action on health and safety grounds, or whistleblowing

✔ The employee asserting a statutory employment right, or refusing to do shop or betting work on a Sunday (if the business is a shop or betting place)

✔ It is also automatically unfair to select an employee for redundancy on any of the above grounds.

Getting It Right: Best Practice for Employee Dismissal

If you've read the rest of this chapter you may have picked up how important it is to behave reasonably and to follow a fair procedure when you are dismissing an employee for any reason. This section considers what is reasonable, and what steps to follow as best practice.

Passing the test of reasonable actions

The simplest way of testing whether you are behaving reasonably is to imagine standing in a court room with up to three Employment Tribunal members, who are a bit like magistrates, questioning you about your actions. What would they think about the case you've presented for dismissal?

If you are considering dismissing an employee, bear the following in mind:

✔ When inviting an employee to a meeting, give them reasonable notice, and arrange a time that fits with their work schedule.

✔ When investigating an allegation against an employee, keep an open mind and establish all the facts before making a decision.

✔ When dismissing an employee make sure you have all the facts, and remain objective.

✔ Make the 'punishment fit the crime' by taking proportionate action.

> ✔ Treat all employees consistently and fairly. Don't discriminate against people based on any protected characteristic, such as age, race or gender.

> ✔ When dismissing someone, give them the notice they are entitled to by law or in their contract, or pay them for it.

> ✔ Consider whether there is any other course of action short of dismissal that you could reasonably be expected to take.

Following the right procedure

At the very least, you must follow the statutory procedure, if you want to be sure that the dismissal is fair.

The minimum steps are as follows:

> ✔ Establish the facts

> ✔ Notify the employee in writing

> ✔ Hold a meeting with the employee allowing them to be accompanied

> ✔ Decide the action (in this case, dismissal)

> ✔ Give the employee the opportunity to appeal and hear the appeal

> ✔ Confirm the reason for dismissal in writing

To protect yourself during the dismissal process, you must:

> ✔ Justify your reasonable belief of facts or allegations which may lead you to dismiss the employee

> ✔ Behave reasonably

> ✔ Only use dismissal if it is a reasonable sanction in the circumstances

You can find the Acas code of practice here: `www.acas.org.uk/media/pdf/a/4/Discipline-and-grievances-Acas-guide.pdf`.

The employee has a right to

> ✔ Reasonable notice of meetings and procedures that might result in dismissal

> ✔ Be accompanied at meetings

> ✔ Put their point of view

> ✔ Appeal if they are dismissed

> ✔ Have the reason for the dismissal in writing from the employer
>
> ✔ Be paid for their contractual or statutory notice period unless they have been *summarily dismissed* (dismissed without notice, usually for gross misconduct)

If you think you may be at risk of dismissing someone unfairly, consider reaching an agreement with them instead of using an outright dismissal. Read more about taking this pragmatic approach in Chapter 17.

Dismissal for capability

If the dismissal is on the grounds of capability (see earlier in this chapter), use the following step-by-step guide to help you follow the correct procedure:

1. **Notify the employee that you are not satisfied with his performance.**

   Notify the employee in writing how his performance is falling short.

2. **Meet with the employee.**

   Invite the employee to a meeting to discuss his performance at work; give him examples of the standards you expect and how he is not meeting them; give the employee an opportunity to share his point of view. If the employee has an illness, you may need to get additional medical information; consider if the employee has a disability and any requirements for you to make reasonable adjustments to support the employee. Give the employee clear performance targets and deadlines to achieve them; set a date for another meeting; follow up by writing to the employee with all the details (repeat this step several times if necessary).

3. **Hold a capability hearing.**

   Invite the employee to a capability hearing, giving him reasonable notice, and the right to be accompanied; hold a capability hearing; give the employee an opportunity to explain why he has not improved his performance.

4. **Provide a written outcome and right of appeal.**

   Decide if dismissal is a reasonable outcome; write to the employee confirming the outcome is dismissal; give the employee the right of appeal; tell him to whom he should appeal and by when.

5. **Hear an appeal if required.**

   Arrange for someone who has not been involved previously to hear the appeal; follow up the appeal finding in writing.

Dismissal for misconduct

If the dismissal is due to misconduct (see earlier in this chapter), use the following step-by-step guide to help you follow the correct procedure:

1. **Notify the employee.**

   Notify the employee of the allegations against her; give the employee the opportunity to consider the allegations and any supporting evidence.

2. **Investigate the allegations.**

   Invite the employee to a meeting to investigate the allegations; give the employee an opportunity to answer the allegations and share her point of view; continue the investigation, interviewing witnesses if necessary, and gathering other evidence.

3. **Hold a disciplinary hearing.**

   Invite the employee to a disciplinary hearing, giving her reasonable notice, and the right to be accompanied; hold a disciplinary hearing; decide if the allegations are found to be true.

4. **Write to the employee to tell her the outcome and give her the right of appeal.**

   Decide if dismissal is a proportionate sanction (this will depend on your business rules, your disciplinary policy, and should be 'reasonable'); write to the employee confirming that the outcome is dismissal and the reason why; give the employee the right of appeal; tell her to whom she should appeal and by when.

5. **Hear an appeal if required.**

   Arrange for someone who has not been involved previously to hear the appeal; confirm the outcome of the appeal in writing.

Dismissal for redundancy

You must follow extra procedural steps if you plan to dismiss an employee due to redundancy. Please read Chapter 17 if you plan to dismiss one or more employees due to redundancy.

Dismissal at the end of a fixed-term contract

A *fixed-term contract* ends automatically at the end of the agreed term, or on the occurrence of a specified event, like the employee completing a project. You must serve the employee with his contractual notice if you want to dismiss someone who is on a fixed-term contract before the end of the fixed term.

If you don't have an early termination clause in the fixed-term contract and you dismiss the employee before the end of the fixed term, the employee can claim breach of contract.

If you dismiss an employee who is on a fixed-term contract, and who has two or more years' service, without giving him the contractual notice, the employee could claim breach of contract and unfair dismissal.

Notice periods

If your employee has more than four years' service when you dismiss her, you have to give her at least a week's notice for every year of service up to a maximum of 12 weeks.

Calculating the Cost of Getting It Wrong

If you dismiss an employee unfairly, he may make a claim to an Employment Tribunal up to three months after his employment termination date.

If the employee claim of unfair dismissal is successful you may have to

- Reinstate the employee in his job or a similar job
- Pay the employee's legal costs
- Pay the employee compensation

The Tribunal calculates a basic compensation amount based on the employee's age, weekly pay and length of service. The Tribunal also makes a compensatory award based on what the employee has lost by being dismissed.

The compensatory award is capped at one year of the employee's salary, or a maximum set by government every year (£78,335 as of April 2015).

If your actions are in breach of an employee's contract, for example by not serving him with the correct notice, you may have to pay up to £25,000.

If you haven't followed a fair process, the Tribunal can increase the compensation amount by up to 25%.

Part II

Maturing in Business: Moving from Managing People to Good HR Practice

Five Stages of HR Maturity

- If you are running a micro business you don't need a lot of rules and procedures. Get the basics in place and keep things simple and flexible.

- As soon as you employ a few more people, you can't personally keep track of all that's going on. Write some ground rules to treat everyone fairly and consistently, and to stay within the law.

- When your business gets bigger, and you hand over some of the management to other people, you surrender direct control. Create HR policies and procedures to keep everyone running in the same direction, and if necessary, to haul them in!

- With increasing maturity comes more complexity. Come up with creative ways to motivate, reward and develop your employees if you want to get the most out of them and keep them in the business for the longer term.

- There will be a tipping point when the volume of employee record keeping and reporting starts to slow you down. Take on a dedicated HR person or service so you can stay focused on the business.

Head to www.dummies.com/extras/hrforsmallbusinessuk for a free article on ways to handle underperformance.

Good HR Practice

In this part . . .

- Keep HR simple and fair
- Use HR tools to help people to do the right things
- Make a difference by using good HR practice

Chapter 6

Setting the Ground Rules

. . . .

In This Chapter
▶ Writing your own rules
▶ Keeping control of the basic policies
▶ Managing absent employees
▶ Writing policies that suit your business
▶ Enforcing you policies

. . . .

*E*very employer must follow, as a bare minimum, a number of statutory rules and procedures (such as paying at least the national minimum wage and providing a safe and healthy work environment). But your business is unique, and you want it to run well, so you may want to develop some of your own rules and policies. This chapter helps you to draw your own rules up fairly and professionally.

Writing Your Own Rules

Whether you employ 2 people or 22, watch out for tell-tale signs that you need to introduce some formal rules and policies.

Look out for the positive and negative indicators that your business is ready to climb another rung of the procedural ladder (and don't worry about that – having more procedures and policies in place usually makes your job a lot easier).

Take a look at Table 6-1. If you can find three or more factors in either column which apply to your business, it's time to start writing some new rules.

Table 6-1	Indicators That You Are Ready for Some New Rules
Positive indicators	*Negative indicators*
Your business has a good reputation and is growing	Your business is struggling to survive and grow
You are regularly recruiting new people	You have to pay new people more than the current employees, to attract them to work for you
	Employees are leaving after a short period of time working for you
	Managers seem to have different standards when they take on new employees
You have a good mix of age, ethnicity, gender and ability among your employees	Many of your employees have similar characteristics
Your business has grown big enough to have other people managing teams	The other managers are not always being consistent in how they treat employees
Your employees are keen to be trained and to progress in their careers	Your employees complain about lack of opportunity
	You have to go outside the business to recruit your managers
Your employees are performing very well and your business is in a competitive arena	Your employees have poor attendance and often come to work late
	You have had to dismiss employees for poor conduct or poor performance
There is a positive, flexible culture where everyone knows what is expected of them	Employees stick to their jobs and won't go the extra mile

In business, staying still is not an option. Even if you are happily ticking all the positive indicators now, put some policies in place before you encounter the inevitable people problems that will arise as you grow.

Shaping your culture through HR policies

In Chapter 3 we described how your personal values and ways of doing business shape the early culture of the business. In a growing and maturing business it will be impossible for you to keep your finger on every pulse.

If you want to protect and nurture the culture you have created, you need to:

- ✔ Let everyone know what you expect from them
- ✔ Delegate some of the management of employees to other people
- ✔ Reward and reinforce employees' positive behaviours
- ✔ Redirect or reprimand employees' negative behaviours
- ✔ Follow through with enforcing the rules
- ✔ Be consistent!

A few core policies form the HR skeleton of your business: they hold up the structure and support the day to day running of the business. These are:

- ✔ Health and Safety Policy
- ✔ Equal Opportunities Policy
- ✔ Disciplinary Policy
- ✔ Grievance Policy

Most of your rules are about what employees do while they are at work, but ironically, some of the most important policies – the ones that put flesh on the bones of your business culture – are the policies about absence!

You may need to write some specific policies for your business, depending on your activities and sector. These policies are like the clothing on the body of your business and are probably visible to outsiders as well as employees.

Making a safe and healthy workplace

You are responsible for protecting the physical and mental wellbeing of your employees while they are at work.

You are required by law to either display the Health and Safety Executive (HSE) approved law poster or to provide each of your workers with the equivalent leaflet: http://www.hse.gov.uk/pubns/books/lawposter.htm

Under the Health and Safety Act 1974, you have a legal obligation to write, implement and communicate a Health and Safety Policy, unless you have fewer than five employees.

And you have to consult your employees about health and safety policy, and tell them if you make any changes.

You must have a *statement of intent* including your commitment to:

- Maintaining a safe and healthy work environment, and to complying with health and safety laws
- Requiring managers and employees to fulfill their legal duties and responsibilities in relation to health and safety
- Regularly reviewing and, where necessary, revising the policy
- Implementing the policy
- Communicating the policy to your employees.

The policy statement must be signed and dated by a senior manager.

Implementation

A statement of intent could be very generic, but the implementation of your health and safety policy is particular to your business. You should specify how the policy will work as outlined in Table 6-2 (your business may need further conditions, of course).

Table 6-2   Health and Safety Topics To Cover in Your Policy

Day-to-day operations	People	Emergencies
Risk assessments (noise, height, new or expectant mothers, manual handling)	Consultation with employees	Accidents
Maintaining plant and equipment	Information and instruction to employees	First aid
Using display screen equipment (computers)	Supervision of employees	Ill-health issues
Safe handling and use of substances	Training, including promoting health and safety awareness	Fire
Providing personal protective equipment		
Machinery maintenance and breakdown		
Driving vehicles		
Monitoring		

Responsibilities

You must specify in your policy who will be responsible for making the health and safety policy happen.

The buck stops at the top of the business, so if you want to make other people responsible for key aspects of the policy, you must tell them and document it in writing. This is known as *delegated responsibility* in your policy.

In particular, make individual people (or the people doing specific jobs) responsible for:

- ✔ Fire safety
- ✔ First Aid
- ✔ Making sure electrical equipment is checked and certified
- ✔ Recording and reporting accidents
- ✔ Reviewing the policy at least once a year and communicating any changes to all employees

Communication

At a minimum you must communicate the statement of intent to all employees.

If there are particular risks in your business, tell employees about the risks, how you are managing them, and what the employees' responsibilities are to manage the risk.

For example, give information and instructions to warehouse staff about the risks of working at height, driving forklift trucks and lifting heavy goods.

You should review and update the policy if there is any significant change to the business, or if you introduce new work methods or equipment.

A senior manager should sign and date the policy when it is published, and every time it is reviewed, even if there are no changes.

Training

You must give training to all employees, to ensure that they can:

- ✔ Understand the health and safety policy
- ✔ Understand their own responsibilities under the health and safety policy
- ✔ Make suggestions for improvements to the policy
- ✔ Report risks or dangers in the workplace

The Health and Safety Executive provides very useful and accessible guidance on managing health and safety in the work place: `http://www.hse.gov.uk/business/index.htm`

Writing your Equal Opportunities Policy

Under the Equality Act 2010 you must ensure that workers are not treated less favourably, or discriminated against, on the basis of having a *protected characteristic*. This legal term is the name for the list of possible reasons why people may suffer less favourable treatment. Following are the protected characteristics:

- Age
- Race
- Pregnancy or maternity
- Disability
- Gender
- Gender reassignment
- Sexual orientation
- Marital or civil partnership status
- Religion or belief

The law protects not only employees but contractors, agency workers, and even potential employees. And if you're tendering for work in the public sector, or charity sector, you will be asked to provide a copy of your Equal Opportunities Policy.

You should have an Equal Opportunities Policy stating:

- Your commitment to ensuring equality, and avoiding discrimination
- That the policy applies to job applicants as well as employees
- That all employees are expected to follow the policy
- The procedure people should follow if they want to complain about discrimination
- That all forms of discrimination are prohibited
- The person who has overall responsibility for the policy in your business

You should give training to all employees and managers in how to apply the policy, and you should regularly review and update the policy.

You can read more about equal opportunities in Chapter 7 and on the Acas website here: `http://www.acas.org.uk/media/pdf/l/e/Acas_ Delivering_Equality_and_Diversity_(Nov_11)-accessible- version-Apr-2012.pdf`

Developing your disciplinary policy and procedure

Your disciplinary policy and procedure gives you a framework to follow when an employee is not performing to the standard you expect or behaving in the way they should at work. The purpose of the policy is to tell employees what you expect of them, and what action you will take if they do not meet your expectations.

Your aim should be to treat all employees consistently and fairly, and to give them a chance to improve their performance or conduct.

 Capability is the term used for an employee's ability to do the job. *Conduct* is the term used to describe behaviour at work.

 According to the Employment Law Act 2008, your disciplinary policy and procedures must be compliant with the statutory guidance:

`http://www.acas.org.uk/media/pdf/k/b/Acas_Code_of_Practice_ 1_on_disciplinary_and_grievance_procedures-accessible- version-Jul-2012.pdf`

Disciplinary policy

Your disciplinary policy should tell employees:

- ✔ That you will treat everyone fairly and consistently under the policy
- ✔ That where possible you will aim to resolve issues informally before starting a formal process
- ✔ What the business considers to be misconduct and gross misconduct
- ✔ What steps you will follow in the disciplinary procedure
- ✔ What sanctions or penalties you may impose on the employee
- ✔ If you have a different policy and procedure for managing capability and conduct
- ✔ The appeal process you will follow

Disciplinary procedure

Your procedure should have a minimum of three steps but you may have more:

1. **Investigation.**

   Find out what happened.

2. **Meeting.**

   Have at least one meeting to give the employee a chance to explain. Allow the employee to have a companion. Confirm the decision and the penalty to the employee in writing.

3. **Appeal.**

   Give the employee the chance to disagree with the decision and or the penalty. Ask someone else to hear the appeal and decide if the decision was fair and reasonable.

You can read more about the procedure in Chapter 7.

Disciplinary sanctions

The principle of disciplinary sanctions is that they are a reasonable and pro-portionate response to the employee's actions. The severity of the sanction, and how long a warning stays on an employee file usually increases with the seriousness or repetition of the misconduct or issue.

You should remove warnings from employee files after their expiry. You can't take warnings into account for future disciplinary action after their expiry date.

Verbal warning

This is a formal conversation, in which you tell the employee what they have done wrong, why you believe that a verbal warning is appropriate, and that you will make a note on their personal file that the conversation has taken place.

Follow up the conversation in writing, and tell the employee that if there are further incidents of misconduct or continuing poor performance, that you may take further disciplinary action.

You could use a verbal warning if you have already spoken to an employee informally for repeatedly turning up late to work, or for a minor breach of your company rules.

Usually a verbal warning stays on an employee file for up to 6 months.

First written warning

This is the first 'serious' sanction. You should describe the nature of the misconduct or performance issue, and whether the warning is following a verbal warning, or if it is the first warning. Tell the employee how long the warning will remain on their file, which is usually six months. Let the employee know that you may take further disciplinary action if there are further instances of misconduct or poor performance.

Give the employee the right to appeal the warning and tell them how to do it.

Second written warning

When you give a second written warning it should be for a repeat of something for which they have already been warned. You can't give a second written warning for poor timekeeping if the first warning was about smoking in the changing room. Include the same elements as a first warning - the reason, the possibility of further action and the right of appeal. Second written warnings are placed on an employee file for 6 or 12 months.

Final warning

Depending on the seriousness of the offence, you could issue a final warning at any stage in the disciplinary process, so it could be a first and final, a second and final, or just a plain final warning. It is one step short of dismissal so it is very serious. You need to warn the employee that a further disciplinary incident could lead to their dismissal.

These warnings are usually placed on the file for 12 months.

If you dismiss an employee without following your own disciplinary procedure, the employee can claim unfair dismissal at an Employment Tribunal. If you lose the case you will have to pay compensation to the employee.

You will have to pay up to 25% extra compensation just for not following the procedure.

Handling grievances from employees

A grievance policy and procedure gives your employees a framework to resolve concerns, problems or complaints they may have with you.

Grievances could include problems with terms and conditions of employment or working practices, health and safety, working relationships, bullying and harassment, or discrimination.

Your grievance policy and procedures must be compliant with the statutory guidance:

```
http://www.acas.org.uk/media/pdf/k/b/Acas_Code_of_Practice_
1_on_disciplinary_and_grievance_procedures-accessible-
version-Jul-2012.pdf
```

Your grievance policy should tell employees:

- ✔ That you will treat everyone fairly and consistently under the policy
- ✔ That where possible you will aim to resolve issues informally before starting a formal process
- ✔ What steps they should follow to raise a formal grievance and with whom
- ✔ If you have a different policy and procedure for managing whistleblowing, bullying and harassment or any other particular issues
- ✔ The appeal process you will follow

You should always aim to resolve issues informally first. Give your managers training in how to handle grievances informally and make sure that they are familiar with the grievance procedure.

Your grievance procedure should follow at least a three step process:

1. **Investigation.**

   Find out what happened/is happening. Ask the employee for details and evidence.

2. **Meeting.**

   Have at least one meeting with the employee to give them a chance to air the grievance. Allow the employee to have a companion. Decide if the employee has good reason for the grievance. Write to the employee with the findings and decision about the next steps.

3. **Appeal.**

   Give the employee a chance to disagree with the findings. Ask someone else to hear the evidence and review the decision.

Managing Employee Absence

As much as your employees love your business and idolise you as their boss (what else could they do, with you now having read *HR For Small Business For Dummies*?!), there will be times when they are not or cannot be in the office.

You will need to manage three main categories of employee absence:

- ✔ Holidays
- ✔ Sickness
- ✔ Other Authorised Leave

Managing holidays

Under the Working Time Regulations, you have to give workers a minimum of 5.6 weeks' paid holiday every year, including the statutory Bank Holidays.

This works out to 28 days per year for someone who works a 5 day week, breaking down as 20 days holiday and 8 bank holidays.

Workers include full time and part time employees, agency workers and casual staff. If you are using agency staff, the agency must pay the workers for their holiday. See the sidebar 'Casual workers and holidays' for more advice.

Calculating holiday entitlement

If someone works part time, the easiest way to calculate their holiday entitlement is to base it on the proportion of a 5 day week that they are working. Table 6-3 shows holiday entitlement at a glance.

Holiday year

The simplest way to manage holiday for all your employees is to decide when your holiday year will run. The most common holiday years run from January to December, or April to March. You could have each employee on their own holiday year, based on the anniversary of when they joined, but this is difficult to track once you have more than a handful of employees.

Casual workers and holidays

If you have casual workers, or people working on *zero hours contracts*, you must pay them for the holiday they accrue. If they are frequently working short, occasional hours, you can reconcile the holiday accrual on a monthly basis, and ask them to nominate a non-working day for which you will pay them the accrued holiday hours.

Zero hours contracts are contracts where there is no obligation for you to provide work to a worker, and no obligation for them to accept any work that you offer them. You can use zero hours contracts to avoid creating an employment relationship with the worker, but you still have to pay them for holiday. For more on zero hours contracts, please flick through to Chapter 12.

Table 6-3	Holiday Entitlement		
Status of worker	*Annual holiday entitlement*	*Monthly holiday entitlement*	*Hourly holiday entitlement*
Full time 5 days per week	28 days	2.33 days	
Full time 37.5 hours per week	210 hours	17.5 hours	
Part time 3 days per week	16.8 days	1.4 days	
Part time 22.5 hours per week	126 hours	10.5 hours	
Casual worker paid by the hour		x	6 minutes 30 seconds for every hour worked

You have to tell your employees in their contracts how much paid holiday they will have each year.

You can set rules about whether employees are allowed to 'carry over' any holiday they haven't taken in one year, into the next. Employers often allow employees to carry over a maximum of 5 days to the following holiday year, as long as they take the extra days off by a certain date.

If you have a rule about carrying over unused holiday, you should tell employees in writing that if they don't take the days off they will lose them, and you won't pay for them.

Holiday accrual

Holiday accrual is the term to describe how a worker builds up entitlement to paid holiday, over time.

You need to know how to calculate accrued holiday so that when an employee joins or leaves the business part way through the holiday year, you know how much holiday to give them.

As you can see from Table 6-3, if an employee is entitled to 28 days holiday per year, this accrues at the rate of 2.33 days per month.

You can make your own rules about how much holiday an employee must accrue before you allow them to take paid holiday, but if the employee leaves, you have to pay them for the holiday they have accrued up to their leaving date.

Employees on maternity, adoption or shared parental leave

Employees on maternity, adoption or shared parental leave accrue holiday during their absence as if they were still at work.

If an employee plans to take a year off for maternity or adoption leave, they will accrue the whole 28 days statutory entitlement to holiday (or more, if your holiday policy is more generous).

You can set the rules about when they should take the holiday, so you can spread the impact on your salary bill. Encourage employees to take some of the holiday before the period of maternity, adoption or shared parental leave, and some after. If their leave period crosses the end of a holiday year, you need to be clear about whether the employee is allowed to carry over their entitlement to the new holiday year.

Employees on sick leave

Employees on sick leave continue to accrue their statutory holiday entitlement no matter how long they are off. They can take paid holiday during a period of sick leave. If they take holiday during a period of sick leave you must pay them at their normal pay rate for the holiday days. Read more about this in Chapter 7.

Approval of holidays

You should tell employees in their contracts or in a policy or handbook how to request time off for holidays, and who will approve them.

Set up a holiday approval process that works for you, and meets the needs of the business:

- ✔ If your business is very busy at a certain time of year you can set rules about when people are allowed to have time off, and for how long.

- ✔ You can have informal or formal rules about who can be away at certain times, for example, only one person from the customer service team can be off at a time.

- ✔ You may need to have certain people covering for each other, so if one manager is away, the other must be working.

- ✔ You may have rules about who needs to work during the Christmas period, to make sure it's fair.

Minimum and maximum limits

You can set minimum and maximum periods of time that employees must take off. Some employers insist that every employee has at least one consecutive period of two weeks off. The cynical view of this arrangement is that it can flush out fraud, errors or other issues that would otherwise stay hidden. It also ensures that you don't get to the end of the year with all your employees desperate to take their outstanding holiday at once.

The more benevolent view is that having two weeks off is more refreshing for the employee.

If you have a policy that employees can take a maximum of two weeks at a time, providing cover in their absence is easier.

You'll inevitably have a request from an employee who wants to get married in Australia or climb Kilimanjaro and needs longer than two weeks. Manage these requests by exception rather than outlining an overall policy in your contracts.

Managing sickness absence

You must tell your employees within two months of them starting to work for you about the arrangements and their entitlement to pay during periods of absence due to injury or sickness.

The simplest way to do this is to include the details in the employment contract.

Statutory Sick Pay

As a minimum you must pay employees Statutory Sick Pay (SSP) for up to 28 weeks if they:

- Have an employment contract
- Have done some work under their contract
- Have been sick for 4 or more days in a row (including non-working days) - known as a 'period of incapacity for work'
- Earn the minimum threshold weekly pay
- Give you the correct notice
- Give you proof of their illness after 7 days off in the form of a *fit note* from their doctor

Employees can qualify for sick pay from more than one job. They could also qualify in one job but be fit for work in another, for example if one job is physical work that they can't do while ill, but the other is office-based.

SSP is set at a weekly limit by Her Majesty's Revenue and Customs (HMRC) and amended each year. Use the SSP calculator to check eligibility at `https://www.gov.uk/employers-sick-pay/eligibility-and-form-ssp1`

Company sick pay

You may offer more generous sick pay than the statutory minimum, which is capped at the same weekly pay for all employees.

Company sick pay schemes are usually based on an employee's actual weekly pay and specify how many weeks you will pay the employee's salary while they are off sick.

You can offer varying levels of company sick pay based on how long people have been working for your business. And you can pay full pay for a certain number of weeks followed by reduced pay, most commonly half pay, for another period.

It's very common for small employers not to pay company sick pay during an employee's probation period.

If you offer company sick pay, you can specify that it is inclusive of the employee's entitlement to statutory sick pay. You can't offer company sick pay that is lower than statutory sick pay

Notice

Set the time limit within which the employee has to tell you that they are sick. Most commonly it is within one hour of their normal start time.

You don't have to pay Statutory Sick Pay if the employee doesn't meet your notice requirements.

Self certification

Ask employees to complete a self-certification form when they return to work, to confirm why they were off sick.

You can create a form, or use the HMRC template:

`https://www.gov.uk/government/publications/statutory-sick-pay-employees-statement-of-sickness-sc2`

Fit notes

You can ask the employee for a fit note from their doctor after 7 days off sick.

The *fit note* is a statement of fitness for work from the employee's doctor stating that they are fit for work, or not fit for work. They may be fit for work of a certain kind, and the GP should advise if there are any limitations on what the employee is fit to do, and the period of time covered by the fit note. The maximum period covered by a fit note is three months.

If an employee has an illness that becomes a disability, you may have to make reasonable adjustments to enable them to come back to work. These adjustments could be shorter working hours or providing special equipment, for example.

Return to work interviews

If you or one of your managers has a return to work interview with every employee after they have been off sick, even if they've only been off for one day, it has a huge impact on absence levels. People are less likely to take a sneaky Friday or hangover Monday if they have to look their manager in the eye and tell a lie about why they were off.

Keep records of employee absence, and the reasons they were absent, so that you can spot any patterns. You may need to take disciplinary action, and your records could form part of the evidence.

You can consider employees who are off work sick for more than 4 weeks as *long-term sick*. As a last resort, you could dismiss an employee who is long-term sick, based on their lack of capability to do the job, but you must follow a fair process before dismissing an employee due to sickness.

If an employee has frequent short term sickness absences, you should talk to the employee, investigate the reasons, and you could request a letter from their doctor to seek an explanation.

Under the Access to Medical Reports Act 1988 and the Data Protection Act 1998, you must have the employee's express permission to request information from their GP.

Write to the employee's doctor and ask if there are any factors about the employee's health which you need to take into account to enable the employee to work. Give the GP as much information as possible about the nature of the work so he or she can take an informed view.

You have a duty of care as an employer to not discriminate against an employee with a disability. Some recurring medical conditions such as depression and epilepsy can be categorised as disabilities.

If you suspect that an employee's frequent absences are not due to genuine sickness, you should advise the employee of your intention to start disciplinary proceedings. Follow the correct disciplinary procedure, covered earlier in this chapter, including the investigation, hearing and appeal steps.

If you dismiss an employee on long term sick or for frequent periods of absence without following a fair process, they could claim unfair dismissal or discrimination at an Employment Tribunal. Read more about this in Chapter 5.

Allowing other time off work

You are legally obliged to give employees time off for a variety of reasons, as outlined in the following sections.

Carrying out public duties

Employees can ask for reasonable time off if they are Justices of the Peace, members of a local authority, police authority or health body, or school/college governors. You can decide if you want to pay them during this time off.

Jury service

You could be in contempt of court if you refuse to provide employees with time off for jury service. You don't have to pay employees while they are on jury service. They can claim loss of earnings and travel expenses from the court, up to a maximum limit.

Trade union duties and activities

Acas provides guidance on time off for union duties and activities for employees who are union officials and union members. You will have to pay for some of the time, but you can make some of the time unpaid.

Read the Acas guidance here: `http://www.acas.org.uk/index.aspx?articleid=2391`

Military training and service

Military reservists may be called to serve in the armed forces but they will be paid by the Ministry of Defense. You can claim financial assistance to cover the costs of releasing a reservist for armed service.

Read more about military service on the Sabre website: `http://www.sabre.mod.uk/Employers/Employing-a-Reservist/Your-rights-and-responsibilities#.VPihn_msXZc`

Parental leave

Women employees have statutory rights to paid maternity leave. Fathers and adoptive parents have statutory rights to paid adoption leave and paternity leave and, from April 2015, may be entitled to shared parental leave. Paternity and adoption leave rights also apply to partnerships of the same sex. You can read more about maternity, paternity, adoption and shared parental leave in Chapter 7.

In addition to maternity, paternity or adoption leave, qualifying employees have the right to take a total of 13 weeks' unpaid leave during the first five years of their child's life.

They can take up to four weeks a year in one week blocks.

Personal and domestic leave

You can decide whether you will give employees time off, paid or unpaid, for personal reasons such as bereavement or illness, or domestic emergencies like fire, flooding or burglary.

Employees have a statutory right under the Employment Relations Act 1996 to take reasonable time off to make arrangements to care for dependents in certain emergencies, and to make funeral arrangements for dependents and attend their funerals.

A *dependent* can be:

✔ The employee's spouse or civil partner, child, parent or someone who lives in the same house (but not a lodger or tenant), or

✔ Any person who reasonably relies on the employee for assistance when they fall ill, are injured or assaulted, or to make arrangements for their care in the event of their illness or injury

What is 'reasonable' is not specified in the legislation as it will depend on the circumstances. One or two days would probably be long enough to deal with most typical emergencies such as making arrangements for a sick child.

The employee is not entitled to have the time off for the whole period of the emergency, only to make appropriate arrangements to deal with it.

Medical and dental appointments

Employees have no statutory right to time off to attend medical or dental appointments. You could ask employees to make up the time they take off, or use some of their holiday. Alternatively you could give the employee unpaid leave.

However, pregnant employees are entitled to paid time off for antenatal care.

Time off for study or training

If employees are pursuing professional qualifications or specialist training from which the business will ultimately benefit, you may want to write a policy giving employees paid or unpaid time off for study and exams.

Employees may also ask for flexible working arrangements to enable them to pursue training courses.

Time off for religious festivals

You are not legally obliged to give employees time off for religious festivals, but if they request holiday to celebrate a festival, and you refuse it without a very good business reason, you could be in breach of the Equality Act.

Time off to look for alternative employment

If you have given an employee notice that their job is redundant, they are entitled to reasonable paid time off to look for other employment. This is usually time off for job interviews.

Writing the Policies Your Business Needs

On top of all the basic policies that keep you legally straight, you may need some rules that are specific to your business. This section looks at some of the most common policies you might want to have in place, but we've also included sidebars for two special cases: Following the Regulations, for financial or professional services, and for care, education, and security.

Following the regulations: Financial or professional services

If your business is performing a *controlled function* or a regulated activity that is specified in the Financial Services and Markets Act, you will need a policy and procedure for recruiting and managing *Approved Persons*. These are people who exert significant influence in relation to a controlled function.

Read more on the Financial Conduct Authority (FCA) website:

```
http://www.fca.org.uk/firms/
being-regulated/approved/
approved-persons/functions
```

If your business is providing non-financial professional services, you may want a policy requiring employees to maintain professional memberships or continuing professional development *(CPD)*.

Protecting people: Care, education and security

If your business is providing services to children or vulnerable adults - the elderly or disabled, for example – you will need a policy and procedure about carrying out background checks before employing people.

Read the guidance here:

```
https://www.gov.uk/disclosure-
barring-service-check/overview
```

If you employ people to provide security, for example door staff or security guards on your premises, you will need a policy and procedure for screening potential security employees. Read the guidance here:

```
http://www.cpni.gov.uk/
documents/publications/
2009/2009024-gpg_pre_
employment_screening.pdf
```

Protecting personal data

If you keep electronic data on employees or customers, you must follow the provisions of the Data Protection Act and put a procedure in place to protect those peoples' privacy.

The data must be secure, accurate and up to date.

If you handle personal data you must register with the Information Commissioner's Office or you could face a criminal charge. Register here:

```
https://www.gov.uk/data-protection-register-notify-ico-
personal-data
```

Upholding intellectual property

If your employees are developing new software, designing products, writing material, or doing any other work that involves the creation of intellectual property (IP), you will need a policy to protect your business IP.

The government intellectual property office (IPO) provides a step by step guide to identifying and protecting your intellectual property: `http://www.ipo.gov.uk/blogs/equip/how-to-identify-business-assets`

Stopping employees from taking your clients or customers

If you employ sales people, specialists, or people providing a person service like hair stylists, there is a risk that when they leave your employment they could 'poach' your clients or customers.

You can put a clause in their employment contract, called a *post termination restriction*, preventing the former employee from stealing your clients. Often this clause applies for up to one year after the employee leaves your business.

You must not impose unreasonable restrictions or time limits, because that would constitute 'restraint of trade' and stop the person from earning a living.

Keeping expenses under control

If your employees are incurring business costs, for example paying for travel to meetings with clients, stationery, or overnight accommodation, write a policy to tell employees what expenses you will reimburse. Tell employees how to claim expenses and when you will pay them.

Tax rules explain how expenses should be treated, and you should follow the HMRC guidance to understand any tax liability arising for you or the employee:

https://www.gov.uk/expenses-and-benefits-a-to-z

Deciding the dress code

If you feel strongly about how your employees are dressed while they are working, write a dress code. It takes only a short time to write and saves you lots of time having conversations with people about how they are dressed.

Avoid any requirements in your dress code which could discriminate directly or indirectly against any groups or individuals.

Read Acas' sartorial guidelines here: http://www.acas.org.uk/index.aspx?articleid=4953

Setting the rules about drugs and alcohol at work

You have obligations under the Health and Safety at work Act 1974, The Transport and Works Act 1992, and The Misuse of Drugs Act 1971 to manage how your employees consume alcohol and drugs at work.

If you write a policy you should focus on

- ✔ Prompt action and support for employees
- ✔ Education for managers to spot problems
- ✔ Being consistent in how you treat employees who are using drugs or alcohol at work

Read the Acas guidance on drugs and alcohol here: `http://www.acas.org.uk/index.aspx?articleid=1986`

Enforcing the Rules

Rules are only valuable if they are kept. If employees break the rules you have set, you should take action.

- ✔ If you are in doubt about the facts of the case, investigate.
- ✔ Depending on how serious the rule breaking is, have an informal word with the employee, or start formal disciplinary proceedings.
- ✔ Follow the steps in the statutory disciplinary procedure, or your company disciplinary procedure.
- ✔ Decide on the sanction or next steps based on

  - What you said in your policy - for example give an informal warning for wearing flip flops if your dress code says you will

  - Having a reasonable response - for example giving an employee a few more days to submit an expenses claim before refusing to reimburse it

  - Being consistent - treat all employees the same under your policies

  - Keeping on the right side of the law - always meet your statutory obligations

To read more about enforcing the rules, flip the page and take a look at Chapter 7.

Chapter 7

Keeping Things Fair

. . . .

In This Chapter

▶ Knowing the rights of your employees

▶ Understanding contracts and equality

▶ Following statutory procedures and creating your own ones

. . . .

The biggest fear of many small employers is that they will have to go to an employment tribunal and defend their actions, and then pay out loads of money on legal fees and compensation. This chapter takes you through the basics of employment law, so you can avoid most of the potential pitfalls. There will always be complex situations where you need specialist legal advice, and when they do arise, it's always better to call in an expert, but this chapter is a good place to start understanding some of the legal principles.

Knowing Your Employees' Rights

A *contract* is a written or spoken agreement that is intended to be enforceable by law. Every one of your employees should have a contract, which helps to define their rights when working for you.

You create an *employer relationship* with someone when you make an offer of a job, and the other person accepts. It's at this stage they become your employee.

Knowing and respecting your employees' rights will help you to:

✔ Create a positive work environment and boost employee performance

✔ Avoid stress for you and your employees

✔ Save a lot of your time

✔ Avoid the cost of compensation payments and legal fees

✔ Protect the reputation of the business.

The trouble with employment contracts is that there are lots of aspects which are enforceable by law, even though they are not written into individual contracts. Read on to find out more.

If in doubt, check out the Acas website www.acas.org.uk or call their helpline on 0300 123 1100. If you have a very tricky question, the Acas helpline advisors may not be able to answer it, but they will advise you that you need to talk to an employment lawyer.

 You may also have people carrying out work for you without them being an employee. Usually known as *workers,* they also have legal rights. Knowing when to treat people as employees or workers will keep you and your business on the right side of the law.

Grasping the fundamentals

Your employees' and workers' rights arise from UK common law, UK employment law and European regulations, and broadly fall into the following categories:

- ✔ Equality of opportunity and treatment
- ✔ Terms and conditions including pay and working hours
- ✔ Time off work
- ✔ Parents' and carers' rights
- ✔ Representation
- ✔ Redundancy, retirement or transfer

 Some employees' rights are explicit in an employment contract, and others are implied:

- ✔ Explicit contractual terms usually spell out the details such as pay, benefits, time off, and company policies.
- ✔ Implied terms may be dictated by common sense, for example, somebody living in India can't fulfill an employment contract for a window cleaning job in Wolverhampton.

An often quoted implied term of an employment contract is one of *mutual trust and confidence* between an employer and employee, which simply means that both parties trust the other, for example not to steal, and not to be violent. The term is most commonly bandied about when the mutual trust and confidence has broken down!

An implied term which has gained some notoriety in industrial relations disputes, particularly in the public sector, is *custom and practice*. This term describes a situation where an aspect of work has become so ingrained that the employer or the employee could reasonably expect that it has become a contractual term. A fairly common example is a 4pm finish time on Fridays, even though the written employment contract stipulates that the working day finishes at 5pm.

Recruiting legally

If you make an offer of a job and the person starts work, you have created an employment contract, which is legally binding.

You must give a new employee certain information about their contract straight away, and other information no later than eight weeks after they start working for you. You can read more about this in Chapter 14.

Withdrawing an offer of employment

If you change your mind and withdraw the offer before the employee starts work, the employee can ask you to pay them for the notice period they would have had in the contract.

If you refuse to pay the employee for the notice period, they could take you to:

- ✔ A civil court and claim breach of contract under common law
- ✔ An employment tribunal and claim wrongful dismissal under employment law

If you lose the case you may have to pay the employee's legal fees as well as the amount you owe them under the contract.

Not making an offer of employment

Applicants for jobs are protected by the Equality Act 2010 all the way through the process, from advertising, through short listing, interviews, any selection tools that you use, to the point of you making a job offer.

Even before someone becomes an employee, you could directly or indirectly discriminate against them, in the way that you do your recruitment:

- ✔ You *directly discriminate* against people if you have selection criteria which would prevent someone with a *protected characteristic* from meeting the requirements of the job. There is a list of protected characteristics later in this chapter in the section 'Providing Equal Opportunities'.

For example, you are directly discriminating against younger and older people if you specify that job applicants should be aged between 20 and 25.

✔ You *indirectly discriminate* against people if they would be less likely to meet the criteria you have set, or be at a disadvantage compared to other candidates, because of a protected characteristic.

For example, if you specify that applicants must live in a certain post code, you may indirectly discriminate against people of certain ethnic origin, religion or belief because they are less likely to be living in that area.

If you don't offer a job to a candidate and they think that you have unfairly discriminated against them, they can make a claim to an employment tribunal, even though they are not your employee. And you may be found guilty even if you accidentally discriminate against people.

There is no upper limit on the amount of compensation you may have to pay if you lose a discrimination case.

Requiring an occupational qualification

If a particular job has very specific requirements that could only be met by a certain type of person, or an *occupational qualification,* you can legally discriminate against people who don't meet the requirements.

For example, a charity employing a counsellor for victims of rape could specify that the role must be done by a woman.

In order to avoid someone claiming that you are being discriminatory, you need to demonstrate (ultimately, if it goes that far, to an employment tribunal) that the occupational qualification is proportionate and necessary for the effective performance of the job.

Base your recruitment decisions solely on objective criteria that are relevant to the job in question, such as competencies, experience, qualifications and skills.

Specifying terms and conditions

You must specify certain terms and conditions in a written statement to employees, which you can read about in Chapter 14. This is known as the *Statement of Employment Particulars.*

Flexible working

Employees who have worked for you for 26 weeks or more have a legal right to request changes to their working conditions, specifically the length and times of their working hours, and their place of work. This is known as a _flexible working request_.

You have to consider the request, and respond within certain time parameters, but you do not have to accept the request. Read more about the procedure for handling flexible working requests later in this chapter in the section 'Following the statutory procedure'.

Pay

Employees and workers have rights about pay, which determine how much and how often you must pay them in various circumstances. This is covered later in this chapter in the section 'Paying fairly'.

Working hours

You must specify an employee's working hours and normal days of work in a contract of employment.

You must also specify whether the employee will be paid for working hours above their contractual weekly hours, and if so at what rate.

Working time regulations

Workers, which is a broad category including employees, agency workers and contractors, have a right not to work more than a 48 hour week on average, over a 17 week period. This right comes from a European Directive: The Working Time Directive; `https://www.gov.uk/maximum-weekly-working-hours/overview`.

If you want workers to work longer hours you must ask them to opt out of these rights, in writing. You can do this by adding a clause into the employment contract, or by asking workers to sign a separate opt out document.

If a worker opts out of the working time regulations, they can change their mind, and opt back in, as long as they give you either 7 days' notice, or up to three months' notice, if they have signed an agreement to give you a specified period of notice.

Workers who are 16 or 17 years old can't normally work more than 8 hours a day or 40 hours a week. You can't average out their hours over the week, and they can't opt out of this rule.

Driving by the rules

If you employ drivers, security guards travelling in a vehicle, or backup driving crew, they are classed as *mobile workers*.

The rules for employers of mobile workers may be found online: `https://www.gov.uk/drivers-hours/rules-for-employers`

You must ensure that they do not exceed the limits of driving hours and breaks between periods of duty. You must keep records of their working hours for up to two years.

Working on Sundays

A person can't be made to work on Sundays unless they and their employer agree and put it in writing. This includes shop and betting shop workers unless Sunday is the only day they have been employed to work on.

An employee can opt out of Sunday working at any time, even if they have agreed to work on Sundays in their contract. The employee must give you 3 months' notice that they want to opt out of Sunday working. They must continue to work on Sundays during the 3 month notice period if you want them to.

If you need employees to work on Sundays you must tell them of their right to opt out, within two months of their start date. If you don't confirm their right to opt out, they will only have to give you one month's notice of opting out.

You don't have to pay a higher rate to employees working on Sundays unless you have agreed to it in the contract.

Working at night

Workers who regularly work more than 3 hours between 12pm and 6am, or who are likely to work some of their annual contracted hours during the night, are *night workers*.

You must make sure that night workers don't work more than an average of 8 hours in a 24-hour period, and keep records of night workers' hours for at least two years. Workers can't opt out of this working limit.

Night workers have a right to a health assessment before you can ask them to work nights, and regularly thereafter. You can find out more here: `https://www.gov.uk/night-working-hours/health-assessments`

Giving time off work

Workers have lots of rights for time away from work, as well as their rights at work. After all, we all need a break now and again.

Paid holiday

Workers have the right to:

- ✔ A minimum of 5.6 weeks paid holiday time per annum
- ✔ *Accrue* (build up) holiday entitlement during maternity, adoption and shared parental leave
- ✔ Accrue holiday entitlement while off work sick
- ✔ Choose to take holiday at the same time as sick leave

5.6 weeks equates to 28 days for a full time worker on a 5 day week. If someone works 6 days per week, the holiday entitlement is still 28 days minimum. If a worker leaves your employment without taking all their accrued holiday, you have to pay them for the days they have accrued but not taken

You can include statutory bank holidays in the total of 5.6 weeks holiday, so you don't have to give the bank holidays as extra time off. You may also ask workers to work on bank holidays as long as you give them other paid days off instead.

You can set the rules about how much notice employees have to give to request holidays, and when they are allowed to take holiday. Read more about this in Chapter 6.

Public and other duties

Employees have rights to time off work, some of which must be paid, to perform public, union and military reservist duties. This is covered in more detail in Chapter 6.

Parental and personal leave

Eligible employees who become pregnant, adopt a child or become the father of a child, or who have responsibilities to care for dependents have rights to paid and unpaid leave. Read more later in this chapter in the section 'Managing parents' and carers' rights'.

Antenatal appointments

Pregnant workers are entitled to paid time off for antenatal appointments. Expectant fathers or the partner (including same sex) of a pregnant woman are entitled to take unpaid time off work to accompany the woman to up to 2 of her antenatal appointments.

You may read the full guidelines for employers here:

```
https://www.gov.uk/government/uploads/system/uploads/
attachment_data/file/361292/bis-14-1063-time-off-to-
accompany-a-pregnant-woman-to-ante-natal-appointments-
employer-guide.pdf
```

Managing parents' and carers' rights

As a small employer, managing parents' and carers' rights sometimes proves quite challenging and may seem unduly onerous. However, it will ultimately save you time, money and stress if you manage these rights well.

Pregnant employees have four main rights:

- ✔ Paid time off for antenatal care
- ✔ Maternity leave
- ✔ Maternity pay or maternity allowance
- ✔ Protection against unfair treatment, discrimination or dismissal

Antenatal care isn't just medical appointments; it also includes antenatal or parenting classes if a doctor or midwife has recommended them.

You can't change a pregnant employee's contract terms and conditions without agreement; if you do you will be in breach of contract.

Risk assessments for new or expectant mothers

If an employee tells you she is pregnant, or has just returned from maternity leave, you must carry out a risk assessment to determine if there are any risks to her health in the workplace that you will need to manage or remove.

If you can't manage or remove significant risks, or provide any suitable alternative work, you must suspend the pregnant employee on full pay.

The Health and Safety Executive provide guidance on how and when to carry out a risk assessment for new and expectant mothers here: `http://www.hse.gov.uk/mothers/faqs.htm#q4`

Maternity and adoption leave

Pregnant employees have a right to take up to 52 weeks of *statutory maternity leave* (SML) no matter how long they have been working for you.

Employees can take up to 52 weeks of *statutory adoption leave* (SAL), if they have been employed by you for at least 26 weeks on the date when they are matched with a child.

The employee must give you the right notice period to request SML or SAL, and must meet certain criteria for some or all of their statutory maternity or adoption leave to be paid.

Statutory Maternity Leave and Statutory Adoption Leave is split into several periods for the purpose of leave, pay and employee rights: check out Table 7-1 for the lowdown.

Table 7-1		**Statutory Maternity Leave and Statutory Adoption Leave**			
	First 2 weeks after the baby is born	*First 6 weeks*	*First 26 weeks*	*First 39 weeks*	*Second 26 weeks*	*Total 52 weeks*
Legal term	Compulsory maternity leave	x	Ordinary Maternity Leave, Ordinary Adoption Leave	x	Additional Maternity Leave Additional Adoption Leave	Statutory Maternity Leave Statutory Adoption Leave
Pay	x	90 per cent of normal pay or SMP if they qualify	Statutory maternity or Statutory adoption pay if they qualify	Statutory maternity or Statutory adoption pay if they qualify	x	x
Work and Job rights	Employee not legally allowed to work	x	Right to return to their exact job and terms and conditions	x	Employee right to return to a similar job and no less favourable terms and conditions	x

Apart from normal pay, you must continue to provide all of the employee's contractual terms – for example holidays and benefits – during Statutory Maternity leave and Statutory Adoption Leave.

If you have a pay review for all employees while someone is off on maternity, adoption or shared parental leave, you must include them in the review. Similarly, if you make changes in the business, especially if they would affect an employee who is off on maternity or adoption or shared parental leave, you must notify them, and if appropriate, consult them about the changes.

Employees can take up to ten *keeping in touch* (KIT) days during maternity or adoption leave without losing any entitlement to maternity or adoption pay. You don't have to offer any KIT days and the employee doesn't have to accept them.

Shared parental leave

Parents of babies born, or children adopted, after 1st April 2015 may be entitled to share the time off work, and the statutory pay.

If both parents are eligible for either statutory maternity or adoption leave or pay, they can split the total 52 weeks of leave and pay between them.

Read the government guidance for employers here: `https://www.gov.uk/shared-parental-leave-and-pay-employer-guide/eligibility`

Time off for emergency care for dependents

Employees have a right to time off for emergency care of dependents but you don't have to pay them. There is no limit on how many times an employee can request emergency time off but you can investigate and may be able to take disciplinary action if the employee's work is affected.

You can read more about how to manage this delicate situation in Chapter 6.

Parental leave

Employees who have worked for you for longer than a year and have parental responsibility for a child under 5 (or under 18 if the child is disabled) can take up to 18 weeks unpaid parental leave before the child's 5th (or 18th) birthday.

Adoptive parents can take parental leave up to the 5th anniversary of a child being placed with them or the child's 18th birthday, whichever comes first.

While your employee is off work, all their employment rights are protected. You can ask for proof of parental responsibility, for example a birth or adoption certificate. The employee must request the time off with at least 21 days' notice.

The employee can take a maximum of 4 weeks parental leave in one year, and must take it in blocks of at least one week at a time. You can ask the employee to delay taking the parental leave, if it will have a critical impact on the business, but within 7 days you must suggest an alternative time for the leave. The new date must be within 6 months of the original request, and you can't change the length of time they have requested.

The government's guidance for employers regarding parental leave can be read here: `https://www.gov.uk/parental-leave`

Managing employee representation and industrial action

You have a general duty to inform and consult employee representatives about health and safety matters, collective redundancies, business transfers and pension scheme changes.

Employees may elect representatives directly or use a union to represent their interests. Elected representatives are entitled to paid time off work to perform their duties, and if necessary, to get appropriate training so that they can perform their duties. Read more about how to consult employee representatives in Chapter 15.

Union recognition

If you employ more than 20 people and more than 10 per cent of the workforce are members of a union, they can ask for that union to be *recognised* in the workplace. This is a formal status which gives the union certain rights.

Industrial action

Employees who are members of a recognised trade union have a right to take industrial action, or go on strike, and not to be in breach of their employment contract. For industrial action to be lawful there must be:

- ✔ *A trade dispute*: a dispute between you and your workers about employment-related issues
- ✔ A properly-conducted industrial action ballot
- ✔ A written notice of industrial action sent to you

Advice from the government about how to handle industrial action can be found here: `https://www.gov.uk/if-your-business-faces-industrial-action/lawful-industrial-action`.

Managing redundancy, retirement and transfers

Employees who are at risk of redundancy have a number of rights about being consulted and about how much you have to pay them. Chapter 17 goes into more detail about managing employee redundancy.

Employees have a right to choose when they retire: if you try to force an employee to retire, you run the risk of unfair dismissal and direct age discrimination. If you try to impose a compulsory retirement age for a justifiable business reason, the age should be the same for men and women.

It is extremely difficult to prove an objective justification for a compulsory retirement age.

Employees who transfer into or out of your business as a result of one business being acquired, merged with or sold by another, have a lot of employment rights under the Transfer of Undertakings Regulations. This is covered in more detail in Chapter 12.

Avoiding the common pitfalls

As you can see, you'll have a lot to remember when it comes to your employees' and workers' rights. We've pulled together some of the key points to remember in Table 7-2. That's right, we're just too kind.

Table 7-2	Staying on Top of Employee Rights
Head in the sand	You will never win a tribunal or court case using ignorance of the law or ignorance of the facts of a case as an excuse.
	If in doubt, use online resources to check your legal obligations as an employer. Start with the gov.uk website or go to acas.org.uk.
	Establish the facts. If an employee claims time off, payment or wants to exercise other rights, you are usually within your rights to ask for evidence of their entitlement.

Look before you leap	If an employee makes a request, and you are unsure of their entitlement, don't answer straight away.
	There are often rules about how much notice an employee must give when making requests for time off, or to exercise many of their rights.
	If you don't have your own procedure, check acas.org.uk for the statutory procedure.
	You may be able to refuse or delay certain requests for business reasons.
A stitch in time	Every year, usually in April or October, the government publishes information about the national minimum wage, statutory maternity pay, and threshold earnings limits.
	Make sure you apply the new rates.
	Subscribe to the Acas newsfeed: `https://obs.acas.org.uk/subscription`
	This will alert you to changes in the law, for example about pensions, or shared parental leave.
One step at a time	Employee rights can appear to be very complex but there is always a statutory procedure to follow.
	Follow the statutory procedure if you don't have one of your own.
	Focus particularly on the deadlines for notifications and when you must respond to employee requests.
	The request won't go away, and if you deal with it correctly you will ultimately save time and avoid legal and other costs.

Playing Fair At Work

There are lots of sporting analogies which could be applied to the workplace. You may have heard employees grumbling about you 'moving the goal posts' or not giving them a 'level playing field'. The great British tradition of fair play is summed up in the phrase 'that's not cricket'.

Some of the rules and behaviours are more obvious than others, and just like in cricket, there are some arcane rules that occasionally surface, and only an experienced umpire could be expected to know how to apply them.

Broadly speaking, if you pay fair and play fair you will avoid most of the serious penalties of hitting your own wicket . . . sorry, getting it wrong.

Paying fairly

In employment as in the rest of life, people get grumpy when they find out that other people have more than them. As an employer, you often have to manage the perception of fairness as much as the reality, but with pay, there are some very important rules you must follow:

✔ You must pay at least the National Minimum Wage, which is an hourly rate on a sliding scale relating to age, and updated in October each year.

You can calculate whether you are paying the NMW and whether you

owe any back payments using the government calculator here:

https://www.gov.uk/minimum-wage-calculator-employers

✔ You should have a policy of paying men and women at the same rate for the same or equivalent work. You can read more about how to compare jobs and manage equal pay claims in Chapter 16.

✔ Employees who are not able to work due to illness or injury may qualify for statutory sick pay after four days of absence. If the employee meets the eligibility criteria, you have to pay them Statutory Sick Pay (SSP) on their normal pay day. You may read the government's guidance on sick pay here: https://www.gov.uk/employers-sick-pay/overview

✔ Employees who become parents are legally entitled to paid time off work if they meet certain criteria. Read all about it in Chapter 4.

Providing equal opportunities

There are good legal and business reasons for providing equal opportunities in your workplace.

Legal reasons

Under the Equality Act 2010 you are legally obliged to:

✔ Protect employees from discrimination because of age, disability, gender reassignment, marriage and civil partnership, pregnancy and maternity, race, religion or belief, sex and sexual orientation

✔ Make 'reasonable adjustments' to ensure that people with disabilities are not treated less favourably than their colleagues

Under the Health and Safety Act 1999 you must provide a safe and healthy work place, which includes protecting the mental health of employees. This means that in addition to your general health and safety duties you must:

    ✔ Ensure that employees are not subjected to bullying, harassment or victimisation

    ✔ Follow the rules for night workers and drivers

According to the Part-time Workers (Prevention of Less Favourable Treatment) Regulations 2000, you are not permitted to treat part-time workers less favourably than full time workers doing similar work. This means in most cases you must offer comparable pay, holiday, promotion opportunities and access to training.

Business reasons

The term _equal opportunities_ is often assumed to mean that everyone should be treated exactly the same.

But in order to really offer equal opportunities, you may have to treat people fairly, but differently, to meet their needs whilst also meeting the needs of your business.

You can claim a competitive advantage by employing a diverse workforce. Your business:

    ✔ Can serve a wider customer base

    ✔ Is more likely to innovate

    ✔ Can build a reputation as a good employer and attract better people

    ✔ May win contracts with public service bodies or charities which have a statutory or philosophical commitment to promoting diversity

You can manage your costs and offer flexible services to customers by employing people who may not fit into traditional working patterns, for example,

    ✔ Term-time only contracts

    ✔ Flexible working arrangements

    ✔ Home-based working arrangements

    ✔ Zero hours contracts

Sticking to contractual terms

An employment contract is legally binding, so if you want to change it you have to inform and consult the employee, and put the changes in writing.

There are four routes to changing an employee's contract:

- ✔ Consensual changes which are changes you agree individually with an employee or through a collective agreement with a recognised union

- ✔ Express changes you can make because there is a clause built into the existing contract; for example, if you have a mobility clause in the contract you can change the employee's place of work

- ✔ Changes because of implied terms, such as the implied term that an employee will follow reasonable instructions

- ✔ Changes you impose by terminating one contract and issuing a new one with the modified terms

Ask the employee to sign a new contract, or a letter confirming the changes.

You can't unilaterally change an employment contract. If you do, the employee can sue you for breach of contract, or resign and claim constructive unfair dismissal.

You should follow a consultation process if you want to change an employee's contract. Read more about this later in the chapter in the section 'Following Procedure'.

Fixed term contracts

If you give an employee a contract with a definite end date it is called a *fixed term contract* and it automatically ends on the date you specified.

If you want to end a fixed term contract before the end date, you must give the employee the notice specified in the contract. If there is no clause for early termination in the contract, you could be liable to pay the employee for the whole remainder of the contract.

If you keep extending fixed term contracts, or you renew them, the employee's service is adding up and they will acquire employment rights just like any other employee after two years' service.

Flexible working requests

Employees may ask to change some of the terms of their contract, as a *flexible working request*. These requests have a legal status and you must deal with requests in a 'reasonable manner'. You don't have to agree to the request, but within three months of the request you must

1. **Consider the application.**

   (You can't just refuse it on principle.)

2. **Hold a meeting to discuss the request with the employee and give them the right to be accompanied.**

3. **Offer an appeal process.**

Read the statutory guidance for flexible working requests here:

```
http://www.acas.org.uk/media/pdf/f/e/Code-of-Practice-on-
handling-in-a-reasonable-manner-requests-to-work-flexibly.
pdf
```

Keeping your promises

In addition to the legal employment contract, there is a *psychological contract* between employers and employees.

This is a term to describe the underlying assumptions and promises that an employer and employee make when they enter into the legal contract.

There is an assumption of trust that the two parties to the employment contract will treat each other fairly, not steal from each other, and act in good faith when representing the other party: exercising *reasonable flexibility*.

An example of reasonable flexibility is where you might expect an employee to stay five minutes after their shift to finish a conversation with a customer, and they might expect that if they are five minutes late to work one day, you won't deduct their pay.

Sometimes the balance in a psychological contract can shift and your employees may seem to be less motivated and flexible.

If this happens, challenge yourself about whether you are keeping your side of the bargain in the psychological contract, and how you might address it. If you promise employees to review their pay, introduce a bonus scheme or to close early one Friday, it is important to either do it, or explain why you didn't keep your promise. People remember!

Following Procedure

Sometimes in a small business you need to react quickly: you want to get from A to D and you don't always have time to go via B and C. More often than not you will save time, stress and money by following the right procedure.

Following the statutory procedure

A *statutory procedure* is one that is set in law and requires you to follow a minimum number of steps.

Table 7-3 outlines the main types of statutory procedure relevant to small business.

Table 7-3	Statutory Procedures for Small Businesses
Discipline and grievance	http://www.acas.org.uk/media/pdf/k/b/ Acas_Code_of_Practice_1_on_disciplinary_ and_grievance_procedures-accessible- version-Jul-2012.pdf
Maternity, paternity, adoption and shared parental leave and pay	https://www.gov.uk/employers-maternity- pay-leave/entitlement https://www.gov.uk/employers-paternity- pay-leave https://www.gov.uk/shared-parental-leave- and-pay-employer-guide
Sick pay	https://www.gov.uk/employers-sick-pay/ notice-and-fit-notes
Pension enrolment	https://www.gov.uk/workplace-pensions- employers
Jury service, time off for reservists, time off for public duties	https://www.gov.uk/giving-staff-time-off- jury-service/overview https://www.gov.uk/employee-reservist https://www.gov.uk/giving-staff-time-off- for-magistrate-duty
Time off for union duties	http://www.acas.org.uk/index. aspx?articleid=2391
Flexible working requests	http://www.acas.org.uk/media/pdf/f/e/ Code-of-Practice-on-handling-in-a- reasonable-manner-requests-to-work- flexibly.pdf
Consultation for redundancies, transfer of undertakings	https://www.gov.uk/staff-redundant/ redundancy-consultations https://www.gov.uk/transfers-takeovers/ consulting-and-informing
Consultation for changes to terms and conditions	https://www.gov.uk/your-employment- contract-how-it-can-be-changed/getting- agreement

Creating your own procedure

For some matters like disciplinary issues or handling grievances you may prefer to write your own procedure, to reflect your company culture.

The key principles of any procedure should be:

- ✔ The purpose of the procedure: why you need it
- ✔ Notice and timing of each step: who must do what and by when
- ✔ Record keeping: what records do you need to meet your obligations
- ✔ Protecting employee rights: for example, to be accompanied, to have the right of appeal, not to be discriminated against
- ✔ Escalation and sanctions: what happens if you or the employee don't follow the procedure

If you write your own procedure for any employment policy, make sure that it meets the statutory minimum requirements.

Chapter 8

Managing and Rewarding Performance

High performing companies take performance management seriously. They know that when designed, implemented and managed well, a good performance management strategy adds value to any business.

A good performance management process ensures that your workforce know what is expected of them, and identifies the skills and tools required to reach those goals. Most importantly, it builds a culture of continuous improvement and drives performance excellence at every level. If you link reward to your company's or individual employees' success you can really drive continued high performance. However be careful linking reward and performance, as this may be perceived as divisive.

Performance Management: What It Is and Why It Matters

Performance management is a framework to translate business strategy into sustainable individual employee performance. If used well, it gives you a prospective and real-time picture of what is actually going on across the business.

Performance management helps executives to address the fundamental business questions of

✔ What are our short-term business expectations in relation to our longer term strategy?

✔ What should be done to meet them?

✔ How do we monitor progress and engagement?

✔ Are line managers able to execute the strategic and operational plan?

✔ What resources and systems are in place to support the sustainable realisation of the short-term objectives?

✔ What reward arrangements, if any, should be put in place to underpin achievement?

An important tool for high performing companies and resulting in numerous positive outcomes if carried out effectively, research has shown that when handled well, performance management can lead to increased employee engagement, a rise in productivity and customer loyalty as well as a significant drop in employee turnover.

Technology is now a key facilitator of performance management. By using technology, companies measure, monitor, and manage their business to optimise performance and achieve goals.

Another important aspect to performance management is that it helps you identify those amongst your team that aren't performing at the required level. A robust and fair performance management approach helps you build the case for fairly dismissing an employee, and if undertaken correctly, can protect you against any claims of unfair dismissal.

Why you should care about performance management

So you might ask, why bother? After all, we have all worked in companies where performance management is perceived by some line managers as an inhibitor to managing the company!

From our experience, companies with weaker performance management programmes are likely to be more inwardly focused and more concerned about yesterday's results than about the future direction of the company. As a result, they are unlikely to have an approach to issues and opportunities that is based upon a good fact base of data and company insight. As a consequence, they are more likely to react to situations, such as the recent economic downturn, with a knee-jerk approach to slashing costs, which may compromise future success in better times.

In contrast, companies with strong performance management programs are better equipped to forecast emerging risks and manage more proactively to mitigate the impact.

Research from professional services firm Price Waterhouse Coopers (in 2009) indicates that companies with strong performance management programs are better equipped to manage costs strategically, and when required can make difficult choices in a way that minimises the impact in the long term.

Succeeding at performance management

There's no silver bullet when it comes to developing and implementing an effective performance management approach, no magical mystical cave to enter to reveal the secrets of success. But experience of working with companies of all shapes and sizes, and in various industries, has enabled us to identify the five key factors that pave the road to success.

The five key factors for successful performance management are:

- ✔ Set clear goals and objectives
- ✔ Get your employees involved
- ✔ Ensure that you and your managers have the rights skills
- ✔ Ensure that the process you follow is simple and effective
- ✔ Ensure that if performance is linked to reward that it is fair

Setting clear corporate goals that articulate what excellent performance looks like is critical to driving performance. Many companies assume that their strategic direction and objectives are understood throughout their workforce, but this doesn't happen by magic.

Take a look at the sidebar 'Setting SMART objectives' for our tips on planning and communicating your business goals and objectives. Be sure to clearly communicate your vision, strategic priorities and business goals, and cascade these to your team. Doing so enables everyone to understand where they fit in, what their personal accountabilities are, and how their work contributes to the bigger picture.

Setting SMART objectives

Setting objectives is easy but achieving them isn't. That's why setting SMART goals - Specific, Measurable, Achievable, Realistic and Timely - is the first step in making your employees' goals a reality.

The acronym SMART has a number of slightly different variations, which can be used to provide a more comprehensive definition for goal setting:

✔ **S** - specific, significant, stretching

✔ **M** - measurable, meaningful, motivational

✔ **A** - agreed upon, attainable, achievable, acceptable, action-oriented

✔ **R** - realistic, relevant, reasonable, rewarding, results-oriented

✔ **T** - time-based, time-bound, timely, tangible, trackable

This provides a broader definition that will help you to be successful in both your business and personal life.

Identification of performance objectives is typically undertaken during or after a business planning process (see Chapter 11 for more details) when the company agrees what needs to be achieved for the following financial year. By clarifying who is delivering what, any duplicated effort or unnecessary work can be identified and addressed.

Designing an effective performance management strategy

Building a performance management process and system that reflects the culture of your company is absolutely critical. For example, in a fluid, young and dynamic company, it would be inappropriate to force in a complex performance management process. The process here should be minimal and brief, with a low degree of emphasis on rules.

Emphasizing what's important

Everyone knows that high performance leads to company success, and yet how often is performance management seen as a once a year process to complete before resuming the 'real work'?

The most important element in managing performance is the quality and frequency of the discussion about performance between a line manager and an employee. Spotting an individual doing it right, or providing constructive, immediate feedback when an individual is off-track is of greater value than any dutifully completed feedback form that is not discussed. Emphasize this fact in all aspects of the process: the way it is launched, communicated, what is celebrated (or not), how forms are written, and so on.

Considering complex performance management issues

Whilst at its heart, performance management is very simple – the delivery of excellent performance from your company and its employees – a number of thorny issues inevitably go side by side with the subject, hiding in the shadows and waiting to jump out and bite you.

For instance a couple of examples of thorns in your business side could be:

- ✔ Whether to have performance ratings, and if so what labels/ numbers to use
- ✔ Whether, and how, to tie performance directly to reward

Consider the pros and cons of these kinds of issues up front in the context of your company and its culture and aims, and make appropriate decisions based on this.

Building the process and system accordingly

If you want to leverage the various benefits of the performance management process, you need to build the process and system accordingly to allow you to exploit these opportunities. For instance, a good online system allows results across your business to be automatically aggregated. This enables key themes and development needs to be extracted and evaluated easily.

Keeping it simple

Many line managers suffer from HR process overload, frustrating their HR colleagues by 'not following the process correctly', 'taking shortcuts', or 'treating performance management as a tick box exercise'. Do everyone a favour, and keep it simple. This may mean compromising some ideals, but remember to tell yourself that the buy-in and commitment you gain will be worth it.

Training employees to implement effectively

Providing training, coaching and support for your employees is critical to the successful implementation and embedding of the performance management approach. Training should focus primarily on the areas many find tricky – how to set objectives, how to give and receive feedback, and how to have difficult conversations, for instance. Don't miss a trick by training managers on the mechanisms, such as the process and forms or online system (which should be simple and self-explanatory), without focusing on these more difficult, but more value-adding areas.

Providing feedback

To effectively manage your business, you need to be skilled at giving out both praise and criticism. While praise is easy to give, it is far more challenging and unpleasant to criticise your employees. Yet the practice of business leadership requires you to occasionally show employees where they need to improve. Thus, it is vital for you to learn how and when to give negative feedback.

The first thing to understand is that people generally respond more strongly to negative events than positive ones. In other words, we are usually more upset about losing £100 than we are happy about winning £100.

So what does this observation mean for you? Put simply, you need to be cautious before providing critical feedback to your employees.

 Acas has produced a great guide for business owners and line managers to help them provide challenging feedback to people that work for them. It can be found here: www.acas.org.uk/media/pdf/0/d/Challenging-conversations-and-how-to-manage-them.pdf

While giving and receiving feedback can be a delicate process, there's no doubting its value in helping to identify issues and solve them. As a business owner you should manage feedback in a positive way so that it can do what it's intended to do: help improve and grow your business.

Here are five tips that can get you on track to giving productive feedback:

- **Create safety.** Believe it or not, people who receive feedback apply it only about 30 per cent of the time. If the person receiving the feedback doesn't feel comfortable, this can cause the feedback to ultimately be unproductive.

  If you don't have the kind of buddy relationship with a colleague or employee that allows you to say virtually anything to each other, then I suggest you add civility and safety into your feedback approach. Don't be mean-spirited. Your feedback usually won't be productive if it's focused on making the other person feel bad or make them look foolish in front of peers.

Instead, create opportunities to build confidence and skills. This is especially effective when people are expecting to be graded. Confined situations in which people know they are being evaluated are good for giving feedback while learning skills.

✔ **Be positive.** Give at least as much positive feedback as you do negative. Positive feedback stimulates the brain, leaving the recipient open to taking new direction. Meanwhile, negative feedback indicates that an adjustment needs to be made and the threat response turns on and defensiveness sets in. You shouldn't avoid negative, or corrective, feedback altogether. Just make sure you follow it up with a suggested solution or development opportunity.

✔ **Be specific.** People generally respond better to specific, positive direction. Avoid saying things like, 'You need to be more talkative in meetings.' It's too ambiguous and can be interpreted in a lot of personal ways. Say something specific and positive, pointed at the task you want accomplished, such as, 'You're smart. I want to hear at least one opinion from you in every meeting we're in together going forward.'

✔ **Be immediate.** The adult brain learns best by being caught in action. If you wait three months to tell someone that his or her performance is average, he or she usually can't grasp the changes needed in order to change direction. It's far too ambiguous and relies on memory. You need to ensure that when giving feedback that you give it frequently.

✔ **Be tough, not mean.** When someone does something at work that is not as you would like and you have to give him or her feedback, start by asking his or her perspective on the situation. You need to try to resist saying how stupid his or her actions were, even if they were!

Conducting a Performance Review

A *performance review* is your chance to give feedback to your employee in a formal or informal meeting, to find out how they think they are doing, and to plan for their future development. They often take place annually.

Regularly-held performance reviews provide you and your team members with an opportunity to:

✔ Discuss what they have achieved over the past months and what they found challenging, and come to an agreement as to how to progress

✔ Begin planning what they will focus on next, agreeing on priorities and on how success will be measured

✔ Identify the development and learning this will require and discuss career development

An alternative view of performance reviews

It would be remiss if it wasn't mentioned that some business owners believe that performance management can cause more issues then it solves!

In some organisations formal performance management are viewed as being negative to corporate performance, an obstacle to straight-talk relationships, and often a cause of low morale at work.

Samuel Colbert, a professor at UCLA, has found some reasons why performance management in organisations can cause more issues then it solves.

Two People, Two Mind-Sets: The mind-sets held by you and your employee in a performance review work at cross-purposes. You want to discuss where performance needs to be improved, whilst your employee is focused on issues such as compensation, job progression and career advancement. You will be thinking about missed opportunities, skill limitations and relationships that could use enhancing, while the employee wants to put a best foot forward believing she is *negotiating* pay. All of this puts the participants at odds, talking past each other. Samuel Culbert proposes that at best, the discussion accomplishes nothing. More likely, it creates tensions that carry over to their everyday relationships.

Objectivity Is Subjective: Some business owners think that most performance reviews are staged as 'objective' commentary. Can you imagine another employee situation where any two managers would reach the same conclusions about the merits and faults of the employee? This is often confirmed when people switch managers; they often receive sharply different evaluations from the new bosses to whom they now report.

Culbert claims that 'this is just further proof that claiming an evaluation can be "objective" is preposterous, as if any assessment is independent of that evaluator's motives in the moment'.

One Size Does Not Fit All: As you will be aware, your employees all come with their own characteristics, positive attributes and imperfections that they use in every attempt to perform their best. Because no two people come similarly equipped, they draw upon the unique pluses and minuses they were endowed with at birth along with life experiences and knowledge they have developed along the way.

However, as you may have already read in a performance review, employees can sometimes be measured along some predetermined checklist of objectives and behavioural competencies. Culbert again proposes that in almost every instance what's being 'measured' has less to do with what an individual was focusing on in attempting to perform competently and more to do with a checklist expert's assumptions about what competent people do.

So this is an alternative view that some might find quite compelling. However, before you rush to 'do nothing' just keep in mind the very positive reasons why performance management can be helpful for you and your company:

- ✔ Performance management allows you to articulate to your employees what needs to be done and why.

- ✔ Performance management helps you deal with employees who are under performing.

- ✔ Performance management can help you reward employees on a differentiated basis if you link employee performance and reward together.

To effectively manage your business, you need to be skilled at giving out both praise and criticism, especially during performance reviews. While praise is easy to give, it is far more challenging and unpleasant to criticise your employees. Yet the practice of business leadership requires you to occasionally show employees where they need to improve. Thus, it is vital for you to learn how and when to give negative feedback to enable you to explore performance reviews to the max.

Of course, performance reviews may not suit everyone – see the sidebar 'An alternative view of performance reviews' – but be consistent in either offering everyone or no one a review.

Planning the review meeting

Building up from a solid foundation is a key ingredient to many a meeting, and performance management meetings are really no different.

The meeting should be structured around the following concepts:

✔ Achievements relating to objectives, behaviours, and any development plans

✔ A general discussion of competence against the role

✔ An identification of problems in achieving objectives or performance standards

✔ Exploring reasons for problems, including factors beyond an individual's control and those that can be attributed to behaviour

✔ Other work-related issues relating to work and relationships with managers, colleagues and, if appropriate, subordinates and clients

✔ An agreement on taking actions to overcome problems

✔ An agreement on any changes to objectives

✔ The review and revision of performance measures

Table 8-1 outlines the typical steps taken to prepare and manage a review meeting.

Table 8-1	Managing a Performance Review Meeting
Step	*Actions taken*
1 **Prepare**	Book in meeting time
	Consider and review the following information before the meeting:
	Relevant information about key business drivers, such as the Business strategy and objectives
	Draft objectives
	Previous objectives
	Personal areas of strength or areas for development
	The appraisee should initiate the process and draft the objectives in the performance development system
2 **Conduct**	Allow sufficient time for a thorough discussion
	The appraiser should set a positive tone and provide sufficient context i.e. the direction of the business and external market influences, where appropriate
	Focus the discussion on the year ahead and create the objectives together, agreeing on:
	What business results need to be achieved by the individual (these form the appraisees' Business Objectives)
	What personal strengths the individual could maximise, or areas in which they could improve in order to achieve their business objectives (these form the Personal Development Objectives)
	How these results should be achieved (the Key Actions and Milestones and the behaviours required to deliver them)
	Think about the factors affecting the individual's performance, for example the environment and support required for success
	Discuss any developmental needs that the team member may have in order to achieve their objectives or overcome any challenges
3 **Review and Agree**	Both the you and your team member must ensure that the objectives are documented and approved

Establishing performance ratings

Companies running performance management programmes often establish performance ratings to confirm how an individual has performed against an agreed list of objectives and / or their peer group undertaking roles at a similar level.

To ensure that employee performance in your company is evaluated in a consistent manner, the process of assessing performance is broken down into different areas of a job and scored according to set guidelines. When all areas have been assessed, this is referred to as an *overall rating*.

This overall rating is sometimes a composite of both *what* work was done and *how* it was done. It is a summary assessment of the employee's total effectiveness on the job for the year.

There are no rules with regard to the number of performance ratings (levels of achievement) that a company might have but it is typical to see three to five different ratings.

Table 8-2 provides an illustration of a typical performance rating scale.

Table 8-2	Performance Rating Scales
Rating	*Description*
Exceptional	Performance consistently exceeds expectations in all dimensions, not only the specific results, but how the results were achieved; the performance is broadly recognized within the community as being unusual and highly valued. A clear role model
Great	Consistently strong level of performance; goals are consistently achieved, and behavioral competencies are generally demonstrated at levels exceeding expectations for the position.
Achieving	Goals are achieved and behavioral competencies are demonstrated at a level consistent with position.
Needs Improvement	Performance sometimes meets expectations; some goals may have been missed and/or expected behaviors may be inconsistently demonstrated.
Poor	Regularly misses commitments and/or regularly demonstrates poor behaviours.

Often the rating scale is used to describe to an employee how well they performed and is communicated towards the end of a performance review meeting.

Dealing with underperformance

So far we've discussed how to prepare for and undertake a review of an employee's performance, and how to provide constructive feedback. However, sometimes the feedback just doesn't work and you need to deal with a performance issue.

In Chapter 5 you find the reasons for fair dismissal of an employee, of which performance is one of them. A robust and fair performance management approach provides the background and detail required to dismiss an employee on the grounds of performance. Intuitively as a business leader you should already be aware of those that aren't performing at the level you need them to; however, do you have the evidence, the facts and data that supports this view?

What is underperformance?

Underperformance or *poor performance* is a failure to perform the duties of the role or to perform them to the standard required by the business. Employers sometime confuse underperformance or poor performance with misconduct or poor conduct. Table 8-3 outlines the key distinctions.

Table 8-3	Poor Performance versus Poor Conduct	
Underperformance typically illustrated as	**Misconduct typically covers**	**Gross misconduct**
Unacceptable standard of work	Continued absence	Violence
Low productivity	Lateness or poor time keeping	Failure to undertake a reasonable management instruction
Poor output	being rude to customers or colleagues.	Theft
Failure to complete objectives		Alcohol or drug abuse whilst at work

What are the possible causes of underperformance?

Identifying the reason for poor performance is important to establish before considering whether you'll take an informal or formal approach to performance management.

Be sure to have asked the right questions and carried out the correct assessments before tackling poor performance; for example:

- ✔ Have you made your expectations clear?
- ✔ Has the employee had sufficient training to carry out the work requirement?
- ✔ Is the workload too high?

There may be other possible causes such as:

- ✔ You hired the wrong person for the job.
- ✔ There may be personal outside influences restricting the person from performing the role.
- ✔ There is ineffective or lack of communication between the person and staff structure/people/colleagues/clients in order to perform the role effectively.

Once you have considered the above, you can set out a plan for improvement.

Creating a Performance Improvement Plan

Acas (Arbitration, Conciliation and Advisory Service) is an independent government organisation devoted to preventing and resolving employment disputes. It takes into account UK employment law when offering advice and guidance.

Acas guidelines state that before considering formal action, you should be able to demonstrate that:

- ✔ The employee is clear as to what is expected of them.
- ✔ You have provided feedback on their performance.
- ✔ The employee is clear about the gap between their performance and the required performance.
- ✔ You have an agreed plan outlining what improvement you expect of them and by when, and the support you have provided to help them improve.
- ✔ The agreed action plan has been in place for long enough for the employee to demonstrate some improvement.
- ✔ You have been clear to the employee about what will happen if their performance doesn't improve.
- ✔ You have a clear audit trail of all of the above.

What if there is still no improvement in performance?

If there is still no improvement in performance after implementing an improvement plan, you may proceed to the formal stage of a disciplinary process which involves:

- ✔ Inviting the employee in writing to a formal disciplinary hearing and giving reasonable advance notice

- ✔ Allowing the employee an opportunity to be accompanied

- ✔ Clearly setting out the reason for the disciplinary hearing

- ✔ Allowing the employee to provide their feedback and any evidence before you make a decision on the level of sanction.

- ✔ Setting out the sanction at the end of the meeting and following up in writing

- ✔ Allowing the employee the right of appeal within five days of receiving the decision in writing

Sanctioning or dismissal?

UK employment law recognises that small businesses may not be able to sustain an underperformer for a lengthy period of time; therefore, the guidance provided in this chapter has taken this into account.

An employee with less than two years continuous service (employed after 1 April 2012) is not eligible to bring an unfair dismissal claim to a court other than that for discrimination or breach of contract.

Please refer to Chapter 5 if you wish to understand how to dismiss an employee fairly.

Linking Performance and Reward

Linking reward to performance can be beneficial to your company and your employees if you undertake it in a robust way. Typically, reward and performance are linked through commission and bonus awards. However, you can link performance and reward through adjustments to base pay.

If you wish to learn more regarding incentive and bonus design, please check out Chapter 4.

Many companies link reward and performance, and the rationale behind such an approach is often as follows:

✔ To motivate employees to deliver higher levels of performance

✔ To convey to employees and potential employees that the company believes in, indeed requires high levels of performance and will consequently pay for it.

✔ Decreased attrition rate, which empowers employee retention in long run and commitment. Due to decreased attrition rate and increased employee retention, recruitment cost is less, which helps in the financial stability of your company.

✔ Employee involvement (Participation Management) is increased, which results in autonomy, more productivity and satisfaction. Employees feel that they are part of a big success, enabling more confidence and innovation in work.

✔ Rather than working on routine jobs, employees volunteer to work on challenging jobs to increase their recognition levels in your company. It enforces healthy competition among individuals to perform better.

✔ Employee gets a chance to learn and enhance their skills, which highlights their development and ability to perform at higher levels.

✔ To support a performance driven culture that 'locks' employees into the success of the company through the rewards they receive.

Working out how to make the link

You need to consider carefully if you have the right circumstances in order to successfully link performance and reward.

The following list provides an indication of some of the factors that need to be in place before a successful link can be made:

✔ Is the nature of work undertaken by your employee / team appropriate to make a link? For some roles, such as sales roles, there is an obvious link, but for others the link might be more difficult to make.

✔ Are your employees in a position to influence their performance and therefore their reward by changing their behaviour?

✔ Are your team clear about targets and standards of performance required of them?

✔ Are the level of rewards proposed meaningful in order to encourage achievement of performance and behavioural change?

✔ The reward should follow reasonably quickly following accomplishment of the task by the employee.

Introducing performance related reward

When introducing a link between performance and reward you should treat the introduction as you would any other internal project or expenditure undertaken.

So you should be clear with regard to the following:

- **Return on Investment:** In simple terms, will the expected uplift of performance from employees cover any additional cost of reward proposed?

- **Solid performance measurement:** Are you certain that you have a robust way of measuring your employees' performance? If not refer to the earlier sections of this chapter.

- **Who assesses performance?** Have you considered to what extent performance or reward decisions might be devolved to your line managers, and if so, what capability do they have to ensure that objectivity and consistency is maintained?

- **How do you propose to communicate your plans?** You should at least put in place a set of guidelines, and where possible for your incentive plans, a set of rules that allows your employees to understand how the incentive plan works and what happens in specific circumstances such as leaving your employment.

Using different types of reward

The types of performance related reward tend to split into two categories:

- Short term reward
- Longer term reward

The *short term* reward schemes tend to be sales incentives, commission payments and quarterly to annual bonus awards.

The *longer term* awards might be the appropriation of shares in your company or adjustments to base salary that are directly influenced by the performance of the employee.

Reviewing base pay

Although you are not legally bound to increase your employees' salaries every year, you might wish to make adjustments based upon the contribution an employee has made during the period under review.

If you intend to run a performance based annual pay review process, it means that you must differentiate pay awards taking into account the performance of individuals over the review period, and typically an employees performance rating influences their salary review adjustment.

One of the really challenging parts of managing people is being able to differentiate levels of performance and the associated levels of reward. This requires you to use your judgement to consider your people in terms of how they perform their role and what they deliver. The performance management process underpins this, and your regular one to ones with your employees should provide a good insight to the year's performance. Make sure that you are focussing on the last 12 months' performance and not considering legacy issues – either good or bad!

A number of other factors should be considered when making salary adjustments, and Figure 8-1 represents some of the factors you may consider.

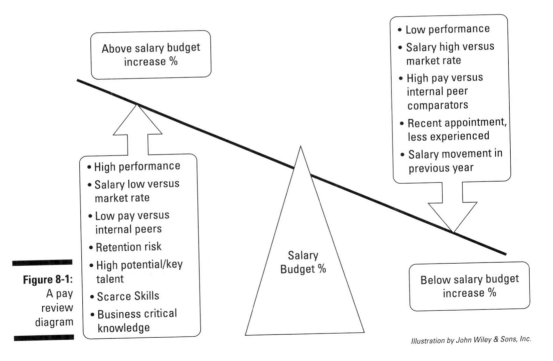

Figure 8-1: A pay review diagram

Illustration by John Wiley & Sons, Inc.

The whole package

When determining the level of increase for each of your employees, you also need to take into account the whole package, particularly in comparison with others doing the same or similar work.

You should consider the level of package versus your understanding of the market value of the role and the spread of salaries within your company. It may be the case that a good performer is already paid well against the market and the peer group so would not receive as high an increase as someone's performance which was not quite as good but whose salary is towards the bottom end of the market and his peer group.

You may not be able to address all of the issues so you should try to prioritise the most urgent cases, for instance highly skilled/valued employees, potential equal pay cases, extreme outliers, or retention of critical employees.

Dancing for beans: Reviewing salary increases

When reviewing pay, you should keep in mind that there are two potential salary review outcomes:

- ✔ Proposed increase to salary
- ✔ No increase to salary

Focus on the final proposed salary and take in account the individual's performance, where their existing salary sits relative internal and external peer group and criticality of retaining the employee rather than just the percentage increase in itself.

Don't forget to justify your salary adjustments and where you can document your rationale with regard to the adjustment made for each employee.

Understanding the legal implications of rewards

Your approach to reward and performance must comply with legal regulations. Typically, employment laws include areas such as minimum pay, and equal pay legislation to ensure that no groups are prejudiced against. There have been high profile cases of female investment bankers winning legal cases against their employers because their bonuses were far less than those paid to male colleagues.

If you don't make a bonus or commission award or you make a mistake then you need to ensure that you undertake the following:

✔ Speak to your employee to explain the misunderstanding

✔ Set out in writing how you have calculated their pay and how you propose to make an appropriate adjustment

✔ Keep copies of any letters and notes of any meetings

Be aware that if a bonus or commission is included in their contract, non-payment is a breach of contract and therefore an employee could resign and can claim constructive dismissal, or indeed refer you to an employment tribunal whilst employed for wrongful deduction of wages.

Chapter 9

Creating a Great Team

The world of football gives us some insight into what makes a great team, but sometimes high profile players and managers hog the limelight and skew our perception of the magic ingredients that lead to success. For every David Beckham, there are often several Nicky Butts working harder with a lower profile.

This chapter offers you some insights into creating, bonding, and managing a great team.

Exploring Models for Describing Teams

In a team sport, team members' jobs are largely defined by the position they play, or their place in the batting or running order. The team goal is very clear – to win the match or race. The boundaries and rules are defined, and an umpire or referee makes sure everyone sticks to them.

In a business team, it's not quite so straightforward, especially for a small business operating in a constantly changing environment.

Recognising successful team behaviours and characteristics

In the quest for the Holy Grail of a perfect team, lots of management theorists have come up with models to describe the characteristics of a high performing team. There are some common themes which help to identify great teams.

The Korn/Ferry Institute created their own team effectiveness model and produced a white paper analysing seven other models of team effectiveness; if you want to know more you can read it here: `http://www.kornferry.com/media/lominger_pdf/teamswhitepaper080409.pdf`

A shared goal

A team is just a group of people unless there is a shared goal and the team shares the responsibility for achieving it.

Khoi Tu, in his book *Superteams* (Penguin, 2012), describes the importance of forging a common purpose for a team. Lombardo and Eichinger's *Team Architect* model labels that common goal as 'Thrust'.

Writing down the shared goal will help you to evolve and crystallise it, and define what it isn't, as much as what it is. And once you're happy with it, that's when you should share it with your team.

In a small business the shared goal may seem very obvious to the owner or manager, but you might be surprised by the results if you try to put that goal in writing for the team without careful thought: for example, if you give your team the simple target of winning every customer who makes an enquiry, you might find you are losing money on every contract.

You should make the shared goal

✔ Clear – so everyone knows what the goal is, and when it has been reached

✔ Inspiring – so everyone cares about reaching the goal

✔ Relevant – to the success of the business

You can read more about goal setting in Chapter 8.

Ken Blanchard, a management guru based in the US, coined a nice phrase (and also created the PERFORM model, described in the nearby sidebar):

> *'Profit is the applause you get for taking care of your customers and creating a motivating environment for your people.'*

Communication

Each team member needs to know what they are supposed to be doing, and what everyone else in the team is doing. It is the team leader's job to give the team the right environment and information to get on with their jobs.

PERFORM

Ken Blanchard created the PERFORM model to describe a high performing team:

Purpose: A high performing team has a strong sense of purpose and a common set of values. They have a compelling vision.

Empowerment: team members are confident in the team's ability to overcome obstacles. They share information and knowledge and help each other. Policies, rules and procedures enable the team to run smoothly. People have the skills and knowledge they need. They have opportunities for growth and authority to act within clear boundaries.

Relationships and Communication: team members communicate openly, listen to each other, share opinions and feel safe in taking risks. They value each other's differences, and if disagreements arise, the team resolves them positively. People are committed to each other professionally and personally and show respect even if they don't like each other.

Flexibility: team members acknowledge that they are interdependent – everyone is responsible for team performance, including sometimes taking the lead on things. The team adapts to changing circumstances.

Optimal productivity: the team produces high quality work and is committed to achieving results. Team members take pride in meeting deadlines, achieving goals, and continual improvement. They hold each other accountable. They have effective decision making processes and problem solving methods. Everyone carries their weight and everyone is proud of team accomplishments.

Recognition and appreciation: team members, the team leader and the organisation regularly recognise and appreciate the team results.

Morale: if all the other ingredients are in place, team members feel optimistic and confident, they overcome challenges, they trust each other and there is a strong sense of team unity.

 When you are managing team communication think about providing

- The tools for good communication so people don't waste time and energy
- The rules and policies people need so they don't have to keep coming to you for the answers
- A forum for communication, up, down and sideways in the team so people can solve problems without always involving you
- A 'feedback loop' so the team knows when it is doing well and not so well

Collaboration

Collaboration is the act of working together to produce something. Just like in a football team with defenders, strikers and a goalkeeper, collaboration works best if people in the team contribute complementary skills and knowledge. If everyone in the business is working independently on tasks without any interdependence, the shared goal will not be achieved and your business will face relegation into the murky depths of non-league.

To enable collaboration you should

✔ Keep reminding people of the shared goal

✔ Give people time, space and the tools to work together

✔ Recruit people into the team who have complementary skills and knowledge

✔ Recognise and reward people who collaborate effectively

✔ Give the team the tools and the freedom to resolve conflicts

✔ Give people time and encouragement to train and develop their colleagues

Adaptability

Successful teams can adapt to new circumstances, or even to a new shared goal, if necessary. Adapting is not just changing the tasks or learning new skills, it's behaving flexibly and embracing change.

To encourage team adaptability you can

✔ Mix it up a little by asking people to do different jobs every so often

✔ Remember to tell the team about new circumstances or changes to the shared goal

✔ Encourage the team to come up with new ways of working

✔ Celebrate when the team introduces innovation

You can read more about training and developing your people in Chapter 13.

Playing the game: Team roles and who plays them

Any group of people typically has a mix of introverts and extroverts, the people with ideas and the practical people, the savers and spenders, the peacemakers and troublemakers.

If you are paying them to work for your business, you want to harness their strengths and direct their energies in the best interests of the business.

In the 1970s Dr Meredith Belbin and a team of researchers at Henley Management College studied lots of teams over almost a decade and came up with the idea that successful teams are ones with a good mix of people playing various team roles. Team roles were defined as 'a tendency to behave, contribute and interrelate with others in a particular way'. They saw that successful teams were ones which anticipated and dealt effectively with problems.

There were nine team roles that had labels and characteristics as shown in Table 9-1. For every strength that a team role brings to the team, they can also bring a weakness, but a good team allows people to play to their strengths and compensates for their weaknesses.

Table 9-1	Belbin's Team Roles	
Team role	*Behaviour that helps the team*	*Allowable weakness*
Plant	Highly creative and good at solving problems in creative ways	Get impatient and don't focus on the detail
Monitor Evaluator	Provide a logical eye, evaluate options and make impartial judgements. Keep meetings to time.	Hold up decisions by over analysing the options.
Resource Investigator	Create and maintain a connection between the team and the outside world	Focus too much on connecting and forget to follow up on tasks
Co-ordinator	Allocate tasks to the right team members and get everyone contributing	Delegate too much
Team worker	Help the team to gel, ensure that everyone stays motivated, and does work for the team	Focus on team morale too much and not get the job done
Implementer	Come up with a practical workable plan and the most efficient way to get the job done	Focus on task too much at the cost of the people
Shaper	Keep the team focused on the goal, and provide the drive to keep going	Show frustration when team is not progressing
Completer Finisher	Check the quality, scrutinise the detail and polish the final article	A perfectionist for whom the job is never quite done
Specialist	Bring expert knowledge or experience	Focus too narrowly and not see the big picture

The most successful teams are ones where every team role is covered. But successful teams don't need to have nine members. People can play more than one role, and most of us do exactly that.

Belbin's theory is that most people have a preference for how they behave, but anyone can 'adopt' a role if the team needs it. This is a *manageable* role – one that uses some of the person's preferred behaviour.

The team leader could play any of the team roles, but it is likely that their behavioural preference shapes their leadership style. In turn, the team leader's leadership style is likely to influence the culture of the team.

Some team role behaviours are easier to spot than others, and you may intuitively know who plays which team role in your team. There are questionnaires and other tools available to work out people's preferences more systematically, if you are interested in exploring this further.

Check out the free resources available on the Belbin Associates website: `http://www.belbin.com/rte.asp?id=396`

Shaping your team

Think about your own behavioural preferences, and those of the people in your current team, and identify any gaps in team roles. Assessing what skills and experience your business needs is tackled in Chapter 2. For example:

- ✔ If there are no new ideas coming through, you may need a Plant.
- ✔ Without a Shaper your team may be constantly missing deadlines.
- ✔ If your customers are complaining about quality, your team may need a Completer Finisher.

If you don't have the full complement of Team Roles in your team, encourage people to play the roles which might not be their first preference, but are manageable. For example, a detail-conscious person who would normally prefer to behave as a Completer Finisher may also be good as a Monitor Evaluator. Get them to keep track of the time in team meetings and ask them to keep a note of the actions everyone has agreed on.

If you are not a Shaper, and you are leading the team, the buck stops with you, so you may need to adopt a more assertive, driving style of leadership than feels completely comfortable.

If too many people are adopting team roles which don't play to their strengths, the team is unlikely to succeed. When you are recruiting the next person to join the team, try to find someone whose strengths and behavioural preferences will fill some outstanding gaps. Add these criteria to the person specification, along with the job related content.

Practising the Art of Communication

When you are recruiting other people to work for the business, you probably have 'excellent communication skills' as one of your selection criteria. If you stop to think what this actually means, it's probably a mix of face to face, phone and written interactions.

Selecting the right communication tool is almost as important as using it well; this section looks at effective communication.

Using meetings to get results

If you consciously think about meetings as a communication tool rather than a time consuming but necessary evil, you will save yourself and the business a lot of time and money.

Setting the purpose of the meeting

David Greenberg, an expert speaker and trainer who works with clients to improve their meeting effectiveness gives lots of common sense tips about how to have effective meetings. One of his top tips is to write down the sentence 'The purpose of this meeting is to . . .'

Before you arrange a meeting, write down the purpose. This will

- Shape the agenda
- Help you to allocate the right amount of time
- Inform the decision about whom to invite to the meeting
- Prompt you to prepare the right material or have the right conversations before the meeting so that the meeting time is productive

Planning for meetings

If you are arranging a disciplinary or grievance hearing or a formal consultation meeting, you must give the employee reasonable notice of the meeting, and give them the right to be accompanied. Read more about employee rights in meetings in Chapter 7. Even for a routine team meeting, it is worth spending a bit of time on preparation and follow up.

Managing the meeting logistics

Whether you are having a regular weekly team meeting, or a one-off meeting for a particular purpose, you can make it more effective by:

- Setting a time limit and appointing a time/clock watcher to let everyone know when there is 10 minutes of the allocated time remaining
- Chairing the meeting with the purpose always in mind
- Starting your meetings on time, even if other people are late
- Taking notes, or if appropriate, asking someone else to take notes
- Keeping 5 minutes spare at the end of the allotted time to summarise the actions and confirm next steps
- Finishing at the right time

After the meeting

If everyone in your team meeting takes away their own list of actions, you may not need to circulate notes or minutes, but you should keep your own record.

Communicating up, down and sideways

As soon as your business has more than about five employees you should think about the best way to manage communication in all directions. If you are all sitting at one bank of desks or in one workshop, you may not think it necessary, but things can go wrong with communication surprisingly often, even when everyone is working in the same room.

The terms up, down and sideways used here are not intended to imply a rigid hierarchy with employees deferentially doffing their caps to you, but merely as directional arrows in the flow of communication!

Communicating up: From employees to you

Even if you are very approachable and open to being interrupted, employees will sometimes need to tell you confidential information or ask you questions that they don't want everyone to hear.

Make it normal to meet your employees on a one to one basis, even if it is for 10 minutes once a week.

If it is not practical to regularly meet all your employees individually, give them a channel of communication they can use, such as

- A regular time slot or lunch hour when you are always available in a meeting room
- Access to a computer at work to send you an email
- An 'open door' policy where any employee can come to see you any time
- Your work mobile number
- An old fashioned 'suggestion box' where employees can put comments or raise questions
- A survey or online 'feedback' tool

Listening is a very important part of great communication, so if you give employees the channel to communicate with you, make sure that you listen, and find ways of letting them know that you've gotten the message.

There are lots of providers of online surveys and employee feedback tools, many of which offer 30 day free trials. Use these to set up a line of communication with your team, where they can feedback either using their name or anonymously.

Communicating down: From you to employees

There should be two kinds of communication flowing from you to employees:

- The information that applies to the whole team
- The information that is specific to individual employees

When you are considering the best method for these communications, as well as the audience, you should take into account:

- Your statutory obligations as an employer
- Whether you need a written record of the communication

✔ The confidentiality of the information, in particular any Data Protection issues

✔ Your external reputation

✔ Any collective agreements you have with employee representatives

You may read more about your statutory obligations for communication and consultation in Chapter 15, and about the Data Protection rules in Chapter 10.

Communicating sideways: Across the team

Even a small team needs to pay attention to communication, so that people have the information they need to make decisions, solve problems and deliver results.

The role of the team leader in sideways communication is to enable it by:

✔ Setting up regular team meetings and ensuring that people share information

✔ Encouraging people to talk to each other regularly between meetings

✔ Ensuring that everyone in the team has access to the information they need from the team leader

✔ Providing guidance about when issues should be escalated

See the sidebar 'Avoiding the rumour mill' for more advice on keeping things calm and sane within your business!

Avoiding the rumour mill

The Greek philosopher Parmenides came up with the idea, in his treatise 'On Nature' in 550 BC, that nature abhors a vacuum.

Your business is a living organism, full of people who abhor the metaphorical vacuum of 'not knowing what is going on'. In the absence of accurate and up to date information people will invent some, to fill the vacuum.

People usually imagine worst case scenarios, and rumours multiply quickly. This is particularly true during times of change.

To avoid the grinding of the rumour mill in your business, you can:

✔ Provide regular business updates, even when the news is bad.

✔ Keep people informed of progress if your business is going through change.

✔ Ask employees what is on their minds when you meet them one to one.

✔ Treat your employees as adults and don't assume that you are protecting them by not telling them the whole story. Trust them to keep your business news confidential.

Writing things down

If there could be just one golden rule for HR in business it would be 'write things down'.

The discipline of writing things down is a good general business practice, but often it is a personal preference rather than a necessity.

In HR, particularly in the context of employee relations or employment law, writing things down is essential.

Contracts of employment

You must provide a contract of employment or *statement of employment particulars* within 2 months of an employee starting to work for you.

You must provide a written reason for dismissal within 14 days when you dismiss an employee.

You must respond in writing to most employee requests to exercise their rights such as flexible working, maternity, adoption and shared parental leave.

Employee performance

Every time you have a conversation with an employee whose performance is not up to scratch, make a note, straightaway. These are called *contemporaneous notes*.

The aim of your note-taking is to keep a record of events should you need to build a case for the future to take disciplinary action.

If you hold a disciplinary or grievance hearing, you are legally obliged to write to the employee confirming the outcome of the hearing and giving them the right of appeal.

If you ultimately dismiss the employee and they make a claim for unfair dismissal at an Employment Tribunal, you will have to produce written evidence to support your decision. Read more about this in Chapter 6.

Policies

When you share policy information with employees in writing, ask them to confirm in writing that they have read and understood the policies. You can show this to an Employment Tribunal, or the Health and Safety Executive, or your insurance company to prove that you have fulfilled your responsibilities as an employer.

Getting your employees to confirm in writing that they've seen policy changes enables you to defend yourself against unjustified claims by employees, avoid statutory fines or support your insurance claims.

Accountability and focus

The written word can be very powerful, especially if you use it as a follow up to a conversation or meeting. If you take the trouble to write something down, you are forced to formulate your thoughts in a more structured way than in a conversation. If you make a note of agreed actions, people are more likely to do what they promised. And if you make a note of a difficult conversation, you can record the facts without the emotion; these facts will stand as evidence after the emotion has receded.

If you ask the other person to confirm that your notes of a difficult meeting are accurate, you are less likely to elaborate or exaggerate.

Leading a Great Team

Earlier in this chapter you find Ken Blanchard's PERFORM model, which describes the many and complex variables that make a successful team. Your role as the leader of the team is to create the right environment and provide the support and resources for the team to flourish.

Providing the team glue

If a team is a group of two or more people working towards a common goal who are mutually accountable for results, there must be some 'glue' holding them together. The team leader has a critical role to play in providing that glue, as outlined in Table 9-2.

Table 9-2		Team Leader Role in a Successful Team
	Team characteristic	*Team leader role to enable the team to succeed*
P	Purpose and values	Provide direction and resources. Provide big picture.
E	Empowerment	Provide opportunities and training. Reward informed risk taking and creativity. Clarify boundaries and let go!
R	Relationships and communication	Share information, give and take feedback, foster trust.
F	Flexibility	Seek and support new ideas, encourage creativity. Demonstrate personal flexibility.
O	Optimal productivity	Ensure that goals are clear. Measure and monitor progress. Manage performance. Support team decisions.
R	Recognition and appreciation	Recognise and appreciate good performance.
M	Morale	Support continuous improvement. Celebrate success.

The theory is all very well but practical ways to support team success are always welcomed! Try the following:

- ✔ Hold team meetings to
    - Share information
    - Provide feedback
    - Hear new ideas
    - Celebrate successes
    - Share problem solving
- ✔ Create a performance feedback system to
    - Build a shared understanding of progress against goals
    - Understand what barriers people are facing
    - Create opportunities for people to learn and develop
    - Ask and challenge the team to continuously improve performance
    - Acknowledge and recognise good work
- ✔ Build trust by being
    - Consistent
    - Fair
    - Prepared to make tough decisions when people don't perform
    - Open, with no hidden agenda

If your team could be performing better, start by giving the team marks out of 10 for achieving its purpose. If you would give the team less than 5 out of 10, you need to take action.

If your team could be performing better, start by looking at the key PERFORM factors that lead to team success. Identify

- ✔ What is missing and put it in place
- ✔ What is getting in the way and remove it
- ✔ What is enabling success and protect it

Don't forget to acknowledge the good things that the team are doing.

Empowering employees

Empowerment is the creation of an environment that releases the knowledge, experience and motivation that resides in people.

The good news is that it is easier for you to empower your team while the business is small than it would be for a manager in a large hierarchical company.

If you say, 'Do as you are told', people will follow your instructions to a fault, even if they can see that your way is not the best way to do the work, or even the best thing to do. In a hierarchical structure, that is what is expected, and rewarded.

If you say 'Own your job', people will take more risks, challenge you more and focus on the result. If people feel ownership for their job and their results, they can take more pride in it.

However, you need to create three conditions for empowerment to succeed:

✔ Share information

- Take some risks and trust people with confidential information – you will build stronger relationships if they are based on trust

- Give people information so they can make better decisions

- Give people feedback about how well they are doing, or not doing so they have a chance to improve

✔ Create autonomy

- Tell people what they can do, not what they can't

- Create boundaries based on people's skill, knowledge and experience

- Stretch the boundaries as people's skill, knowledge and confidence grows

- Give people the big picture, so that they can see where they fit in

- Discuss and agree on people's goals rather than imposing them

- Make sure that people understand which decisions are theirs, and which ones stay with you as the manager

✔ Don't rely on hierarchy

- If you admit that you don't know all the answers, but you have a strong vision of where you want to get to with the business, share the problem with the team.

- If you have given people enough information and a sense of empowerment, the team will help you to solve the problem.

Delegating tasks and responsibilities

As the business grows you will probably want to delegate some of your work to others, but it is sometimes difficult to let go of business critical activities, for fear that other people – mere mortals – might get it wrong.

Delegation is the temporary or permanent assignment of responsibility and accountability

✔ For specific outcomes or achievements

✔ To a specific individual or team.

If you follow the discipline of delegation, you can let go of the work without feeling you have also let go of control. Table 9-3 gives some advice on relaxing into the fine art of delegation.

Table 9-3	A Model of Delegation	
Step	*Do*	*Don't*
Planning	Delegate to the right person who has the skills, time and authority to do the work.	Don't give out assignments haphazardly.
	Spread delegation around and give people new experiences as part of their training.	Don't always give tasks to the strongest, most experienced or first available person.
	Build in contingency time.	Don't wait to delegate the task until it gets to 'crisis' time.
Discussion	Tell them what results you need and by when.	Don't tell the person how to do it.
	Make sure the quality standards and the outcome are clear.	
	Ask 'What else do you need to get started?'	
Let go	Delegate the authority along with the responsibility.	Don't make the person keep coming back to check in with you.

(continued)

Table 9-3 (continued)

Step	Do	Don't
Support and coach	Ask questions, give support, make suggestions if the person gets stuck.	Don't do the work for them.
Audit	Build in time and agreed audit points to review and check everything is going well. Ask for progress reports.	Don't keep checking in between the agreed audit points.
Accept only finished work	Reiterate that the work must be complete.	Don't accept a job partially done.
Show appreciation	Give praise and appreciation. Give constructive feedback to help the person to learn.	Don't forget!

Dealing with adversity

If Martin Luther King Jnr had it right, 'The ultimate measure of a man is not where he stands in moments of comfort and convenience, but where he stands at times of challenge and controversy.'

We can safely assume he measured women by the same standard, and in the context of running a business, Martin Luther King Jnr's statement is certainly true.

In HR, the most common times of adversity, likely to give you sleepless nights, consume a lot of your time, and cost the business money, are when:

- ✔ An employee is not performing well in their job
- ✔ An employee engages in misconduct, whether it is minor or serious
- ✔ An employee makes a complaint about you or someone else in your business
- ✔ You need to cut costs and you think you need to cut jobs
- ✔ An employee has an accident or injury at work
- ✔ You need to cover for an employee on long term sick, maternity, adoption or shared parental leave
- ✔ Your employees take industrial action
- ✔ An employee makes a claim to an Employment Tribunal

Even in the most successful businesses, these situations will arise. How you handle these 'people issues' in your business informs your culture, and impacts on the motivation and morale of the rest of the team.

In most HR situations you can save time, legal fees, compensation payments and your reputation by

- ✔ Establishing the facts
- ✔ Following a fair process
- ✔ Respecting employee and worker rights - in the spirit as well as by the letter
- ✔ Being consistent in how you treat all employees
- ✔ Fulfilling your statutory obligations as an employer
- ✔ Taking reasonable and proportionate action
- ✔ Behaving with integrity and keeping your promises

If you slip up along the way, because, let's face it, none of us is perfect, accept that you're wrong and try to redeem the situation. Tomorrow is another day, with its own highs and lows!

Chapter 10

Setting Up HR in Your Business

....

In This Chapter

▶ Deciding who should carry out HR roles

▶ Making sure that your managers are up to the job

▶ Keeping and protecting employee data

▶ Avoiding problems when outsourcing HR responsibilities

....

'Human Resources': step back from your job for a moment, and at face value this is a very odd term and not very 'human'. However, as business has become more sophisticated, and employees have become more discerning and aware of their rights, we should all recognise that the people in your business probably give you the best competitive advantage. In that sense they really are 'resources' and worth managing well for you to get the best value out of them.

This chapter is of most use if you own or manage an established small or medium sized business, and you're consolidating the way that the business works, how you deliver to customers or how you manage your employees.

Recognising When You Can't Do it All Yourself

The Chartered Institute of Personnel and Development (CIPD), the professional body for HR, has identified some of the signs that a business needs dedicated HR support. If you recognise some or all of these signs in your business, it is time to think about how you 'do' HR.

Some of the indicators the CIPD give are:

- ✔ As a business you are becoming more forward looking and systematic
- ✔ You don't have enough time to spend with every single employee, to inspire them directly with your vision and values
- ✔ The business is visibly doing well and employees are wondering when they might have a share of profits, or performance related pay

Other factors you should consider are:

- ✔ You have one or more managers with teams and you want to make sure that everyone is treated the same
- ✔ Each team needs to see how they fit into the bigger picture and how their targets contribute to your overall business performance
- ✔ Employees are asking what training and career development you can offer
- ✔ You are offering more complex or higher value services or products to customers than in the early days of the business
- ✔ The business has grown to a size where some people's work is to support internal customers or colleagues, for example a management accountant or sales support team
- ✔ The structure of the team or individual jobs may need to change to meet the needs of the business
- ✔ The value of your time and how it should best be spent

Letting Your Managers Know What They Have to Do

Whether your managers are promoted from within the ranks or recruited from outside the business, you should make it clear to them what their responsibilities are in relation to their teams. Without this information, even the best manager will struggle to do her job effectively.

Managing recruitment

Give your line managers a strong steer about your expectations. Even if a manager is experienced at recruiting people, spend at least some time agreeing on the job brief, the milestones and budgets.

If the manager has not recruited before, invest some of your time at the beginning to:

- ✔ Talk through the process step by step, agreeing target dates, and who will do what. Be clear about whether you want to meet one or more of the candidates during the process.

- ✔ Agree on the main outline of the job, and the skills and experience required.

- ✔ Advise where you have advertised or found candidates in the past.

- ✔ Tell them the kinds of questions you find useful at interview (see the top 10 interview questions in Chapter 20).

- ✔ Talk about what kind of personality and experience will best complement the rest of the team, and reinforce the company culture.

- ✔ Ask the line manager to use an interview template and scoring matrix to keep a record of each interview.

- ✔ Agree on the budget for advertising or agency fees and the target salary, including any flexibility you are willing to give.

Ask the manager to write a job description and person specification which you can sign off on before they start the recruitment. You may read more about job descriptions and person specifications in Chapter 2.

If you want to have the final say on the appointment, make sure that the manager understands this. If a manager, acting on behalf of the business, offers the job to a candidate, the offer is legally binding.

If your manager breaks the law by unfairly discriminating against a candidate, or not checking an employee's right to work in the UK, the business will be liable for the offence. Make sure that all managers understand their responsibilities.

Working together

Once you create a 'layer' of management between you and the rest of the employees, you lose some direct control over how people are working day to day. However, you can still influence the culture of the business by giving your managers a clear indication about what you expect in relation to

- ✔ Managing late comers and people who are off sick

- ✔ Maintaining standards of work in the office/workspace

- ✔ One to one meetings

- ✔ Team meetings

- ✔ Setting goals and managing people to meet them

Keeping things fair

Chapters 6 and 7 cover the basic policies and procedures you need to have in place to keep on the right side of the law. As with recruitment, your business is liable if one of your managers fails to follow the correct procedure. Read more about following procedure in Chapter 7.

When you promote or appoint a manager, make it clear to them what their responsibilities are in relation to:

- Organising Health and Safety in their work area/team, including:
  - Carrying out risk assessments for pregnant or new mothers
  - Manual handling training
  - Employees wearing personal protective equipment
  - Reporting accidents
  - Following fire evacuation procedures
- Ensuring that there is no bullying, harassment or discrimination going on in their team
- Following the disciplinary procedure without fail when investigating misconduct or poor performance
- Handling grievances raised by their team members, including trying to resolve matters informally in the first instance
- Approving holiday and other leave requests
- Managing sickness absence, especially carrying out return to work interviews after periods of absence
- Consulting employees about proposed changes to their jobs
- Following the correct procedure and behaving reasonably when dismissing employees
- Keeping records

Even if each of your managers is successful in following all the rules within his or her own team, you need to keep the bigger picture in mind, and make sure that all the managers are being consistent.

Managing great teams

Chapter 9 covers the key factors that lead to high performance in a team. A shared goal is the most important determinant of success.

When the business grows, teams and individual employees may lose sight of where they fit in the business.

Your managers' most critical role is to give everyone in their teams a clear idea of the shared goal.

Hold your managers accountable for sharing the overall business targets with their teams, and helping them to see where their work fits in. If you are ready to share some of the profits, or to give performance related pay to your employees, you will need to set clear targets and rules.

Your managers will have to communicate the targets, and manage people to achieve them. If everyone is succeeding, the manager's job is quite straightforward. Nobody minds giving people good news. Conversely, if some people are not performing well, you need to give your managers the training and the tools to manage the situation.

Parting company

In Chapter 5 you find the HR adage that people don't leave their job, they leave their boss. If a lot of employees are leaving from one team, there might be a problem with the manager.

Try to find out why people are leaving so you can do something about it. Train your managers so they have the skills to handle resignations or dismissals without compromising the business.

Ask your managers to do *exit interviews* when people leave the business. These are short conversations, sometimes no more than 10 minutes, where the manager asks a set of standard questions about why an employee is leaving, where they are going next, and if possible, details of their new job and salary. Ask the managers to keep notes; review the notes every quarter, to see if any patterns exist.

If you have more than one manager, ask them to do the exit interviews for people who leave from the other teams, as the employee is more likely to be honest if they are leaving because of their manager.

If you have concerns about people leaving one team more quickly than from other teams, you may find the answer in the exit interview notes.

You won't be able to claim a defence of not knowing what was going on if you have given your managers the authority to dismiss employees. It is your responsibility to know what is going on and to oversee if effectively.

Make sure that your managers are aware of employee rights, and your obligations as an employer. When managers take any action, they are representing the business.

Record Keeping and Protecting Confidentiality

You must keep certain information about all of your employees, and rules are in place governing how you must keep this info confidential. These rules are regulated by the UK Border Agency and HMRC (known to many as the friendly, smiling tax office).

Whether you keep physical or electronic records, to meet UK Border Agency and HMRC rules, you should have for all employees a record of:

- Name, address, date of birth, National Insurance number
- Evidence of a name change (if there has been one)
- Evidence of permission to work in the UK
- A signed contract or statement of employment particulars within two months of the start date (see Chapter 14 for all the gory details)
- A signed opt-out of the Working Time Regulations if the employee works more than 48 hours on average in a 17 week period (see Chapter 7)

Data protection

The *Data Protection Act 1998* protects people's rights in relation to the information that is stored about them electronically, and in 'relevant filing systems.' The Act defines *personal data* as that which could identify an individual living person, and could include their name, date of birth and address. The Act also describes *sensitive data*, which may include racial or ethnic origin; political opinions; religious or other beliefs; trade union membership; health; sex life; criminal proceedings or convictions.

As an employer you hold personal data about your employees, and probably some sensitive data, about your employees. Even if you haven't entered it onto a computer system, if an employee could be identified by – for example, someone using an alphabetic index or filing system – that is considered to be a 'relevant filing system', and the Data Protection rules will apply to you.

Having ownership of personal or sensitive data means that you are a *Data Controller,* who determines how personal data will be handled and used, or a *Data Processor*, who obtains, records or holds information or data or carries out any operation on that data, including adding it to a file.

If you are a Data Controller you must register with the Information Commissioner's Office and pay a small annual fee. You can complete a self-assessment to find out if you should register: `https://ico.org.uk/for-organisations/register/self-assessment`

As a Data Controller or Data Processor, you must follow the eight enforceable principles of good information handling. If you do not, employees or contractors may take you to court and claim for damages and sometimes distress caused by your breach of the Data Protection Act.

The eight principles ensure that personal data is

- ✔ Fairly and lawfully processed
- ✔ Processed for specified and lawful purposes and not in any manner incompatible with those purposes
- ✔ Adequate, relevant and not excessive
- ✔ Accurate and up-to-date
- ✔ Not kept for longer than is necessary
- ✔ Processed in accordance with the data subject's rights
- ✔ Kept securely
- ✔ Not transferable to countries outside the European Economic Area without adequate protection

Most of these principles are self-explanatory but you should:

- ✔ Get employees' and contractors' explicit permission to process their data. The simplest way to do this is to include a clause in the employment contract or service contract.
- ✔ Make sure that no unauthorised parties, for example marketing partners, have access to the data
- ✔ Review data regularly and destroy out of date records

✔ Follow the Information Commissioner's (ICO) guidance on how long to retain employee records and interview records for candidates

More info is available here: `https://ico.org.uk/for-organisations/guide-to-data-protection`

✔ Keep physical records in locked storage

✔ Make sure that managers keep personal data, including notes of one to one meetings, in a secure place

✔ Keep electronic data in password protected files and folders

✔ If you use a third party to process data, make sure they are not storing it outside the EEA, or if they are, that they are approved by the ICO

Medical records

If an employee is off work on a long term sickness absence (no strict definition is applied, but often employers treat more than four weeks as long term) or has frequent short bouts of absence, you may want to seek a medical opinion before making a decision about what action to take.

Under the Access to Medical Reports Act 1988, you must get the employee's written permission to write to their doctor asking for a medical report.

The employee has the right to request that they see the report from the doctor before it is sent to you, and to refuse you access to it, if they don't wish to share it.

If an employee refuses to give you access to their medical report, you could justify making a decision in the absence of the information, and if the employee subsequently claims that you treated them unfairly, you can show that you behaved reasonably by seeking the relevant information.

Personal circumstances

If you work in a small business, it is likely that you will become aware of employees' personal circumstances, some of which they may not want to be general knowledge among their colleagues.

The implied term of *mutual trust and obligation* in the employment contract means that you should be careful not to share any information which might cause distress to the employee, and which they could reasonably have expected you to keep 'under your hat'.

At best, you run the risk of demotivating and upsetting an employee, and at worst, you might give the employee a reason to claim discrimination if you share information about a protected characteristic.

An employee who has caring responsibilities for someone with a disability is 'associated' with the person for whom they are caring, and could claim discrimination if they think they are being treated less favourably than their colleagues because of it.

Letting Go of the Reins

As your business grows and becomes more complex, you will reach a point where you need some expert knowledge, most commonly with the disciplines of marketing, legal, finance, IT and HR.

If you are not an expert yourself, you face the choice of:

✔ Recruiting an expert

✔ Training someone who is in the business already

✔ Buying in the services of marketing agencies, lawyers, accountants or freelance consultants

✔ Outsourcing the work to a specialist provider

You may hit a point of growth in the business when it seems like you need more expertise in all five management disciplines at the same time, and it is unlikely that the business can afford it.

Spend an hour doing a *SWOT analysis* for the marketing, legal, finance, IT and HR in your business. A SWOT analysis is a simple four box grid, where you identify the Strengths, Weaknesses, Opportunities and Threats facing the business; have a look at the example in Figure 10-1.

Once you have created your SWOT analysis, work through it as follows:

1. **Go back to your business plan and remind yourself where you want to take the business in the short and medium term.**

2. **Use the SWOT analysis to identify where your biggest threats and opportunities lie.**

3. **Identify any risks that could fundamentally put the business in jeopardy**

Strengths	Weaknesses
Great team, good mix of people and good working atmosphere	Recently, new employees leaving after 2–3 months
3 apprentices doing really well	Not sure if we have all the HR paperwork up to date
2 new managers showing potential to take on more responsibility	A few employees in one team having a lot of time off sick
Opportunities	**Threats**
New warehouse with better transport links and facilities available 5 miles away	New service contract for big customer and not enough staff
Chamber of Commerce offered to help with getting Investors in People status	Competitor on the same factory estate paying more to their employees
Funding available from local Council for taking on more apprentices	Best manager just notified she is pregnant

Figure 10-1:
Sample SWOT Analysis of HR in your business.

Illustration by John Wiley & Sons, Inc.

4. **Think about how you can use the strengths you already have in the business. In HR terms, that means looking at the people you've got, their skills, experience and potential.**

5. **Consider your budget.**

6. **Consider the costs and benefits of each alternative, where possible, allocating a financial measure.**

As this book specifically looks at HR, break your analysis of the SWOT chart down into the following component parts:

✔ Administration: contracts, letters, files, holiday and sickness records

✔ Legal compliance: procedures, policies, employee rights

✔ Employee relations: disciplinary, grievance, consultation, negotiation

✔ Reward and recognition: pay, benefits, awards, bonuses, motivation

✔ Development: training, career progression, developing managers

✔ Strategy: HR and people planning to fit with the business goals

Some of these elements of HR could be done by one person, but it is difficult for one person to do it all or to be interested in doing it all, so you may decide to keep some of the HR activities in-house, and to outsource or use experts for other elements. Table 10-1 throws up the sort of alternatives you may wish to consider.

Table 10-1	Letting Go of Your HR Responsibilities	
Alternatives	*Costs*	*Benefits*
Recruit an expert	Recruitment costs	Likely to be more self-sufficient
	Additional salary, Employers NI, benefits	Quicker to address issues and risks based on experience
	Work space and equipment	Dedicated resource to focus on HR priorities
	HR/Payroll software costs	
		Fresh perspective
Train someone in the team	Training fees	Familiar with the business
	Opportunity cost of time away from other work	Motivating to offer career progression
	May need to increase salary	More flexibility in the business to cover multiple roles
	More management time while they get up to speed	
	Need to keep investing in training/updates	
Buy in specialist advice	Premium rates for expertise	Only use it when you need it; flexible
	Takes time to get up to speed with business	Lower risk of making mistakes and likely to have professional indemnity insurance
	You need to know what questions to ask/help you need	
	May be tied into a contract	Fresh thinking and up to date expertise
	May invalidate insurance if you don't follow the advice	
Outsource to a specialist provider	Ongoing retainer costs for the duration of the contract	You can specify the service to include administration, advisory and payroll
	Take time to get up to speed	
	Proscriptive administration processes to follow	Strong data protection and legal compliance.
	Few provide on-site support; service may feel impersonal	Professional advice often covered by indemnity

Linking HR and Payroll

There is an inescapable link between HR and payroll that is really obvious in a tiny business, because you probably keep all the records in one place, and one person keeps track of all the administration.

If your accountant (or an external payroll provider) is running your payroll, you need to put controls in place to make sure that

- ✔ Employees are paid correctly, with the correct deductions
- ✔ Fraud is prevented
- ✔ Records are accurate for HMRC real time information reporting

HMRC introduced Real Time Information reporting in 2014 so that all payments received by employees, including wages, benefits and tax credits, are tracked centrally, linked to National Insurance number. Most employers, with very few exemptions, must complete an online return to HMRC at the end of every month.

You can check here to see if you are exempt: `https://www.gov.uk/find-out-which-employers-are-exempt-from-online-payroll-reporting`

Deductions from pay

There are certain deductions which you are legally entitled to make, including tax, National Insurance and any attachment of earnings or deduction of earnings orders issued by a court, usually in relation to child maintenance or the payment of penalty fines.

You are not allowed to make any other deductions from an employee's pay unless you have his or her explicit permission to do so.

The easiest way to cover yourself in case you accidentally over pay somebody, or you want to deduct money from their pay for unauthorized absence or damage to company property, is to include a clause in the employment contract, seeking the employee's permission to make certain deductions.

Statutory payments

When employees go on maternity leave, or request adoption or shared parental leave or have time off work for sickness, you have to make the appropriate statutory payments.

You must ensure that employees provide you with the right paperwork to back up the payments. Keep copies on the employee file for later reference, and send the originals to the payroll provider or HMRC.

You will need the employee's maternity certificate, or MATB1 form if you are reclaiming maternity pay, for example. `https://www.gov.uk/recover-statutory-payments`

Benefits

Most benefits that you provide to employees will have a tax liability, so you must provide the details of any benefits like medical insurance, the use of a company car, company mobile phone, or travel expenses to HMRC so that the employee pays the right tax.

Avoiding the Pitfalls of Outsourcing HR and Payroll

If you decide that outsourcing HR and or payroll is the way to go, you will find a plethora of providers offering services.

Here are ten key questions to ask yourself before committing to a contract with an external service provider:

- Is there any flexibility built into the contract, to grow as your business grows? Often this is expressed in number bands, for example 1–10 employees or 10–50 employees.

- What software is the provider using to manage your data and provide the administration or payroll service? Make sure that you have a demonstration of the system. Some systems have built in 'workflows' to automate certain processes.

- What are the monthly charges, and are there any hidden additional costs you could incur?

- Who will be your key contact? There may be only one person providing the service, or at the other extreme you may be directed to a call centre.

- What data security measures do they have in place? Check if they are registered with the Information Commissioner's Office as Data Controllers, and ask about their back up and disaster recovery provisions.

✔ How much will the service be tailored to your business? Some outsourced service providers have very proscriptive processes, forms and deadlines. Others are more flexible.

✔ Ask for at least two client references and if possible, make a visit to the service provider's office or call centre.

✔ How well will the provider fit with your culture?

✔ How long is the contract and what are the break and notice clauses?

Part III
Growing People and Teams

Five Growing Pains for Small Businesses

- ✔ **Letting go:** Watch out for the signs that it's time to let go of some of the day-to-day running of the business so you can focus on the bigger picture. Recruit great people you can trust, with the skills you need, so you can let go without too much pain.

- ✔ **Stretching up:** Create a structure that allows people to try new things, and support them while they learn. Invest in training people for the skills you will need in the future, not just for now.

- ✔ **Expanding out:** During rapid growth, keep the communication flowing. Make sure that everyone stays connected and focused on the right things.

- ✔ **Hitting the ceiling:** Watch out for hermit crab syndrome. If people feel cramped and under-appreciated they might start looking for a new home. Show people how they can grow within the business.

- ✔ **Losing a tail to save the body:** You might need to sacrifice part of the business, and that means some of the people, for the long-term benefit of the whole business. Use the right processes and treat people fairly to minimise the pain for the leavers and the people left behind.

Interested in finding out more about attracting and retaining top talent? Head to www.dummies.com/extras/hrforsmallbusinessuk.

In this part . . .

- ✔ Put HR strategy at the heart of your leadership
- ✔ Create a flexible, responsive business
- ✔ Grow your future managers and leaders

Chapter 11

Leading Your Growing Business

*W*hat does it mean to lead a growing organisation? What issues will you encounter, and how do you navigate your way through? Such simple questions, but we've devoted a chapter to answering them! Many of the issues discussed in this chapter reflect common and best practice.

Anyone who is a leader recognises that it can be a lonely place and can often be a temporary position if you don't undertake it with vigour and commitment. You may not know it, but if you're an entrepreneur at the helm of a growing business, you're quickly approaching a crossroads. At some point in the not-too-distant future, if your business is flourishing, it will become too big for you to manage it in the way you have always done and therefore it becomes imperative that you develop leadership skills in order to continue to grow. This chapter helps you to make that transition.

Making the Transition from Entrepreneur to Leader

Most small businesses are founded and operated by a person with an entrepreneurial mind-set. You haven't set out to create a business: you believe you are gifted at what you do and you believe you can do it better than the company you work for currently, or you see an opportunity that is not being filled today.

So you start a journey to create a company and serve some customers. Then you become overloaded and so you find another person like you who becomes your first employee, and your leadership journey has begun.

Over time you gradually add a few more people whilst running the business through direct interaction with each of your team members. Most people can do that for a while and even make all the decisions along the way. But at some point in the future, often when you have grown to employ 10 or more employees, things begin to break down. *You* have become a bottleneck because everything has to go through *you*. You have always made all the decisions, after all, it is your business. But unfortunately that approach doesn't scale and soon things are really a problem and the staff and customers begin to express dissatisfaction with a company that they were previously very happy with.

What has to change to move you from entrepreneur to leader? Much of the change is a mind shift. It is understanding that rather than working 'in' the business 24/7/365, you have to spend significant time working 'on' the business as well. The key is that the transition should begin. Until that happens, no progress can be made. Accidental entrepreneurs seldom have business training, so even with a desire to make a change they often struggle knowing what that means.

Staying involved whilst delegating decision making

In its beginning stages, a company *is* its entrepreneur. Because the entrepreneur is the creator of the enterprise, he frequently experiences a very strong emotional attachment to the business, not unlike that of a parent to a child. As a result, entrepreneurs often feel the need to exercise complete control over every detail of the business, being driven by the fear that if they don't do something, it won't be done correctly.

Entrepreneurs who want to be able to scale successfully need to learn how to delegate, pushing decisions as far down the organisation as possible so that they can focus on high-level problems like determining the company's overall direction and long-term goals. At this stage, set clear emotional and practical boundaries. You can no longer equate yourself with the company; you can no longer be all-powerful and all-seeing.

Being able to delegate responsibilities is a critical skill for making the most of your personal effectiveness. Delegating, however, can be somewhat tricky - you have to be firm, yet trusting with the person you're delegating your responsibilities to.

When looking to delegate to your team you should take account of the following:

- **Forget your ego.** A big mental road block to delegation is that 'If you want something done right, then do it yourself.' You're not the only person in the world who can do it right. You *may* be the only person who can do it right at this very moment, but if you train someone, they'll probably be able to do it right, too.

- **Stop waiting for people to volunteer.** If you're reluctant to delegate work, you may have a minor case of martyr syndrome - you're probably overwhelmed, and you often wonder why people don't ever offer to help. Let go of any frustration you might have over people not offering a helping hand; remember that it's ultimately your job to communicate your needs and therefore seek help!

- **Delegate the objective, not the procedure.** This is the key to not becoming a micro-manager. Set clear standards for what kinds of results you're looking for, and show the person how you do it, but tell them that they can do it any way they want, as long as it's done well and it's completed on time.

- **Allocate the resources necessary to complete the task.** You may have resources available that are necessary to complete the task but the person given the task may not be able to access them. Things like password protected data and specialised equipment can be vital to the completion of this task, so make sure that your helper has whatever he or she needs to succeed.

- **Be patient and accept that there will be mistakes.** The person to whom you delegate *will* make mistakes while he or she is learning how to do a new task. It's part of the learning process. If a task or project doesn't turn out the way you wanted it to it's your fault, not his or hers.

- **Recognise your helper when it counts.** Delegating tasks to someone else is necessary if you are to be an effective leader. However, it's counterproductive when you delegate a task, let your helper work hard on it, and then take all the credit for yourself. Recognise and praise the efforts of others on your behalf.

Building trust

One of the biggest mistakes you can make as a leader is to assume that others trust you simply by virtue of your role or title. Trust is not a benefit that comes packaged with the nameplate on your door. As we know if you are a parent, trust must be earned, and it takes time.

As a leader, you are trusted only to the degree that people believe in your ability, consistency, integrity, and commitment to deliver. The good news is that you can earn trust over time, by building and maintaining eight key strengths (all the 'C's'):

- **Clarity:** *People trust the clear and mistrust or distrust the ambiguous.* Be clear about your mission, purpose, expectations, and daily activities. When you are clear about your expectations, you are more likely to get what you want. When you are clear about priorities on a daily basis, you will find your team will become more productive and effective.

- **Compassion:** *People put faith in those who care beyond themselves.* Think beyond yourself, and never underestimate the power of sincerely caring about another person. People are often sceptical about whether someone really has their best interests in mind.

- **Character:** *People notice those who do what is right ahead of what is easy.* Leaders who have built this pillar consistently do what needs to be done when it needs to be done.

- **Contribution:** *Few things build trust quicker than actual results.* You can have compassion and character, but without the results you promised, people won't trust you. Be a contributor who delivers real results.

- **Competency:** *People have confidence in those who stay fresh, relevant, and capable.* You should keep learning new ways of doing things and stay current on ideas and trends. Arrogance and a been there done that attitude prevents you from growing, and compromises others' confidence in you.

- **Connection:** *People want to follow, buy from, and be around friends – and having friends is all about building connections.* Trust is all about relationships, and relationships are best built by establishing genuine connection. Ask questions, listen, and above all, show gratitude –it's the primary trait of truly talented connectors.

- **Commitment:** *People believe in those who stand through adversity.* Your team trust you when they see commitment and sacrifice for the greater good. Commitment builds trust.

- **Consistency:** *In every area of life, it's the little things – done consistently – that make the big difference.* The little things done consistently make for a higher level of trust and better results. The great leaders consistently do the small but most important things first. They make that call and write that thank you note. Do the little things, consistently.

Without trust in the workplace, communication and teamwork erodes. Additionally, morale decreases while turnover rises. These are all Bad Things.

Shifting from reactive management to strategic planning

Reactive management refers to a situation in which you can't – or don't – plan ahead for problems or opportunities. Instead, you react to them as they happen. As a result, you're always a step behind. You don't have time to look ahead to pre-empt problems, so they seem to happen out of the blue.

In contrast, proactive management happens when you plan ahead to avoid or manage problems.

Why reactive management happens

You might be in a reactive state for several reasons. For example:

- A crisis may have forced you to change or abandon your plans. You need to make short-term decisions to cope with a fast-developing situation.

- Your organisation may have poorly planned processes or policies. You need to spend your time fixing these or working around them, instead of planning for the future.

- You may find a reactive management style exciting. People can enjoy the buzz that goes along with it.

Making the shift to strategic planning

To many people, _strategic planning_ is something meant only for big businesses, but it is equally applicable to small businesses. Strategic planning is matching the strengths of your business to available opportunities. To do this effectively, you need to collect, screen and analyse information about the business environment. You also need to have a clear understanding of your business - its strengths and weaknesses - and develop a clear mission, goals and objective.

The core components of a strategic plan are to:

- **Determine where you are.** For an accurate picture of where your business is, conduct external and internal audits to get a clear understanding of the marketplace, the competitive environment, and your organisation's competencies (your real – not perceived – competencies).

- **Identify what's important.** Focus on where you want to take your business over time. This sets the direction of the business over the long term and clearly defines the mission (markets, customers, products, and so on) and vision.

From this analysis, you can determine the *priority issues* – those issues so significant to the overall well-being of the enterprise that they require the full and immediate attention of the entire management team. The strategic plan should focus on these issues, so:

1. **Define what you must achieve.** Define the expected objectives that clearly state what your business must achieve to address the priority issues.

2. **Determine who is accountable.** This is how you're going to get to where you want to go. The strategies, action plans, and budgets are all steps in the process that effectively communicate how you will allocate time, your people, and money to address the priority issues and achieve the defined objectives.

3. **Review. Review. Review.** It's not over. It's never over. To ensure that the plan performs as designed, you must hold regularly scheduled formal reviews of the process and refine as necessary.

Planning plays an important role in any business venture. It can make the difference between the success or failure of your business. You should plan carefully before investing your time and, especially, your money in any business venture. A strategic plan is a document used to communicate with your team the business goals, the actions needed to achieve those goals and all of the other critical elements developed during the planning exercise.

Two factors now make strategic planning even more important: globalisation and technological innovation. Technological advances have levelled the playing field for smaller businesses that want to compete with larger ones, but they have also accelerated the pace of change and the degree of uncertainty every business owner has to live with. You need a way to assess the big picture, and that's where strategic planning comes in.

Though the primary purpose of a strategic plan is to help you chart the smartest possible path to growth, there are other benefits. A good plan ensures that every member of your team is working toward the same goals, and helps you be smarter about budgeting, hiring, resource allocation, and succession planning. If you're looking for external financing, it can reassure lenders that you have both a vision and a specific plan to achieve it.

Strategic planning comes in many shapes and forms; however, the strategic planning process should include a *situational analysis*. This consists of looking at the current external and internal environment the business finds itself in, formulating business objectives and strategies based upon the environmental assessment, and developing procedures to implement and evaluate the strategic plan.

Strategic plans for your business should cover a three-to-five year period, but if the business or its environment is highly dynamic, a shorter period may be advisable.

Getting the Right People on the Bus

In the classic book *Good to Great*, Jim Collins says, '. . .to build a successful organisation and team you must get the right people on the bus.' His research shows that great companies and organisations do this. They get the right people and put them in the right seats.

But a question you should be asking yourself is 'Who are the right people?' After all, in order to get the right people on the bus you must identify who the right people are, right?

Getting the wrong people off the bus and the people in the right seats is a lot harder than it seems. Chapter 5 helps with regard to determining how people should leave your business.

You will quickly find that if you're filling the bus with the right people in a small company, there's likely no baggage and people are jumping from seat to seat. However, as you grow, it becomes more and more important to look in the rear view mirror and see how things are settling out.

These principles are worth consideration when rearranging your bus:

✔ **Just because someone was the right fit at the last stop doesn't mean they are the right fit at every stop.** Companies outgrow employees. Employees outgrow companies. It happens. Get over it and don't hold onto people for compassionate reasons. Also accept that great people will leave, and it is critically important to acknowledge this point. However, if they have had a great experience with you they become advocates of you and your business, and you never know, they might want to come back!

✔ **Measure employee contribution versus aggravation.** You may live with more aggravation from your highest performers, but their contribution tends to exceed issues that nag and distract the company. But don't let the contribution versus aggravation equation get out of balance – even for your top performers. Deal with it through a balanced review of their contribution, look at their behaviours in equal light to their measurable achievements and form an all round view of their value to your business. After all, why have a high performing sales manager if he continually bullies his team, leading to employee turnover and therefore additional cost.

✔ **Make deliberate decisions.** If you suspect that someone is no longer a good fit, make the decision to exit them quickly, but do not make knee jerk reactions and do not let an issue linger. Be deliberate, decisive, and move on. If you have any compassion at all it will be insanely painful to ask someone to leave the bus, but, it will inevitably be better for both the business and the individual. Do both of you a favour and have the hard conversation.

> ✔ **Asking someone to change seats can be tricky.** Do not ask someone to get out of a seat without assigning them a new one to sit in. Develop a plan, define clear success criteria, and persevere. Any ambiguity when moving seats is a disaster. The more time the employee is walking in the aisle, the higher the probability that you'll need to swerve, they will fall over and someone will get hurt. Before you do it, make sure that you're not taking the easy road because you don't want to have to ask them to get off!

Recruiting to match your values and your culture

Company culture, sometimes referred to as organisational culture, is an integral part of any company's identity, as it dictates how business is conducted, the way decisions are made and how employees treat one another.

At small businesses in particular, each employee can have a sizable impact – either good or bad – on the organisational culture. Most small business owners can tell stories of past hires, employees who, despite having impeccable credentials and great interviews, just didn't fit in or rubbed people the wrong way.

The impact of these at a small business can be significant, including training and equipment outlays as well as the 'softer' costs of diminished morale, not to mention increased uncertainty in the workplace.

See Chapter 3 for further details regarding establishing the culture of your company.

Recognising the things you aren't good at

Perhaps one of the most important reasons to recruit new staff is to put in place a skill or competence in your business that either supplements what you do or even perhaps is so specialist in its nature that it would be foolish to believe you would have it yourself.

Obvious examples would be Finance, Human Resources, Marketing or sales skills. So it is therefore critical that you recruit experts in these areas that have knowledge and experience that is greater than your own.

Chapter 2 gives more guidance for recruiting the right people at the right time.

Recruitment is one option; outsourcing to specialists can in the short term also be a beneficial option, because it may:

- ✔ Reduce and control operating costs
- ✔ Improve company focus
- ✔ Gain access to world class capabilities
- ✔ Free internal resources for other purposes
- ✔ Share risks with a partner company

In the early days, cost or headcount reduction were the most common reasons to outsource. In today's world the drivers are often more strategic, and focus on carrying out core value-adding activities in-house where an organisation can best utilize its core competencies.

Ensuring that everyone is going to the same destination

You need to make sure that you get the agreement and buy-in of all those who are going to make the journey with you. Anyone who has travelled with children who are being taken somewhere they don't want to go will appreciate this. You may still achieve your goal, though they object, but the entire process will be painful and you may even wish you hadn't gone at all. Get everyone involved and make sure they feel that they have been consulted and listened to, because the effort of involving them upfront is a lot less than the effort of dragging them along behind you fighting every step

So how do you ensure that everyone is going in the same direction and most importantly that the direction they are going is your desired destination? It is actually relatively simple, and links directly with the strategic planning you need to undertake.

The strategic planning exercise allows you to chart the smartest possible path to growth. By undertaking this exercise you should arrive at the targets and objectives your business will need to achieve in order to grow. The targets might be financial or they might be associated with developing a new product or service that enables you to grow.

You need to translate the big hairy organisational targets into a series of objectives and targets that reflect your progress along your journey. Once you have created the targets you then need to delegate them to your team.

Keep the individual employee objectives SMART (Simple, Measurable, Achievable, Relevant and Timely). In Chapter 8 you discover how to align your business goals to those of your employees.

Don't forget to check progress along the way. Regularly checking your progress has a number of benefits. It allows you to spot early when you are off course, making any corrections only minor ones, saving time and resources. It builds confidence in those people taking the journey allowing them to think, 'Yes, we are making progress', 'We are on track', and so on. It reaffirms that you made the right decision in choosing your goal and course of action. It also builds a momentum of its own, encouraging people to keep going and put the effort in because they see that effort isn't wasted.

An important point to remember is when you get to your destination, celebrate your success! How many times in life do you reach the top of the mountain and rather than taking the time to admire the view, appreciate your achievements and thinking about what you have learnt from the journey, someone shouts up "Look! There is the next mountain and it is even higher and steeper than this one. Let's go everyone!"?

When you achieve your goal make sure you make the time to enjoy it. Take a relaxing breath, enjoy your new surroundings and savour the smells and flavours of the proverbial food and beer, because the next time the going gets tough and you ask people to dig deep, those memories will sustain them and keep them going. That shared experience builds a strong, resilient team.

Understanding That Leadership Is a Lonely Place

Leadership is lonely. You may or may not believe that great leaders are motivated by making the right decisions for the greatest good of the business and teams they lead. You may already find support systems, emotional and spiritual fulfilment, and validation outside of the work setting through family, friends, and external coaches/advisors. However, all of this is purely theoretical unless you really do understand that leadership really is a lonely place.

The best leaders have confidantes who can give it to them straight, speak truth to power, and keep them in the know. Stanford management professor Robert Sutton warned against those in charge becoming more self-absorbed and less attuned to others' perspectives precisely when they need outside information the most.

You also need to be aware that one person's isolation or loneliness becomes a larger problem when it leads to poor decision-making, negativity, fatigue and frustration. And who wants to work for you if you are an unhappy person?

So how do you deal with this? Here are our ideas on dealing with loneliness at the top:

- ✔ **Find a peer group.** You will struggle to find equilibrium. Find people in similar positions who are battling similar circumstances that you can discuss confidential issues with. It will have a significant impact on your business and your well-being.

- ✔ **Get a coach or a mentor.** One of the reasons a coach is helpful is because he or she can discuss issues with no vested interest in your decision — unlike nearly everyone else in your life. A good coach helps you see blind spots and get underneath issues, not just attack them at the surface.

    Often, you can find a mentor who serves the same function in an unpaid relationship. Finding a leader with past experience relevant to yours, who is motivated to be your mentor, can be a big advantage. That person knows how hard it is to be in your shoes because they were there once. Perhaps it's why they'll jump in to help you now.

So in the end don't just accept that it is a lonely place, and that in reality life may appear to suck! Take the initiative and tackle the issue as you would any other business problem.

The Buck Always Stops With You. . . check out this definition of accountability from the *Merriam-Webster Dictionary:*

> *The quality or state of being accountable; an obligation or willingness to accept responsibility or to account for one's actions.*

Defining accountability may be easy, but how many of you actually live up to it? It would appear that we live today in a society where we demand privacy for ourselves and accountability from everyone else!

However, you know as a business leader that ultimately your actions do lead to outcomes for which you cannot avoid accountability. So how do you ensure that everyone on your business feels accountable for their actions?

Basically you ask them and you demonstrate time and time again the following:

- ✔ **Face your own lack of accountability.** In order to improve your behaviour, you must identify and analyse your weak points. So first, look back at your leadership and pinpoint times when you've failed to hold yourself, or your team accountable. If you know when and how you're most likely not to have taken accountability or held a member of your team to account will help you make sure it doesn't happen again.

✔ **Take ownership of all problems (and stop playing the blame game!).** It's pretty simple: If you're a leader, the buck does stop with you . . . regardless of whether the results are good or bad. We have all blamed external problems, for example a financial downturn, or a client leaving for reasons that you perceive are beyond your control, but the reality is these things happen! Your job is to ensure that you have a steady pipeline of replacement clients to mitigate the inevitable losses.

As a leader, your job is to do everything you can to fix every single problem. If you don't, the other person isn't the weak link; you are. The next time you find yourself in this situation, don't point fingers. Instead say, 'Let's all concentrate on helping me fix our problem'. See yourself as the accountable party. And as soon as you realise there's an issue, ask yourself how you allowed this to happen. Getting to the bottom of things in an honest and timely manner will give you the most direct route to the solution, even if it's not comfortable.

Believing That People Really Are Your Most Important Asset

Not all people are valuable assets, but the vast majority could be if only they were managed properly. The problem is very, very few managers or HR people know how to do that.

Many companies, even those with HR departments, do a very poor job of managing their employees, a poor job of unleashing the full potential of employees. A considerable store of creativity, innovation and productivity exists in every person, and the management challenge is to unleash that supply and apply it to the goals of the business.

So what do you do to demonstrate that you really believe your people are your greatest asset rather than pay lip service?

✔ **Embrace people as your most valuable asset.** You should fully recognise your people as your most valuable asset. Realise your best performing employees will come from the ranks of the most engaged, and understand that employee engagement drives business outcomes. It's important to keep in mind that it's through your employees that customer loyalty is built. Also, it's through them that products and services get delivered, and profits and growth are achieved.

✔ **Help leaders lead.** Today's fast-paced business environment demands significantly more leadership than in past years. People in management positions play a vital role in engaging people and getting results. You need to set the pace and tone, communicate expectations, get people actively involved in running the day-to-day business, and provide regular coaching and feedback so your employees can keep the momentum going and make needed course corrections.

✔ **Develop your people to be the best they can be.** Always remember, people want to do a good job. They want to participate in a winning business, where they know they can make a difference, have influence over their future, and feel appreciated for their efforts. Employees thrive on performing meaningful work and knowing that what they do contributes to the success of the business. Don't forget to communicate to them how they are doing.

✔ **Embrace learning and growth.** Your employees need to know you value them as much as you do any customer. One way to show them is to invest in their professional development. When you ensure that they have the skills and information they need to perform well in their job, they know you care. When you take the time to reinforce what they've learned in training, they know you support their success. When you teach them everything you know and strive to help them become the best they can be, they know you value them and their contributions.

Making cash or growing people

Many entrepreneurs seem to view employee training and development as more optional than essential . . . a viewpoint that can be costly to both short-term profits and long-term progress.

The primary reason training is considered optional by so many business owners is because it's viewed more as an expense than an investment. This is completely understandable when you realise that in many companies, training and development aren't focused on producing a targeted result for the business. As a result, business owners frequently send their people to training courses that seem right and sound good without knowing what to expect in return. But without measurable results, it's almost impossible to view training as anything more than an expense.

Now contrast that approach to one where training's viewed as a capital investment with thoughtful consideration as to how you're going to obtain an acceptable rate of return on your investment. And a good place to start your "thoughtful consideration" is with a needs analysis.

As it relates to training and development, a needs analysis is really an outcome analysis – what do you want out of this training? Ask yourself, 'What's going to change in my business or in the behaviour or performance of my employees as a result of this training that's going to help my company?' Be forewarned: this exercise requires you to take time to think it through and focus more on your processes than your products.

As you go through this analysis, consider the strengths and weaknesses in your company and try to identify the deficiencies that, when corrected, represent a potential for upside gain in your business. A common area for improvement in many companies is helping supervisors better manage for performance. Many people are promoted into managerial positions because they're technically good at their jobs, but they aren't trained as managers to help their subordinates achieve peak performance.

Determining your training and development needs based on targeted results is only the beginning. The next step is to establish a learning dynamic for your company.

In today's economy, if your business isn't learning, then you're going to fall behind. And a business learns as its people learn. Your employees are the ones that produce, refine, protect, deliver and manage your products or services every day, year in, year out. With the rapid pace and international reach of the 21st century marketplace, continual learning is critical to your business's continued success.

To create a learning culture in your business, begin by clearly communicating your expectation that employees should take the steps necessary to hone their skills to stay on top of their professions or fields of work. Make sure you support their efforts in this area by supplying the resources they need to accomplish this goal. Second, communicate to your employees the specific training needs and targeted results you've established as a result of your needs analysis.

Third, provide a sound introduction and orientation to your company's culture, including your learning culture, to any new employees you hire. This orientation should introduce employees to your company, and provide them with proper training in the successful procedures your company's developed and learned over time.

Every successful training and development program also includes a component that addresses your current and future leadership needs. At its core, this component must provide for the systematic identification and development of your managers in terms of the leadership style that drives your business and makes it unique and profitable. Have you spent time thoughtfully examining the style of leadership that's most successful in your environment and that you want to promote? What steps are you taking to develop those important leadership traits in your people?

Financial considerations related to training can be perplexing, but in most cases, the true budgetary impact depends on how well you manage the first three components (needs analysis, learning and leadership). If your training is targeted to specific business results, then you're more likely to be happy with what you spend on training. But if the training budget isn't related to specific outcomes, then money is more likely to be spent on courses that have no positive impact on the company.

In many organizations, training budgets are solely a function of whether the company is enjoying an economic upswing or enduring a downturn. In good times, companies tend to spend money on training that's not significant to the organization, and in bad times, the pendulum swings to the other extreme and training is eliminated altogether. In any economic environment, the training expense should be determined by the targeted business results you want, not other budget-related factors.

To help counter this tendency, sit down and assess your training and development needs once or twice a year to identify your needs, and brainstorm how to achieve your desired results effectively and efficiently.

Your employees are your principle business asset. Invest in them thoughtfully and strategically, and you'll reap rewards that pay off now and for years to come.

By tying training directly to a quantifiable factor, such as improved productivity or process improvement, you can come up with a figure that reflects the value of the training to your company's bottom line. Choosing the right factors to measure, both before and after training, enables you to show how training has resulted in benefits to your employees and your company. You can measure this return on investment of the training as follows:

1. **Choose discrete items to measure, based on what type of training is being offered and what areas of your business it is designed to impact.**

   If the training is intended to teach a new, faster process to make widgets, for example, your baseline criteria to measure against are how long it takes the average employee to make one widget and at what cost.

2. **Measure how long it takes the average employee to make the widgets before the training.**

   If the average number of widgets produced per employee is 60 per 40-hour, five-day work week, the employee averages 12 per day, or 1.5 widgets per hour.

3. Calculate the company's pre-training, per-widget production cost.

It costs the company £180 per week per employee for all costs, including wages, materials, equipment, facilities, distribution and overhead. The employee makes 60 widgets each week, so each widget costs the company £3 to make. The same 60 widgets are sold for £4 apiece, for a profit of £1 each, or £60 per week. Over the course of a 50-week work year, assuming the standard two weeks of vacation time, the employee makes enough widgets to earn the company £3,000 in profits.

4. Provide the process improvement training to the employees, at a cost of £1,000 per employee, for this example.

If the training is successful, you should expect to see a greater number of widgets produced per employee, per hour. Measure the amount of time it takes the employees to make widgets after they have successfully completed the training program. If the employee now makes 80 widgets each week, or 16 widgets per day, the average number of widgets produced per employee is now two per hour. This reflects a 25% increase in per-hour production by the employee following the training – a clear improvement.

5. Calculate the new per-widget production cost.

Since receiving the training, each employee is now averaging two widgets per hour. The weekly per-employee operating costs are the same – £180 per week – but the employee is now producing 80 widgets each week, so the cost per widget drops to £2.25. The widgets are still sold for £4, but since the production cost has dropped, the per-widget profit is now £1.75. So the employee is now producing a profit for the company of £140 per week, for a total profit of £7,000 per year – another clear increase.

6. Figure out the net benefit to your company.

In this example, the benefit is the increased profit produced for the company by the employee over a year. Before training, the annual profit produced was £3,000 per employee, based on 3,000 widgets a year making £1 profit each. The employee now makes 4,000 widgets each year, at a per-widget profit of £1.75, so the total annual profit from that employee's widget production is £7,000. The increased profit is £4,000.

7. Calculate the ROI for that employee's training, using the standard formula.

Use the net benefit – increased profit – and training costs noted above. In this example, ROI (percentage) = ([£4,000 – 1,000]/1,000) × 100, or (3,000/1,000) × 100, or 3 × 100, for a percentage return on investment of 300. This training can thereby be shown to have been effective and worthwhile, since you are getting a return of £3 for every £1 spent on training.

Keeping the right people

Your employee turnover rate can be an important indicator in telling you if your workforce plans are effective. To put this at its most basic, if you have recruited people you want to keep, and they are leaving, or if you want people to go, and they are staying, then you have a problem!

An employee quits his or her job whenever they face problems at the work-place and are not satisfied with their work. The job must be challenging enough and the employees should learn something new every day for them to stick to it for a long time. It is the responsibility of you and your managers to ensure that the team members are contented with their work and share a good rapport amongst themselves.

When people are badly managed, there can be unhappiness, reduced efficiency and high staff turnover. When the people that work for you resign, they often leave poor managers, not your business.

Businesses with high potential for turnover send out warning signals, according to Gallup research, but managers and executives must know where to look. These are the top five predictors of turnover:

- ✔ **The immediate manager.** If employees report that their manager's expectations are unclear; or that their manager provides inadequate equipment, materials, or resources; or that opportunities for progress and development are few and far between, watch out: trouble is on the way.

- ✔ **Poor fit to the job.** Another sign of trouble appears when employees perceive that they don't have opportunities to do what they do best every day.

- ✔ **Co-workers not committed to quality.** Watch for employees who perceive that their co-workers are not committed to a high standard of work.

- ✔ **Pay and benefits.** Engaged employees are far more likely to perceive that they are paid appropriately for the work they do (43%), compared to employees who are disengaged (15%) or actively disengaged (13%). And pay and benefits become a big issue if employees feel that their co-workers aren't committed to quality; they may feel entitled to extra compensation to make up the difference or to make them feel like they are truly valued by their employer.

- ✔ **Connection to the business or to you and your management.** Another key sign that turnover may be looming appears when employees don't feel a connection to your business mission or purpose or its leadership.

So what can you do about this? The answers are relatively straightforward but not always easy to apply. The majority of successful employee retention is associated with your leadership of your business.

Research by the leading Human Resources consultancy HAY has indicated that the following five actions and leadership behaviours make a significant difference to the engagement and therefore retention of your employees:

- ✔ **Employees like certainty.** They need reassuring that the firm they work for is well-led and heading in a positive direction.

- ✔ **People want to be able to reach their potential at work.** They want to know that there are opportunities to learn, grow and progress.

- ✔ **Staff need to feel valued,** especially if they are to deliver more with less in difficult times.

- ✔ **Employees need to feel that they are working for a tightly run operation,** one that will support them to work smarter as well as harder, and where colleagues pull together to help each other.

- ✔ **You must unleash the force for good** by allowing your staff to do their jobs effectively and to influence how work is done.

What to take away from these points? Clearly, delegation is important to your personal success as the leader of your business, but you must also remember that delegation breeds contentment and engagement in your team. Delegation profits everyone.

Chapter 12

Getting the Structure Right

. . . .

In This Chapter

▶ Planning ahead to enhance your business

▶ Building flexibility into the way you work

▶ Creating space for growth

. . . .

*P*icture an old-fashioned stagecoach thundering along a dusty road. It's designed to carry six passengers inside, some luggage on the roof, and a driver on a high seat holding the reins and directing the horses. You're the driver. You can pile on some extra luggage for one of the passengers and charge them a bit extra. You can take a turn off the main road to pick up an additional passenger and squeeze them in for a fee. You can even drive the horses an extra few miles to the next coaching inn before you feed and water them. You can push your luck for a few days but if you keep this up, the axles will creak, the horses will slow down and the passengers will start to complain. There's a point at which you need to provide a second coach, even if it's not full.

This chapter is about how to construct the right vehicle, whether it's the stagecoach described here or the bus described in Chapter 11, to carry you and your team to your destination.

And in case you're wondering (we think you probably are), we've not gone completely crazy with this analogy between your business and a stagecoach; check out the sidebar, 'A vehicle for your business ideas' to find out more.

Joining Up Your Business Plans and Your People Plans

In the early days of your business, you do everything in your power to grow your revenue without increasing your costs, but if you pile on extra production, extra customers and extra working hours every day, without increasing your resources, something will snap.

A vehicle for your business ideas

On a 'Start your own Enterprise' course for business novices, a warm up exercise to get people thinking about how they would describe their business idea links us back to the analogy of the stagecoach. The trainer asked everyone to imagine that their business was a vehicle, and to draw a picture of it. Predictably, some people drew a bus, with themselves in the driving seat, and lots of smiling customers going along for the ride. One person drew a vertical take-off plane, with one seat for the pilot. He was planning to make lots of money out of an Internet business he would run from his bedroom. He was going to move fast, work alone, and go straight to the top. Another drew a fluffy cloud drifting across a blue sky to describe her holistic therapy business – she wanted her clients to feel as though they were floating on a cloud. Then there was the chap who drew a bicycle with a basket on the front to represent his environmentally-friendly local delivery business.

The potential entrepreneurs were really surprised by how much their drawings inadvertently revealed about their values, goals and dreams. More to the point, the drawings revealed a lot about how these people planned to structure their businesses. Some of their companies would never grow beyond the owner's personal input and pedal power. Others could grow larger, either by simply increasing in size, or by replicating a simple structure multiple times.

In Chapter 11 you read about using your strategic plan to map out the road ahead, and plot the milestones you want to hit along the way. In Chapter 8 you discover how to link your employees' goals to your business goals, and how to encourage and reward people for meeting these goals. Chapter 2 looks at the signs that your business might be ready to take on employees. This section offers further detail and ideas.

Sizing up your people

When you recruit for each new job in the business, write a job description and person specification. Writing a job description forces you to be specific about what the business needs, and what gaps you are trying to fill with the new job. The person specification is simply your tool to measure up the candidates against the skills and experience you want them to have to do the job. You can read more about this in Chapter 2.

In the early days, when money is tight and you are building your customer base, you will probably recruit behind the demand – each time you take someone on you are running to keep up rather than building future capacity. At some point, if you want to grow the business beyond its current size, you will need to take a leap of faith, and recruit ahead of the immediate business need. That is where your strategic plan comes in.

Let's use the example of an office cleaning services company. The owner wants to double the sales revenue in the next five years. He might not need twice as many sales people to hit the target, but he will need more resources. The next few sections demonstrate what he needs to think about – but of course this isn't just relevant to an ambitious office cleaning service; it applies to your business too.

Measuring up current resources

Working out who and what is needed to support the business growth is a key HR skill. It starts with understanding what is happening in the current sales (or other relevant) team. Consider the following:

- Calculate the number of people and the total time they are spending on sales

- Calculate the conversion rate from sales calls through appointments and proposals to signed contracts

- Identify if the average conversion rate is different for each individual in the team

- Identify the factors which might affect individual performance – geography of the 'sales patch', types of clients, size or type of contract, employee experience, personal effectiveness, training, style of the manager, incentives on offer

- Calculate what time is being spent by other people supporting the sales effort – for example a sales administration team sending out proposals, a telesales team identifying warm leads, a marketing person managing the website and social media, an apprentice researching local businesses

- Add up the total people time and cost of generating the current sales revenue

- Calculate a ratio to reflect the relationship between sales revenue and the total cost of sales

- Estimate any spare capacity in the current team to take on more work

Generating more sales revenue is only one part of the growth equation. If the cleaning company owner keeps piling on new customers without adding to his cleaning team and renewing the equipment, he will lose customers and staff as quickly as he can find them.

Estimating spare capacity

Estimating spare capacity is probably the trickiest aspect of this process. Unless people are sitting around twiddling their thumbs, it can be difficult to tell whether they have capacity to do more work.

You could do some simple checks every so often to make sure that the team are not just looking busy on Facebook or Internet shopping. Wander through the workspace and have a look at people's screens. You could look at people's Internet history or just log in to their emails if you have admin access.

Before assuming that you need to recruit lots more people, think about the processes and people you've already got in place and whether you could improve efficiency. The cleaning company owner could check the van routes to optimise the travelling time for his cleaning teams.

Factors you should consider include:

✔ How technology or improved processes might make the current team more efficient

✔ Whether training would help people to work smarter

✔ What incentives you have in place to encourage people to get better results

✔ Whether the managers or team leaders are pro-actively managing their teams' performance, particularly if people are under performing

Measuring people's contribution

There are some aspects of your business which are easy to quantify in time and money terms and others which are less straightforward. The ones that can be expressed in numbers are often called *Metrics* or *Key Performance Indicators. You* can use them to keep track of the most important aspects of your business as it grows.

If you measure the *baseline,* which is your starting point, while the business is still small, and set the improvement targets from there, you're more likely to be realistic about the numbers, because you are still in touch with many of the day to day activities.

Set simple metrics that are easy to measure without lots of complicated reports that add to people's workload. Some examples of metrics you could set for various people in your business are

✔ Number and ratio of sales calls to appointments and signed contracts

✔ Productivity rates – number of rooms cleaned, boxes packed, blogs published, adults trained, children's faces painted

✔ Creditor days and debtor days – average length of time that incoming and outgoing invoices are outstanding

✔ Monthly net profit

✔ Satisfaction ratings from customers or clients

If you measure the key metrics of your business over a prolonged period you will be able to track the impact of any actions you take, such as providing training, or installing a new telephone system.

Your metrics tell you where your business is now, and your strategic plan tells you where you need to take it over the next 3 to 5 years. Now all you have to do is construct the vehicle to take you there.

Getting ahead of the growth curve

If you are planning for a step change in the business, rather than growing organically, at times you'll need to employ new people, incurring higher costs and earning lower profit margins in the short term, to create the capacity to grow your margins in the medium and long term.

Following the stagecoach analogy earlier in the chapter: if your coach will only hold six passengers, and you want to carry seven passengers, you need to invest in a second coach and horses and another driver. You may lose money on that passenger route in the short term but if you never acquire the second coach, your profit will always be limited by how many passengers you can transport in one coach.

However, improving the capacity of your business is not just about employing more people. Step back and think about the skills and knowledge your business needs as it grows. You may be able to tap into more of your current employees' potential. Part of your role as the leader of the business is to support your employees to grow, so that they contribute to the increasing capacity of the business as it grows.

Shaping your team to do the business

You could probably describe fairly quickly which aspects of your work take up most of your time, which parts you love and which parts you would hand over in a flash, given half a chance. Most of your employees would be able to describe their own jobs in those terms too, if you asked them.

For each job in your business, imagine it split like this:

25%	The new and stretching stuff that keeps the job interesting
50%	The day to day stuff that must be done, and is quite interesting The 'core' of the job
25%	The familiar but dull stuff that could go to someone else

In a growing business, you can create opportunities for everyone to spend more time on the top 25% of their job, and less time on the bottom 25% of their job. Think of all the jobs as part of the bigger picture.

One person's familiar but dull can be another person's new and stretching, as demonstrated in Table 12-1.

Table 12-1		Stretch, Core, and Familiar Business Tasks					
Manager		*Customer Service Role*		*Receptionist*		*Intern*	
Stretch 25%	Creating a new service agreement						
Core 50%	Managing the team						
Familiar 25%	Training new colleagues	Stretch 25%	Training new colleagues				
		Core 50%	Taking customer orders				
		Familiar 25%	Routine customer complaints	Stretch 25%	Routine customer complaints		
				Core 50%	Meeting and greeting visitors		
				Familiar 25%	Taking and directing calls	Stretch 25%	Taking and directing calls
						Core 50%	Data input
						Familiar 25%	Scanning files

Keeping employees engaged

Keep talking to your employees about what they like doing, what they hate doing, and what they hope to do in the future.

Think pro-actively about changing the shape of people's jobs to keep every job interesting, and to grow the total sum of skills and knowledge in the business.

If the business is static, and you're not recruiting lots of new people, you can still mix it up between jobs so that people get a new challenge every so often.

Don't raise employees' expectations of interesting work and career progression unless you can deliver. It's better to stay silent than to disappoint people. Check out the sidebar 'Motivation for Millennials' to see what makes these particular employees tick.

Making time for learning

If the business is constantly busy and everyone is working flat out, they won't have space in their heads or time in their working day to learn new things.

In a small business you need to keep things fluid, and not have too many rigid processes, but you can create an environment that supports growth by

- ✔ Allocating a budget to pay for external training if that is required

- ✔ Encouraging employees to train each other

- ✔ Allocating space and time for employees to learn new skills

- ✔ Delegating some of your familiar but dull stuff to other people who will learn from doing it

- ✔ Regularly reviewing job descriptions and talking to people about how their jobs could change

- ✔ Looking at the people you have in the business before you recruit from outside. Let your current employees hand over some of their familiar but dull work to the new person who will find it interesting and stretching.

You can't expect people to just pick up the skills and experience they need to do more complex work if you don't give them any training.

Motivation for Millennials

A recent London School of Economics (LSE) study of '*Millennials*' or people born between 1980 and 2000 indicates that they make up 50% of the global work population. 83% of 'Millennial' responses to an attitude survey indicated they had thought about leaving their current job, and only 23% of them planned to stay longer than 3 years. The most important factors affecting their job satisfaction were

- Decision-Making Autonomy
- Workplace Communication
- Impact of Work Tasks
- Skill Development
- Shared Values
- Social Support
- Opportunities for Career Progression
- Technological Infrastructure
- Physical Amenities and non-money 'extras'

Money and job security didn't feature in the top nine factors affecting Millenials' job satisfaction! If you were born before 1980 you may be frustrated that your younger employees have an entitlement culture. It might seem to you that these employees expect everything at work to be geared around their personal satisfaction, just like life outside.

The LSE survey results tell us what is important to typical employees in their twenties. They want meaningful work, the opportunity to develop, and good relationships with colleagues. The Millennials are really no different from their older colleagues, but they are often more vocal about their expectations, and they are prepared to vote with their feet if the job doesn't cut it.

Don't take it personally if one of your 'Millennial' employees decides to up and leave. You may even have ticked all their job satisfaction boxes, but you just couldn't beat that ticking clock.

Building in Flexibility

You can keep your business fluid and ready for change by paying attention to how you structure it, the ground rules you set, the behaviours you encourage, and the contractual relationships you use.

Setting the structure

Always have in mind the next stage of growth for the business and build some room for expansion into the structure.

- Write job descriptions with some flexibility built in so you can ask people to do different tasks and cover for holidays or busy periods.
- Create project teams that mix people from different parts of the business so they can build relationships, understand each other's jobs and come up with the optimum solutions to problems.

✔ Create part-time or job-share roles so you can attract a wider pool of candidates and accommodate flexible working requests.

✔ Consider outsourcing non-core activities, with service level agreements that allow you to scale the service up or down as the business changes.

Using processes and policies

Think of your HR policies and processes as tools. Use them to provide a framework that supports people to work flexibly:

✔ Use a variety of recruitment methods so you are not always fishing in the same pool of candidates and you bring in fresh blood and new perspectives.

✔ Open up new vacancies to internal candidates so that people can see there are opportunities to progress – if you fill the job internally you can recruit to replace the successful person – you might even save some money.

✔ Encourage employees to suggest improvements to working processes and give them recognition or reward if their ideas save the business time or money.

✔ Invest in training people for new skills so you can use them in different ways and in different parts of the business

✔ When you write new policies, like your flexible working or shared parental leave policies, approach them as enablers of flexibility in your business, rather than as a legal duty change the emphasis from rules to possibilities!

Encouraging a culture of flexibility

How you behave and how you expect managers to behave sets the tone for your business.

Be mindful of the following:

✔ Show personal flexibility so that you are role modelling the behaviours you expect employees to demonstrate.

✔ Encourage employees to take measured risks and avoid a blame culture when people make mistakes.

✔ Encourage managers to think creatively about how they organise the work in their teams and how they manage the people in their teams.

✔ If you have people working remotely, give them the tools and technology to enable great communication, and don't assume that it will all work smoothly without some effort from you and your managers.

✔ Celebrate and reward examples of employees showing flexibility.

Using contracts creatively

In Chapter 2 you can read about the pros and cons of employing people or using contractors to do certain work, but contracts may be used in other ways to achieve flexibility for the business.

If your primary vehicle is a coach or a camper van, some of the following contract variants are like the luxury upgrade that offers a smoother ride, or the pop up tent that gives you additional capacity when you need it.

Employee Shareholder status

If you are running a successful business with good future prospects, you may be able to attract high calibre people with particular skills into your business at a salary you can afford by offering them Employee Shareholder status.

The employee is effectively exchanging some of their employment rights for shares in the business. Employee Shareholders:

✔ Share the risks and the potential successes as the business grows

✔ Are more likely to focus on the bigger picture when they are doing their jobs

✔ Can influence business decisions, depending on their voting rights

✔ Are more likely to stay in the business so that they can reap the rewards

Employee shareholders work on an employment contract and own at least £2,000 worth of fully paid up shares in the business. You must give the Employee Shareholder 'fully paid up' shares, without asking them for any payment in exchange. They have lots of the same employment rights as other workers, but there are some important rights they don't have, so their Statement of Employment Particulars is different to the standard one.

The statement must specifically refer to the employment rights the Employee Shareholder doesn't have, such as the entitlement to statutory redundancy pay, and the right to claim unfair dismissal (except on the grounds of discrimination or health and safety). It must also include details about the types of shares, voting rights, and other technical aspects of the share ownership.

Your business must be limited by shares, and you must have the consent and authorisation of shareholders in the business or the parent company to issue the shares. If you are not trading your shares publicly, you will need to have a formal valuation. You can get this from the Shares and Assets Valuation department of HMRC: `https://www.gov.uk/share-valuations-exchange-shares-for-employee-rights`

If you offer an existing employee the opportunity to become an Employee Shareholder, they don't have to accept.

You could end up with three kinds of employee rights to keep track of: Employee Shareholders, employees with more than 2 years' service and employees with less than two years' service (for more on length of service see Chapter 5).

Share ownership and the selling of shares comes with tax implications. HMRC provides guidance for employers and employees: `https://www.gov.uk/government/publications/guidance-on-the-income-tax-treatment-of-employee-shareholder-shares`

You can read more about the Employee Shareholder scheme here: `https://www.gov.uk/employee-shareholders`. The Employee Shareholder scheme and rules are quite complex, and you may need to seek legal and financial advice to put it in place. You must pay for each potential Employee Shareholder to receive qualified advice about the proposed agreement, and give them 7 days to think about it after they have received the advice.

Agency workers

In the past, using temporary workers or *temps* from an agency was simply a relatively expensive but ultimately flexible way to deal with peaks and troughs in workload.

For short term peaks in workload, especially in an emergency, or for technical roles where you need someone to hit the ground running you may still find that a temp from an agency is the best solution.

Since the implementation of the Agency Worker Regulations, agency workers are now entitled to the same access to facilities such as your canteen, childcare and transport as a comparable employee. You must also tell them about job vacancies.

After a 12 week qualifying period, agency workers are also entitled to the same basic conditions of employment as if they had been directly employed by you on the first day of the assignment. This specifically covers pay, bonus, commission and holiday pay, but does not include redundancy pay, contractual sick pay, and maternity, paternity or adoption pay. Agency workers are also entitled to have the same holiday as comparable employees in your business.

Some recruitment agencies give their workers an employment contract, and pay them between temporary assignments with clients, so if one of those temps was placed in your business, they would not be entitled to the equal pay and equal treatment with your employees, since they are employees of the agency.

If you think that you may need to use a temp for 12 weeks or longer, make sure you discuss with the agency what kind of contract is in place, and if there will be any change in the rate they charge after 12 weeks. You may find it would cost less to recruit someone to work for you directly on a temporary contract.

Annualised hours contracts

An annualised hours employment contract specifies a number of working hours across a whole year, commonly split into *rostered* hours, which are set and communicated in advance, and *reserve* hours, which can be called in depending on workload. The actual hours the employee works is likely to fluctuate from week to week or month to month.

The advantages to your business are

- ✔ If you have a very variable workload across the year you can avoid paying overtime or temp costs

- ✔ If there are predictable times or seasons when you will be busy, you can nominate these as rostered hours for more people, giving you certainty that you will have enough employees available to work

- ✔ You may be able to attract a wider pool of employees who want to use the down time to travel or study, or want to match their working pattern with a partner's working pattern or their childcare arrangements

- ✔ If you pay employees a regular salary every month for annualised hours, you can smooth the cash flow impact across the year, even if the workload is fluctuating each month

If the proportion of reserve hours in the contract is very high because you want to have optimum flexibility, you need to have a good system to track the hours worked, and make sure that you call employees in to work all their contracted hours.

Policies and procedures should be created to manage how employees are called in, what notice they can expect, whether they can refuse a request to work reserve hours, and to ensure that you are treating everyone equally.

If employees are on reserve but not working for long periods of time, you and your managers need to keep in touch with these employees, to keep them engaged and informed, especially about any changes that are happening in the business.

Employees are still entitled to the benefits, holiday pay and other terms and conditions that apply to more traditional contracts.

Zero hours contracts

The term *zero hours contract* has been demonised in the media and by various politicians accusing employers of exploiting their workers. There is no legal definition of a zero hours contract, but the CIPD have quoted the following definition in their Labour Market Outlook survey:

> An agreement between two parties that one may be asked to perform work for the other but there is no set minimum number of hours. The contract will provide what pay the individual will get if he or she does work and will deal with the circumstances in which work may be offered (and, possibly, turned down).

Just like any other contract or policy, how you apply it determines whether or not you are exploiting your employees or workers.

The advantages to your business of using zero hours contracts are

- ✔ You only have to pay people to work when you need the work to be done

- ✔ You may attract a pool of candidates who do not want to be tied down to fixed hours or days of working because of study, other jobs, or caring responsibilities

- ✔ If you have workers rather than employees it may be cheaper because you don't offer the full range of benefits enjoyed by your employees, and you may pay a lower hourly rate

You should be clear about the status of the person – as an employee or as a worker, and construct a zero hours contract to reflect that status. Monitor how the relationship is working in practice, and if the true status is not reflected in the zero hours contract, you should consider either changing the contract, or changing how you manage the relationship. You can read more about the differences between employees and workers in Chapter 2. If you opt for a worker status contract, there is no obligation for the person to accept work when you offer it, and they will probably be less committed to the business.

If you offer a zero hours employment contract, you have more control over the person, and can require them to be available when you need them, but the employee has the same rights as other employees, after the relevant qualifying periods. You must adhere to at least the statutory notice requirements to terminate the contract. The employee may expect to have access to training, and you have to pay for any employee benefits – which may incur a disproportionate cost for the amount of work they do for you.

Whether you have workers or employees on zero hours contracts, you must pay them at least the National Minimum Wage, pay them the statutory holiday entitlement of 5.6 weeks per year, and if they meet the minimum requirements as a 'qualifying employee', pay them statutory sick pay.

You must pay people on zero hours contracts for time they are working, training during working hours, travelling while at work (but not commuting to work) and for time when they are required to be at or near the workplace available for work. This does not include time waiting at home to be called for work, and you don't need to pay them for rest breaks.

You should specify in the contract how you will request and confirm hours of work, what entitlement the employee or worker has to turn down work, and whether there is an ongoing relationship between you, even when the person is not doing work for you. If the contract includes an exclusivity clause preventing the person from working for other employers, you need to consider whether that is reasonable, taking into account the volume of work you are giving them. You should not include an exclusivity clause if someone is a worker rather than an employee.

Creating Space for Growth

You can build clauses into employment contracts to make it easier to move people around or ask them to be flexible when the business changes. If your strategy is to grow by acquisition, to move into new service areas, or even to dispose of non-core parts of your business, there are some very stringent rules about how you take your employees on that journey.

Relocation and redeployment

You may never need to use one, but if you include a *mobility clause* in your contract of employment, life will be a lot easier if you want to change an employee's work location, either because you are moving a whole business or team, or you just want to move their job.

Mobility Clause

A mobility clause is one where you specify the primary place of work, but that the employee may be required to work at other locations. You may wish to specify the alternatives by category or by geography. For example you could specify a requirement to work at other company locations or client sites, or to work in a location within 10 miles of their current workplace, or anywhere in the United Kingdom.

You must exercise the clause within the constraints of mutual trust and confidence inherent in the employment relationship. This means that you must consult the employee about the proposed change, give them reasonable notice, and take into account any of their reasonable objections. If you don't follow these steps the employee could leave and claim constructive unfair dismissal at an Employment Tribunal.

Ultimately, if you can objectively justify the need to exercise the mobility clause, the provisions of the clause allow for a move to the proposed location, you engage in meaningful consultation, and follow the correct procedure, including giving appropriate notice, and an employee refuses to move, you can dismiss them for 'some other substantial reason' and avoid a redundancy payment.

Statistically, more women are secondary wage earners than men, so it is possible, depending on the circumstances, that a woman could claim indirect sex discrimination if you enforce a mobility clause.

Working outside the UK

If an employee is normally employed in the UK but you want them to work abroad for a period of more than one month, you need to include in their employment contract, or give them a separate letter, confirming:

- ✔ The period for which the employment abroad is to last
- ✔ The currency in which the employee is to be paid
- ✔ Any additional pay or benefits, including how you will handle pension contributions
- ✔ Terms relating to the employee's return to the UK

To avoid any misunderstandings it is a good idea to confirm what expenses they are entitled to claim, and whether you will make a contribution to their personal phone charges.

If you are sending an employee to work in a country outside the European Union, check the work visa requirements with the host country embassy before you send them!

Rebuilding after redundancy

Sometimes if you change the way you do business, move location or restructure a team, you may need to make some jobs redundant, to free up the money to pay for the new jobs that you need.

In Chapter 17 you can read about how to manage a redundancy process fairly.

Remember the survivors after you have been through a redundancy process. Whether the people who are left were put at risk themselves, or were watching from the side-lines, their morale and confidence is likely to be shaken.

There are two ways you can help to minimise the negative fallout from redundancies.

- How you treat the departing employees leaves a legacy:

  - Give them reasonable time off to look for new jobs and go for interviews.

  - If you can afford it, pay for them to have outplacement support, particularly if they have been out of the job market for a while, so they can get advice about their CV and interview skills.

  - Don't allow your discomfort with the situation to appear as if you don't care – have a leaving do if it is appropriate and give them a good send off.

- Equally important, and often forgotten, are the remaining employees

  - Recognise that they may have more work to do.

  - Provide training if people need new skills.

  - Keep communicating about the good things that are happening in the business.

Transfer of Undertakings

When a business changes owner, the employees are usually protected by the Transfer of Undertakings (Protection of Employment) Regulations, commonly referred to as *TUPE* (pronounced two-pee).

The primary principle of the regulations is that employees of the business being acquired, automatically transfer across to the new employer on the same terms and conditions, and maintain their continuity of employment.

TUPE provisions apply in two situations:

✔ A business or part of a business moves from one employer to another, including a merger where a new entity is created.

✔ A service provider changes. This could happen when:

- A service being provided within a company, like cleaning, catering, (or HR!) is transferred to a contractor.

- A service being provided by a contractor, as above, is brought into a company.

- A service contract moves from one service provider to another.

The nature of the service must be fundamentally the same before and after the transfer. Where the contract is for the provision of goods rather than services, TUPE does not apply.

Whichever party you are in a transfer, the *transferor* handing over employees or the *transferee* receiving them, you have obligations to your employees.

Before the transfer of ownership or contract takes place, the employer must inform employees or their representatives about anything relating to the transfer which might affect them, and aim to reach agreement on proposed changes. At a minimum the employer must inform them

✔ That the transfer is happening, when it's happening and why

✔ How the transfer will affect them

✔ Whether there will be any reorganisation

✔ How many agency workers they are using and what types of work they are doing

If you have 10 employees or fewer you can consult with them directly if you don't already have employee representatives. You can read about how to elect and consult with employee representatives in Chapter 15.

If any of your employees don't want to transfer to the new employer they can refuse, and resign. This is not a redundancy. If the new working conditions are significantly worse than the old ones, the employee can resign and claim constructive dismissal, but they may not succeed, depending on the particular circumstances.

The fundamental principle of the TUPE Regulations is to protect people's jobs and terms and conditions. Table 12-2 outlines your responsibilities as an employer.

Whatever your vehicle, and whatever changes your business is going through, remember your employees – whether they are hanging by their fingernails from the stagecoach roof or clutching the pommel of the crankiest camel in your caravan, your success depends on them!

Table 12-2	Employer Obligations During and After a Transfer of Undertakings
Transferor (transferring employees out)	**Transferee (receiving employees in)**
Informing and consulting affected employees about the changes	Informing and consulting affected employees about the changes
Can't change employee terms and conditions to match those of transferor, even if employees agree	Can't change terms and conditions just by reason of the transfer
	Must have agreement of employees to any changes, even improvements to terms and conditions
	Must justify any proposed changes based on economic, technical or organisational grounds
	After the transfer, could change terms and conditions to be less favourable if it will protect jobs. Must be with agreement of employee representatives.
Follow provisions of any collective agreements up to transfer date	May not have to follow some aspects of collective agreements if not involved in the negotiation. Can negotiate new collective agreements after one year if the overall contract is no less favourable
Can allow the Transferee to consult employees prior to a transfer about redundancies which may arise after the transfer	Can't make employees redundant just by reason of the transfer
	Must justify any redundancies based on economic technical or organisational grounds and follow correct consultation process

Transferor (transferring employees out)	Transferee (receiving employees in)
Pension provisions apply up to the date of the transfer	Doesn't have to replicate previous pension arrangements
Must provide the Transferee with Employee Liability Information (ELI) – details of all current employees at least 4 weeks before the transfer	Must take on any legal obligations relating to the employees, including claims arising from historic actions of the Transferor, but may negotiate a financial indemnity as part of the commercial negotiations for the transfer
Name, date of birth, main details of employment including start date, salary and benefits	
Disciplinary, grievance and legal action relating to employees in the last 2 years	
Potential legal action employees might take	
	May need to pay employees outstanding wages if the Transferor has become insolvent and owes employees money.

Chapter 13

Training and Developing Your People

*W*hether you're an entrepreneur keen to get on with your next big idea, or a manager in a small business stretching limited resources, investing time and money in training and developing your people will ultimately pay off in the long term.

This applies not only to developing your employees' abilities and enthusiasm, but also to identifying the next generation of managers from within your company rather than recruiting management talent unused to your company culture. This chapter focuses on how you can give people the skills and knowledge to progress their careers and benefit your business.

Investing in the Future of Your Business

Your business will reach a point where lots of new work needs to be done but you can't afford to take on a new person. If you've recruited people to do a particular job, like driving the delivery van or developing JAVA script, it's tricky to suddenly ask them to start handling some of your sales enquiries.

The secret of maximising existing talent is to build in flexibility everywhere – in your structure, in the kind of people you recruit, and in your ways of working. Think of your business as an amoeba, which is a shapeless, single-celled organism that moves by stretching out one part of itself like a 'false foot' in the direction of travel, and then flowing the rest of itself into the new position. It responds to external stimuli, protecting itself from predators and finding food. Each part of the cell has a job to do, but when the cell moves, all the parts flow in the direction of travel.

If you applied this analogy to your business, you would give your van driver the skills and knowledge to actively start the selling process if he meets a potential customer in the loading bay. Your JAVA developer may not be a natural sales person, but if she answers the phone when there is no one else in the office, she needs to know what to say in response to a sales enquiry.

In simple biological terms, if a single-celled amoeba can respond to a stimulus and flow towards food in order to absorb it, what's stopping everyone in your business from responding to opportunities to grow?

Recognising the barriers

Following are some common barriers to a small business having the ultimate responsiveness and flexibility:

✔ People don't know what's expected of them.

✔ People don't recognise the external stimulus for what it is – they answer the phone but may not think of it as a sales enquiry.

✔ People think they have a certain job, and helping to grow the business is not part of it.

✔ People don't know what to say or do in response to the sales enquiry so they pass it on to someone else.

✔ People are conditioned by education and traditional ways of working to stay in their comfort zones.

✔ There is no incentive for people to step outside their comfort zones.

✔ The managers, possibly including you, are the ones who grow the business and come up with the new ideas. They don't expect anyone else to push things forward.

✔ People don't know what the direction of travel is, so they just flow behind the main body, because it's easier.

Removing the barriers

If you have recruited the right kind of people and empower them to succeed, anything is possible. Some of the barriers to success may be created by you or by other managers in the business.

✔ Give people information about your plans for the business.

✔ Tell all your employees about your pricing, your products and services so they can answer simple enquiries.

✔ Tell your employees that everyone's job is to grow the business.

✔ Give employees a reason to step outside their comfort zones – it could be an incentive, or some praise, or a simple thank you!

In Chapter 2 you can read about recruiting people with the right skills and attitudes. In Chapter 9 read about building a great team, and in Chapter 12 you can read about recruiting people who show flexibility and how to shape your team to do the business. All of these will help to break down barriers to success.

Developing the Skills and Knowledge for the Future of Your Business

Humans and other animals, in their simplest form, respond to stimuli to avoid danger, to eat and to reproduce. Your business is the same in many ways – although go easy on the eating and reproduction during working hours. You need to equip your people with the skills, knowledge and confidence to protect and grow the business.

To do so, you'll often need to invest in external training courses, but you can also use your own and other employees' expertise to provide briefing and coaching. Table 13-1 shows some of the positive triggers that highlight the need for training, and Table 13-2 shows some negative triggers that call for training as well.

 Tables 13-1 and 13-2 are not intended to oversimplify the complexity of your business, but to highlight the importance of equipping your team to respond to and sometimes to anticipate the changes in the external environment which will impact your business. Check out the sidebar 'Training needs analysis' to see how often you should review your team's needs.

Table 13-1	Examples of Positive Triggers for Training in a Growing Business	
Trigger (positive stimulus)	*Skills and knowledge your people need to respond*	*Tools you provide to build skills and knowledge*
New customers or suppliers	Technical knowledge of your product/service	Team briefing from you or other employees
	Terms and conditions of your product/service	Coaching
	Relationship building skills, Sales skills	External training courses
	Telephone, face to face and written communication skills	
	Data handling skills	
	Knowledge of your business structure, roles and responsibilities	
	Knowledge of your standards/expectations and contract/payment terms	
	Quality Assurance knowledge	
New product or service idea	Assessment of impact on existing business/customers	Briefing from experienced employees
	Financial evaluation and business modelling skills	Training courses
	Process design skills	
	Research skills	
	Marketing knowledge	
Acquisition of another business	Legal knowledge	Training courses
	Negotiation skills	Formal education
	Data analysis and financial evaluation skills	Coaching
	Project Management skills	

Table 13-2	Examples of Negative Triggers for Training in a Growing Business	
Trigger (negative stimulus)	*Skills and knowledge your people need to respond*	*Tools you provide to build skills and knowledge*
New competitor	Marketing knowledge	Formal education
	Financial analysis skills	Training course
Customer complaints	Knowledge of your complaints procedure and escalation route	Briefing from you or other employees
	Complaint handling skills	Coaching
	Knowledge of your terms and conditions	
	Ability to assess and recommend changes to service/product offering/ ways of working to avoid future complaints	
Cash flow issues	Credit control skills	Coaching
	Cash flow forecasting skills	Training
	Negotiation skills	Formal education
	Communication skills	

Training needs analysis

Depending on the length of your business cycle, or how long it takes for you to convert a sales enquiry into money in the bank, you should pause at least once a year and assess your team's ability to meet the current and predictable future needs of your business. At its most thorough, this is called a *training needs analysis*, but if you have a small business, you can do this mini skills audit in 15 minutes on one side of A4.

If your business cycle is short, for example if you are launching new products or services every month, and the lead time from engaging with a customer to closing a sale is short, you will probably need to do your mini team audit more often than once a year.

Formal education

If you are operating in a regulated market, selling professional services or manufacturing pharmaceutical products, for example, you may need to employ suitably qualified people, with legal, financial or quality assurance qualifications. As your business grows, you may need more than one qualified person, but if you think ahead, you can grow your own and save a lot of money.

Professional institutes such as ACCA for financial accountants, http://www.accaglobal.com, or CQI for quality assurance professionals, http://www.thecqi.org, offer training and accreditation which can be undertaken while people are working.

Some professional bodies require a degree as an entry level qualification, so you can recruit a graduate, start them at the bottom and pay all or part of their fees in exchange for a commitment from them to stay with you for a determined period, or if they leave, to pay back your investment.

Depending on the institute and the training body, you may need to release the employee from work one day a week, and it is usual to offer some paid time off for exams.

External training

If you have a very limited budget for training, prioritise the most pressing gaps in the business that you need to fill, and don't compromise on paying for good quality training.

Then invest some of your time in researching low cost training options!

Cheap and cheerful training

Have a look at YouTube videos, for example, about how to deliver great customer service. Decide which one best fits your culture and ask the team to watch it. In an office you can get everyone watching at the same time while having a sandwich lunch, and then poke fun at the trainer's irritating foibles.

Check out https://www.youtube.com, and type in a few key words for the training you desire plus the word 'tutorial'.

YouTube is not the only place to find free or cheap online training: TED is a non-profit organisation set up to spread good ideas globally. Tune into TED talks on a wide range of topics from promoting innovation to managing conflict: https://www.ted.com.

You could also subscribe to an online training company for a monthly or annual fee, and download technical training videos on topics as diverse as Excel data modelling and website design. Check out `http://www.lynda.com`, for example.

Finally, try logging on to Harvard Business Review online and read articles about many aspects of running and growing a successful business. Share links to interesting articles with your team to prompt discussion and promote learning. You can find it here: `https://hbr.org`.

Other ways to access specialist knowledge

The old adage is true, that 'nothing is for nothing', but if your team are prepared to put in the time, they can get some 'free' expert knowledge.

Here are some examples:

- ✔ **Networking events:** Professional institutes such as the Chartered Institute of Marketing offer relatively expensive 3 day courses, all the way up to accredited diplomas, but they also often run free taster events or networking events with expert guest speakers.

- ✔ **E-books:** Many professional advisors create E-books as a marketing tool, and if you search the internet for particular topics you will no doubt land on some relevant links. Usually you will have to provide your email address, as the advisors will want to follow up to win your business but you can unsubscribe as soon as you have downloaded the 'Top ten tips for writing a compelling business case' and given it to your IT manager to stop him bothering you to pay for a new server.

- ✔ **Create a library:** Depending on your workplace, you may have a space for a shelf of reference books and a screen for online training.

 Set goals for people to read certain books/articles or watch particular videos and then have a discussion at a team meeting. Encourage your team to use the space, by offering an hour of paid working time if they invest an hour of their own time.

Briefings

Briefings can be individual or team based, and are primarily about conveying knowledge or facts.

If you invest time, either your own or that of another experienced employee, in planning the content, briefings can be a really powerful way of setting consistent standards and maintaining quality.

Create simple one page briefings for information such as:

- ✔ Fire evacuation procedures for new employees
- ✔ Customer complaint handling procedures
- ✔ Your key product or service features
- ✔ How to check in a delivery
- ✔ Security or data handling protocols for your business

Ask employees to sign a record that they have been briefed and they understand their responsibilities.

If you are seeking ISO (International Standards Organisation) accreditation, some of these briefings can be the building blocks for you to demonstrate consistency of standards.

Writing down the information may seem laborious but it gives you the freedom to ask other people to do the briefings in the future.

If an employee isn't meeting the required standard, you can refer to the briefing as part of your evidence when you start managing their performance.

Interns and apprentices

During recent challenging economic times, the prevalence of internships has increased, as a route for desperate graduates to gain some work experience and for businesses with limited resources to access some free labour.

Apprenticeships go through phases of popularity and decline, often linked to the colour of the current government, but in recent times there is a consistent call from business for the re-establishment of Apprenticeships as a route to building a skilled workforce for the future.

Interns

The term *intern* is used loosely, and often with the assumption that the intern is a friend or family member doing unpaid work. Most commonly interns are new graduates or school leavers with little experience of work, who want to pursue a professional career.

If you have an intern in your business to do a job, rather than to just observe and learn, you must pay them at least the national minimum wage.

An excellent internship is one which benefits your business while the intern is gaining valuable work experience.

As with most things in life and in business, there are no shortcuts to excellence. Investing time in setting up an internship properly and recruiting and selecting interns carefully will pay off in the long run:

- ✔ Recruit your interns as you would do for a 'proper job', and select the best candidate based on their attitude and skills rather than just based on a friendship or relationship

- ✔ Have an intern agreement outlining the length of the internship, the hours of work, their reporting relationship and their rate of pay

- ✔ Give the intern a proper introduction to your business and give them a clear understanding of what you expect of them

- ✔ Give the intern clear responsibilities, and some variety in their work

- ✔ Give the intern time off to go for job interviews, or training courses that will help them to get a permanent job

- ✔ Allocate a manager or mentor to oversee the work of the intern

- ✔ Give the intern feedback about their work so that they can learn from mistakes and build on their strengths

- ✔ Be clear with the intern about whether there may be a permanent role for them with your business, and what process you will use to fill it

Have a look at some guidance about how to run great internships at `www.work-experience.org` or `www.internocracy.org`.

Apprentices

Apprenticeships are work-based training programmes which will lead to a nationally recognised qualification. Apprentices must be aged 16 or over and will normally work 30 hours a week and attend a local college or specialist training provider, one day per week.

For your business they are a really cost effective way of employing people to meet a current workload demand, but more importantly, to build the skills and loyalty of your future team.

Apprenticeships take between one and four years to complete, depending on the level.

You can offer apprenticeships to new or existing employees. You could receive funding from the National Apprentice Service (`www.apprenticeships.gov.uk`) depending on your sector, and the age of the Apprentice.

Setting up an apprenticeship scheme is straightforward, and lots of help and advice is available to support you:

- Check what apprenticeship framework you want to use – these are sector specific and cover everything from science and engineering to sports coaching and hairdressing: `www.gov.uk/government/publications/apprenticeship-frameworks-live-list`

- Register your interest in setting up an apprenticeship scheme with the National Apprentice Service:

  `http://nas.apprenticeships.org.uk/employers/employer-online-enquiry-form.aspx`

- Find a training provider or college to provide the training. They will provide the qualification and carry out the assessments:

  `http://nas.apprenticeships.org.uk/employers/find-an-apprenticeship-training-organisation.aspx`

- Check with the National Apprentice Service if you are eligible for a grant. If you have less than 50 employees and your apprentice is aged 16–24 you may qualify for a grant of £1,500. You can support up to 5 apprentices.

- Advertise your apprenticeship vacancy in local schools, colleges and on the government universal jobmatch site: `https://jobsearch.direct.gov.uk`

- Select your apprentice and give them an apprenticeship agreement confirming the length of the apprenticeship, their working conditions, the training you will give them and the qualification for which they are aiming. You can write your own agreement or use a template:

  `https://www.gov.uk/government/publications/apprenticeship-agreement-template`

You have to pay Apprentices at least the national minimum wage. And remember that they must be allowed one day a week to study for their qualification.

Read more about all the steps above on the government guidance website `https://www.gov.uk/take-on-an-apprentice`

Coaching and Mentoring

The terms coaching and mentoring are often used interchangeably, and they do share some common threads. Both techniques use one to one conversations to support someone to develop the skills and knowledge to improve their work performance.

Coaching your people to success

Coaching focuses on improving people's performance at work by developing specific skills and aiming for certain goals.

There are several ways of looking at it:

✔ A coaching 'intervention' is a specific step by step approach that helps the person being coached to identify a challenge or issue, consider alternatives and come up with the best solution.

✔ A coaching style of management is one where the manager keeps asking questions rather than providing solutions, so that the person being coached comes up with their own answers.

✔ A coaching culture in a business is one where people are encouraged to come up with their own solutions and allowed to make mistakes and learn from them, and works best when managers are trained to provide coaching to their teams.

Thinking about coaching in a sports context, the Coach may never reach the levels of excellence of the sports person they are coaching, but they know what great looks like, and they know what's required to get there.

The essence of coaching is for the coach to help the other person to come up with the answers. You can use the GROW model to keep a coaching conversation on track. Take the example of coaching an inexperienced employee to handle a customer complaint:

		Questions to ask
G	Goal	What are you trying to achieve?
R	Reality	What is the customer complaining about?
		What actually happened? Is the customer right?
		What will the impact be if we don't resolve the complaint?
O	Obstacles	What could get in the way of resolving the complaint? Is there any history with this customer or other customers that we need to take into account? What is our policy?
	Options	What are the options for resolving the complaint? What would the impact be?
		What can you not do?
W	Way Forward	What are you going to do?
		When will you do it?
		How will you do it?

You might invest half an hour in this conversation, and spend most of the time wondering why you didn't just pick up the phone to the customer yourself and resolve it in five minutes. However:

- ✔ The employee will own the conversation with that customer and want a positive outcome much more than if you had just told them to call the customer and offer them 5 per cent off their next bill.

- ✔ The longer term payback for the 30 minutes of your time is that the employee is now equipped to handle future complaints with minimal involvement from you.

If you give your managers training in how to adopt a coaching approach, and encourage them to coach rather than instruct their team members, you will unleash every employee's potential. Over time, your business will benefit from everyone being empowered to do a better job.

Many models of coaching exist, of course, and the sidebar 'Heron's interventions' describes another way of looking at coaching.

Heron's interventions

John Heron is a renowned writer whose theory of interpersonal 'interventions' was first published in 1973 when he was helping doctors to train the next generation of General Practitioners.

His model suggests there are six main ways in which people interact, ranging from Prescriptive ('Do as I say') to Coaching ('Try this'). In Chapter 3 you can read about Ken Blanchard's Situational Leadership theory, which suggests that you should adopt different management styles with each employee depending on the situation, and their experience and confidence. Like Blanchard, Heron suggests that the most appropriate style will depend on the situation and the person.

What these and many other management theories recognise is that coaching is the most time consuming, but ultimately the most effective way to help people learn certain skills. Some examples of where coaching is most effective are:

- ✔ Helping technical experts to develop better ways of handling people

- ✔ Supporting someone with potential but limited experience to practice key skills

- ✔ Encouraging a newly promoted person to take a more strategic perspective

- ✔ Helping someone to handle conflict or who is in a difficult working relationship to achieve a positive outcome

Mentoring the next generation

Mentoring uses similar questioning techniques to those in coaching, often to help the person being mentored to look at things from a wider or longer term perspective.

As a mentor your goal is to build the employee's skills and knowledge for the future, rather than solving a particular short term challenge, which is usually the focus of coaching.

Mentors ask questions such as:

- ✔ 'Where do you want to get to in your career in a few years' time?'
- ✔ 'How realistic is that, with your current experience?'
- ✔ 'What experience/skills will you need to have?'
- ✔ 'How might you get that experience or those skills?'
- ✔ 'What barriers are in the way?'
- ✔ 'What options do you have?'
- ✔ 'Who do you need to speak to/ask for help?'
- ✔ 'What are you going to do in the medium term/short term to help you to reach your goal?'

In large businesses, the senior management team often mentor more junior people, helping them to deal with organisational politics, or supporting the more junior employee to plan their career path.

In a small business, you or other senior managers may be thinking about planning for your succession.

Mentoring can be a really effective way of developing the next generation of managers. A line manager is focused on what the employee is doing day to day, while a mentor is thinking longer term.

It is best if you can be a mentor to someone whom you are not directly managing, because it is difficult to wear both hats simultaneously.

If you are in a very small business you may also need to consider how it looks if you offer to mentor one person, and not another.

If you are in a very small business without the luxury of spreading the mentoring between a few senior people, you could ask someone from another business to act as a mentor for one of your employees, and offer to do the same for them.

Growing Your Own Managers

The most common pitfall into which you could stumble as the business grows is to promote people into jobs as managers, without proper consideration.

The *Peter Principle* is well known in business. In the 1960s, Laurence J Peter was working at the University of California, and published a theory that people are promoted to their level of incompetence, because they are selected for promotion based on their past work, rather than on their predicted ability to do the higher level work. A great IT developer finds himself managing a team even though he lacks the people skills to do it well. A fantastic sales person is promoted to Sales Director, and people wonder why he is such a rubbish manager when he is so 'great with people'. The answer is that he is great with customers, and how he got to be a fantastic sales person was by being completely focused on his own targets, possibly at the cost of other people in the company.

Of course your Head of IT needs to know about IT systems, and your Sales Director needs to know your customers, but there are some other fundamental behaviours and attributes that all your managers will need to display. Some of them are personal preferences, and almost all of them can be learned over time. Table 13-3 outlines what to look for or develop in a successful manager.

Table 13-3	Behaviours and Attributes of Effective Managers
Role of the manager	*Behaviours or attributes managers need*
Setting goals for the team, and measuring progress against them	Ability to translate the business goals into realistic targets
	Ability to analyse data
	Well organised and systematic
	Impartiality to distribute work fairly
Giving people feedback about their performance – good and bad	Clear communication skills
	Empathy
	Courage to have difficult conversations

Role of the manager	Behaviours or attributes managers need
Supporting development of individual team members	Ability to adopt a coaching style
	Commitment to developing others
	Patience
	Longer term vision
Supporting team members to work effectively together	Collaborative personal style
	Understanding of your business processes
	Ability to manage conflict between team members
	Ability to identify barriers to collaboration and to remove them
Taking action for continuous improvement	Listening
	Encouraging people to share ideas
	Being decisive
	Using good judgement when solving problems
	Being accountable for team performance

Whether you are creating the first or the tenth manager job in your business, write a job description and person specification (read about these in Chapter 2). Consider the behaviours and attributes outlined above and any others that will be particularly important for the manager of the team in question. You can also include specialist or technical knowledge if it's important.

Look at the current team and consider if any of them are ready to be promoted to manager. Compare them against the priority list of attributes.

If you're not sure whether someone meets the criteria, don't promote them until you have gone through a proper process.

You may have somebody who is not ready now, but could be ready within 6 months with a bit of help.

If more than one person is ready for promotion (or they think they might be!), advertise the job, and select the best person using a range of selection tools.

Taking your managers on a journey

A huge range of management and leadership training is available and the quality is variable. Sending a newly promoted manager on a one day course for £199 is very unlikely to transform them overnight.

At best they will pick up a few trite management phrases and tips for how to be a better manager. At worst they will think they now know everything about management and start practicing on everyone around them, including you.

Be clear about your expectations

If you promote someone to a managerial role in your business, don't assume they know what you expect.

- ✔ Give the new manager some clear goals to achieve in the first three months, for themselves and for the team

- ✔ In the early days, make yourself accessible to the new manager so they can run things by you, and test out their ideas – use a coaching style to help them to come up with their own solutions

- ✔ Tune in to conversations and try to pick up from the team how well the manager is doing

- ✔ After three months, have a formal review of the manager's performance. Give them feedback about what they've done well and how they could improve. Focus on the people skills as well as the tasks

Providing support and training

If you can afford it, send the manager on a management training course with a reputable provider.

Rather than assuming that a short management course will cover everything the new manager needs, try to identify specific gaps in their skills or knowledge and invest in filling those. A very common gap in new managers' knowledge is finance, and there are some great Finance for Non Financial Managers courses on the market.

Discuss what you want the new manager to learn before they go on the course, and review the learning with them when they come back. Ask them what they are planning to do differently following the training.

If your training budget is limited, you could recommend that the new manager reads articles about management in books, magazines or online, or listens to some TED talks (see the earlier section 'External training' for more details).

Giving managers the tools to manage

If you expect your managers to deliver a great team performance, you need to give them some basic tools:

✔ Information about the business, and how their team contributes to overall business performance

✔ Team targets – for example financial, productivity, complaint resolutions

✔ Disciplinary and Grievance policies and procedures and training in how to use them

✔ Clear guidelines about their delegated authority – for example their limit of authority on finances, people and business decisions

You can read more about setting team goals and rewarding performance in Chapter 8.

Reaping the benefits

Some of the benefits to your business of growing your own managers are:

✔ You save the cost of external recruitment.

✔ You may be able to pay a lower than market rate salary to a newly promoted manager – but be careful as this can backfire by demotivating people if they feel undervalued.

✔ You build loyalty, and retain good employees because they see the potential to develop their careers by staying with your business.

✔ You retain critical business knowledge, and managers who are promoted from within often have more credibility with employees than external hires.

✔ If you promote the right person and give them the right support, they can have a big impact on the motivation of the rest of the team – they will be more productive.

✔ Someone who has grown with the business is more likely to behave in a way that fits your business culture.

✔ Promoting your managers from within creates a good impression on your customers, suppliers and other stakeholders.

Part IV
HR and the Law

Five HR Fundamentals

- ✔ **Know your employees' rights.** Always start with the employment status, which tells you which rights apply. Some rights are based on length of service; others apply from day one, or even before, in the case of discrimination.

- ✔ **Treat people fairly and equally.** Before you make a difficult HR decision, imagine yourself on the stand at an Employment Tribunal defending your actions. Investigate the facts, behave reasonably and act in good faith.

- ✔ **Follow the correct procedure.** Don't take procedural shortcuts; they are rarely worth it. Some things just take time, and following the right steps will ultimately save you time and will definitely save you money.

- ✔ **Communicate and consult.** People will put up with a lot if you tell them what is going on, ask for their opinions, and listen to their ideas. You will build trust and ultimately come up with a better solution.

- ✔ **Follow through.** Don't make idle threats or promises and not follow through with action. You will engender mistrust, demotivate the people who work hard and follow the rules, and ultimately undermine your own leadership.

Check out this book's Cheat Sheet at www.dummies.com/cheatsheet/hrforsmallbusinessuk for tips on how to hire your first employee, including minding all the legal requirements for doing so.

In this part . . .

- ✔ Keep out of trouble by knowing your way around the law
- ✔ Respect your employees' rights from when they join to when they leave
- ✔ Manage your money within the rules

Chapter 14

Hiring People

. . . .

In This Chapter

▶ Attracting people to work for you

▶ Selecting the right person

▶ Offering someone a job

. . . .

*E*ddie Cochran once sang, 'There are three steps to heaven'. He could equally have sung 'There are three steps to recruiting people', which although less memorable would also have been correct. Perhaps Eddie could have had a career in HR?

Such speculation aside, these steps are:

✔ Attracting the right kind of people to apply

✔ Selecting the right person for the job

✔ Making an attractive and legally binding offer of a job

Attracting People to Work for Your Business

Mutual attraction is important, so when you write a job advert, describe your business and your culture as well as the job and the ideal candidate.

Using the right words

Keep your messages clear and simple so your potential job candidates don't get bored.

Think about the people you want to target, and use appropriate language to draw them in.

In your descriptions, avoid using words or phrases which could suggest that you intend to discriminate against people either directly or indirectly, based on a protected characteristic, such as age, disability, race, religion, nationality, gender or marital status. Be aware of the two types of discrimination:

- ✔ *Direct discrimination* is where you explicitly exclude certain categories of people by using a phrase like 'We are recruiting for people to join our young and friendly team,' which is telling older people not to bother applying. You're excluding grumpy people, too, but that's acceptable because they're not protected by the Equality Act (which gives them something extra to grumble about!).

- ✔ *Indirect discrimination* is trickier to spot, so it's easier for you to fall into the trap. A phrase like 'local jobs for local people' might seem completely neutral, but depending on the area where you are advertising, you may be indirectly discriminating against people from ethnic groups that are not represented among the residents of your local area.

Be careful about the job title you advertise – if you use a title like 'waiter' or 'stewardess', you are discriminating against one of the genders. If you find it impossible to avoid using a job title that implies that only one gender should apply, you should also include a statement that you welcome applications from suitably qualified men and women.

Table 14-1 shows you some words and phrases to avoid, and any circumstance in which it would be acceptable to use them.

Table 14-1	Words and Phrases To Avoid in Job Adverts	
Word or phrase	*Why you should avoid it*	*When you could use it*
Recent graduate	Indirectly discriminates against older people and people of other nationalities with a different educational system	For a job that specifically requires a degree for a reason. Otherwise use a phrase like 'graduate degree or equivalent'
A minimum of 10 years' project management experience	Discriminates against younger people	Don't use it at all. Use a phrase like 'a track record of delivering projects of varying size and scope'
At least 21 years old	Discriminates against younger people	When job has a legal age requirement, for example age 18 to sell alcohol, or you have an over 25 insurance policy for driving company vehicles

Word or phrase	Why you should avoid it	When you could use it
Agile, nimble, quick on your feet	Could discriminate against older people and people with physical disabilities if it's not relevant to the job	When the job requires a particular physical fitness, for example to climb ladders
Hours would suit a return to work Mum	Discriminates against men and older or younger women	Don't use a phrase like this – just state the hours
We work hard and play hard, 24/7	Indirect discrimination against women who are more likely to be main carers and less flexible with working long hours	Take out the implication that people have to be available 24/7. Use a phrase like 'We work long hours and there are lots of opportunities to socialise'
Italian waitress wanted	Direct discrimination against all non-Italians and men!	You can use a phrase like 'Italian-speaking waiting staff'

Genuine Occupational Requirement

You may be able to justify asking only certain people to apply for roles, if the job genuinely requires a certain characteristic. The Institute of Advertising Practitioners' guidance says that you can rely on using a *Genuine Occupational Requirement*, 'where the essential nature of the job calls for a person of that sex for reasons of physiology (excluding physical strength or stamina) or in dramatic performances or other entertainment, for reasons of authenticity'.

You could justify recruiting a female carer to provide personal care to elderly women in their homes, or require a male actor for a particular role, as a genuine occupational requirement.

In these cases, you must specify in the advert that you intend to apply the genuine occupational requirement; otherwise, an unsuccessful applicant could claim that you discriminated against them.

Equal opportunities statement

You don't need to use an equal opportunities statement by law, but it creates a great impression if you use a phrase like 'We are an equal opportunities employer and welcome applications from all suitably qualified people regardless of their race, sex, disability, religion/belief, sexual orientation or age'.

You could keep it really simple and say, 'We are an equal opportunities employer'.

Looking in the right places

Having a diverse, or varied workforce has been statistically proven to lead to business success through improved innovation, decision making, customer insight and flexibility. You will only attract a diverse pool of people if you look in different places.

You can read more about the various ways to advertise your vacancy in Chapter 2.

Social media

If you advertise your vacancies on social media, using your LinkedIn, Facebook or Twitter accounts you can cast your net quite wide while also building your brand awareness.

Bear in mind that although 33 million adults use the Internet every day in the UK, according to an Office of National Statistics survey, 62 per cent of adults aged 35 to 44, and only 40 per cent of adults aged 45 to 54 use social networks to communicate online.

This means that you should have at least one other way of reaching potential candidates, to ensure that you don't indirectly discriminate against older people or people with disabilities who don't use mobile technology.

Job Centre Universal job match

It doesn't cost you anything to register as an employer and post your vacancies on the Universal job match system. By registering with the Job Centre you also demonstrate that you are considering a diverse range of candidates, if you ever have to defend against a discrimination claim.

You can register as an employer here: `https://jobsearch.direct.gov.uk/register`

People from outside the EEA and Switzerland

The UK Visa and Immigration department has created the shortage occupation list, of types of job for which there is a short supply of skilled people in the UK. If you are trying to recruit for one of these jobs, you may want to cast your net quite wide, and sponsor a visa for someone to come from outside the *EEA* and Switzerland to work for you.

The *EEA* is the European Economic Area and includes all the EU countries, plus Norway, Iceland and Lichenstein; people from these countries (and Switzerland!) can work in the UK without a work visa.

The shortage occupation list may be found here: `https://www.gov.uk/uk-visa-sponsorship-employers/job-suitability`. You'll need to jump through lots of hoops to be approved as a sponsor, advertise the job and be really sure there is no one suitable in the UK before you can make the offer. You can see the steps here: `https://www.gov.uk/uk-visa-sponsorship-employers`

Recruitment Agencies

For certain specialist jobs, or for seasonal or high turnover jobs, you might save time and money by using a recruitment agency.

If you use an agency to provide you with temporary workers in agriculture, horticulture, shellfish collecting, forestry or food processing and packaging they must be registered with the GangMasters Licensing Authority. See the sidebar 'Specialist recruitment agencies' for other agency requirements.

Using a recruitment agency doesn't remove your legal responsibility as an employer to avoid discrimination. You must be confident that the agency is not discriminating against any candidates in their selection processes, even before they present the candidates to you.

Employee referral schemes

Whilst diversity is valuable, there's also a lot to be said for sticking with a winning formula. If your current employees have friends or family who might make great employees, you could reward them for a successful introduction. Just be careful that you don't inadvertently build in discrimination by recruiting in your own likeness.

Specialist recruitment agencies

It is an offence for you to use an unlicensed labour provider. You can check the list of licensed labour providers here: `https://www.gov.uk/gangmasters-licensing-authority`

Agencies providing nursing or domiciliary care must be licensed with the Care Quality Commission. `http://www.cqc.org.uk`

Companies and the individuals working for them who are providing security services must be licensed with the Security Industry Authority. `http://www.sia.homeoffice.gov.uk`

The ingredients of a good scheme are:

✔ Offer the referral scheme to employees who have a minimum of 6 months' service with you so they have a solid track record

✔ Pay a fixed amount for the introduction, whatever the level of job

✔ Only pay when the introduced employee has successfully passed their probation period – it's in everyone's interest that the job works out well

✔ Limit the pay out to one or two introductions per employee to avoid creating a family dynasty or unmanageable group of best mates!

✔ Make sure you check that the person being referred has the right to work in the UK – you should check this for all your employees

✔ Don't take any shortcuts with references or background checks so that you can't be accused of discrimination or favouritism

Universities, Colleges and Schools

If considering an apprentice, intern or school leaver to learn the ropes, contact your local colleges and schools.

If you want to build a longer term relationship with the school or college, you could offer to speak at their careers days, and create a simple leaflet inviting the young people to get in touch about job opportunities when they finish their studies.

You may need Saturday or casual workers, and what better place to find them than in your local college or school. You then have a pool of tried and tested potential future employees to draw from as your business grows.

Remember it's not just the kids you can find in schools! If you don't need full time workers, you could advertise school hours only work in the nearest primary school, and recruit local parents.

By recruiting locally you can build a loyal workforce with a low turnover of staff which saves you money in the long run.

Always pay the National Minimum Wage, at the appropriate level for the age of employee.

If you want to offer a job to a student who has come from outside the EEA to study in the UK, you must check their visa to see if they are allowed to work. Read more at the end of this chapter.

Selecting People

If you draw from as wide a pool of people as possible, you are more likely to find the right one for the job. Advertise in several places rather than just one. The disadvantage of this is that you have to spend more time reviewing and responding to the applications.

These simple tips save you time at the beginning of the process:

- ✔ In the advert, use a phrase like 'if your application is shortlisted we will be in touch in the next few weeks but we won't be able to respond to every application in person'.

- ✔ If you are using an online job board to advertise, use their filter questions to eliminate unsuitable applicants straight away. Only use objective filter questions you can justify, to avoid being accused of discrimination.

- ✔ Direct all the applications to one central place, ideally a dedicated email address, so you are not trying to keep track of multiple groups of applications.

If you are recruiting locally, especially if you also have a lot of local customers, try to respond to all the applications. You are managing your business reputation as much as you are trying to fill a vacancy.

Table 14-2 shows how to use the job description and person specification as the basis for deciding the selection tools to use for an office administrator role.

Table 14-2	How to Choose the Right Selection Tool	
Responsibilities – job description	*Skill or knowledge required – person specification*	*How to find out if they have it – selection tool*
Managing online events diary, room bookings and shared calendars	Diary management experience	CV
	Personally well organised	Interview questions
Opening and directing post and general emails to appropriate team members	General awareness of how business works	References

(continued)

Table 14-2 *(continued)*

Responsibilities – job description	Skill or knowledge required – person specification	How to find out if they have it – selection tool
Ordering office and catering supplies within a tight budget	Basic negotiation skills	CV
	Knowledge of suppliers	Interview questions
	Basic research skills	Simple test at interview stage
Inputting customer data on sales system Printing and sending out invoices and tracking payments received	Knowledge of your sales system or other database/sales systems Basic financial knowledge	CV Technical questions at interview
Organising monthly events including invitations, speakers and hospitality	Event management experience	CV
	Protocols about speakers and hospitality	Competency based interview questions
	Self confidence	Simple test
	Good communication skills	How the candidate communicates with you during the process
	Calm under pressure	Psychometric profile
	Basic budgeting skills	References
Handling telephone and face to face enquiries and complaints	Self confidence	CV
	Good communication skills	Competency based interview questions
	Calm under pressure	References

Managing the process of elimination

Think of the process of elimination as a funnel, with a wide and varied selection of candidates going in at the top and only one or two very strong candidates coming out at the bottom.

Start with the job description and person specification. Read about how to write them in Chapter 2.

If you have already done the thinking about the job that needs to be done and the skills and experience required to do it, you can more easily decide the best way to select the right person.

Whether you prefer the Latin 'course of life' *(curriculum vitae)* or the French 'summary' *(resume)* the most useful place to start filtering your candidates is with their own statement of what they've done in their careers so far.

Create three physical or electronic piles for 'no', 'maybe' and 'yes' to sort the CVs for the next stage of the process.

No, maybe, yes

You can look for key indicators about the candidate in their CV, whatever the job you are trying to fill. Use these indicators to eliminate candidates immediately, if they are critical to the role:

- ✔ Accuracy, spelling, layout and grammar
- ✔ A statement in their personal profile that they are looking for a job that is fundamentally different to the one you advertised
- ✔ No mention of the minimum educational qualifications you have stipulated, or an equivalent from another country
- ✔ No evidence that they have relevant experience which could transfer across to the role you are trying to fill

Even if you feel strongly that everyone should be able to spell and use correct grammar, don't eliminate people who have applied for a job that doesn't actually need good spelling and grammar. You could be discriminating against people who don't have English as a first language, or who have a disability like dyslexia. You might miss out on some great talent.

Some clues in a CV might indicate that the person isn't right for your vacancy, but you may need to investigate further if the CV otherwise looks strong:

- ✔ A history of changing jobs frequently without any indication of reasons
- ✔ Gaps between jobs that are not explained by education, sabbatical or caring responsibilities
- ✔ A mismatch between the job titles and the responsibilities described on the CV
- ✔ A declared disability which may impact their ability to do the job
- ✔ Information you know to be inaccurate, for example dates of employment or education that don't add up.

Don't eliminate an applicant based on their nationality, age, gender, disability, marital status, or any assumptions you make about them based on their name, where they live or when and where they went to school.

If someone declares a disability you have a legal obligation to consider them, and if they are the best candidate in every other way, you must consider any reasonable adjustments you could make, both during the selection process and ultimately to enable them to do the job. Read more about making reasonable adjustments in Chapter 7.

Handling the rejections

If you have time, create a template email to reply to unsuccessful candidates and include a phrase like 'we had a large response to our advert and we have shortlisted a number of candidates who have more relevant experience' as an explanation of why they were unsuccessful.

For data protection reasons you can't just send out a mass email with everyone's address in it, but you could use 'bcc' to protect the identities of the other unsuccessful candidates.

Considering the 'maybes'

If you have a good pile of 'yes' CVs, you may not need to worry about the maybes, but if you think you might have a few gems in the pile, it is worth spending a few minutes reviewing them.

For a candidate who has gaps between jobs or frequent changes of job, you could arrange a quick telephone conversation, or send them an email asking them to explain, and then reject or shortlist them based on the answer.

For inconsistencies in the CV or other vague concerns, you should probably shortlist the candidate for interview and ask a few targeted questions face to face – you will be better able to read their reaction as well as establish the facts.

Taking the next step

In Chapter 2 you can read about some of the selection tools you could use to shortlist candidates. Whilst most people value interviews as the best way to choose people for jobs, you should use them wisely and consider adding some other selection tools.

If someone has declared a disability, you should ask them what adjustments, if any, they would find helpful to enable them to participate in the selection process.

Selection interviews

The best way to ensure that you are fairly assessing candidates against the requirements for the job, and fairly comparing them to each other, is to have a core set of interview questions that you ask every candidate for a particular role.

You can add specific questions for individual candidates; for example, if someone is living in Wolverhampton and the job is based in Luton, you can ask if they would be prepared to move house if they got the job.

You can find some good examples of core questions in Chapter 20.

Competency based interviews

Competency based interviews are designed to test the candidate's ability to do the job, by illustrating how they have done similar jobs or dealt with similar situations in the past.

When you are deciding on your questions, go back to the person specification and think about the skills, abilities and attitudes you need the person to have in the role.

Ask the candidate to describe a situation they faced, how they handled it, and what they learned or what they might do differently next time – for example, for a sales role you could start with a general question like:

> *'Can you describe a time when you have convinced a customer to spend more money than they originally intended?'*

If the candidate spends too long describing the situation rather than what they did, ask a follow up question like:

> *'What did you specifically do or say that made the customer change their mind?'*

And follow up with a question like:

> *'Would that approach work for all customers, do you think?'*

> *'What other approaches have you used in the past, to influence customers?'*

This set of questions not only tests the candidate's selling skills, but also gives you an insight into their level of self-awareness, flexibility and confidence. These 'soft skills' are often the ones that will differentiate a great sales person from a mediocre one.

Technical questions

People will often over-estimate their level of technical skill to make their CV look good. Don't be afraid to ask a few pointed technical questions at interview to flush out the bluffers. For example if they claim to have advanced Excel skills, you could ask them a technical question about pivot tables or how they have used macros to handle data.

Simple tests

For some skills, the best way to find out whether candidates have them is to create a simple test. Typing a letter, creating a report from a database or proof reading for errors in a technical document are all good examples of tests that can be done in 10 or 15 minutes as part of your selection process. This gives you a higher level of confidence in your selection decision and some tangible evidence to support it.

Getting other opinions

As your shortlist reduces to a small number of candidates, consider asking colleagues to be involved in the final decision.

If you are confident that two candidates could both do the job, you could ask them to come for coffee or lunch to meet a few people from the team. If you involve more than one other person in the decision, decide beforehand what you will do if they each prefer a different candidate!

Psychometric profiles

You can read more about psychometric profiles in Chapter 2. They focus mainly on identifying candidates' behavioural preferences. These tools may be useful to identify whether a candidate would enjoy working in your company culture, and the type of work that they will be doing. Someone who hates to work to tight deadlines will probably not be successful in a job where everything needs to be done quickly.

References

Some people like to take up references before the interview, but that involves more work, so we recommend taking up references only for your preferred candidate. You can read more about how to take up references in the section 'Taking up references' later in this chapter.

Avoiding discrimination

The key principles to follow to avoid discrimination in recruitment are

✔ Cast the net wide and use a number of methods of advertising the role to include a varied range of people

> ✔ Don't use words in your job adverts that exclude or discriminate against people with protected characteristics
>
> ✔ Shortlist people against a list of objective criteria – focus on the skills and knowledge that are required to do the job
>
> ✔ Use the most appropriate selection tools to find the best person for the job, and if possible, use more than one tool
>
> ✔ Be consistent in how you treat everybody at each stage of the selection process but be prepared to adjust your process for a candidate with a disability
>
> ✔ Don't make assumptions, or even ask questions to test your assumptions about people's child care responsibilities, marital arrangements, or any other aspect of their lives that do not relate to the work.

Some employers check candidates' social media profiles as part of their background checking, either before or after making a job offer. If you use this information as part of your decision making process, and you are not checking every candidate's profile, you could be accused of discrimination. If an older employee doesn't have a social media presence, they might be at an advantage because they can keep their private lives to themselves!

Keeping records

The best way to keep your selection process objective is to create a scoring matrix for the criteria you are using, and to give each candidate a rating. Table 14-3 shows a well filled out example.

Table 14-3	Sample Scoring Matrix	
Criteria	**Score/10**	**Comments**
Business Development experience Breadth and depth – including small and medium sized enterprises	8	Has done a lot of cold calling, meetings and so on and really understands the challenges of small businesses. Not sure how much actual success she has had at last role – she blames the model – high cost to employer and charity not using a sustainable model
Understanding of sales cycle and own selling style	6	Understands need for cold calling, meetings, investment of time and energy and persistence. (Not sure if she is a 'closer')
Experience of working with young people with poor employment records	7	Set up enterprise scheme for young people, currently mentoring young people, and works at another charity

(continued)

Table 14-3 *(continued)*

Criteria	Score/10	Comments
Experience of creating guidelines / protocols	6	Helped marketing team to do it. Has good understanding and good writing skills – something she could do
Telephone style and communication throughout the process including presentation of CV and covering letter	8	CV and covering letter strong. Nice telephone manner, very warm, builds instant rapport. Emails professional and timely.
Evidence of collaborative working style and joined up working	7	Gave good examples of how it should work. Was trying to improve it at last job – should she have made more of a difference? Not sure in such a short time
Understanding of third sector – impact reporting, outcomes, target groups	6	Passionate about giving young people a chance. Knows about importance of targets, and real outcomes rather than statistics – not deep understanding of impact reporting as a concept
Apparent fit with our company ethos	8	Ethical, talked about not over promising, managing expectations, being patient, building relationships, understands small business challenges
Direct line management experience or experience /knowledge of working in a small business	5	Doesn't enjoy line management, prefers to have colleagues than people reporting in to her. Has not directly managed young people or a small business herself although she has worked in them
Fit with logistics of job requirements – availability for fixed term contract period	8	Would ideally like to start before Christmas. Looking at a few other opportunities
Total	69/100	Minimum score of 75 for 2nd interview

You need to keep a record of the applicants for a role and any notes you take at interviews, including any scoring matrix you may use, for three months, just in case an unsuccessful candidate wants to make a claim of discrimination.

Data protection and destroying records

You should only keep relevant information for a reasonable length of time, to be compliant with the eight principles of the Data Protection Act (read more about these in chapter 10).

Some of the information about candidates, like name and address, and details about

their health or criminal records, for example, which you collect during the selection process, is sensitive information, which means that you must keep it securely and confidentially, and when the time comes, destroy it carefully.

The other advantage of keeping a good detailed record is that if you make a job offer and the candidate turns you down, or they are unsuccessful during the probation period, you can go back to your notes and decide if you would make an offer to one of the other strong candidates. If a month has gone by you might not remember all the details of the interview.

Check out the nearby sidebar 'Data protection and destroying records' for advice on how long to keep your interview paperwork.

Making a Job Offer

If you make a verbal offer of a job to someone and they accept, that is a legally binding agreement. The person can start work with you based on this agreement. However, you should protect yourself and your business by having the agreement in writing.

By law you must provide a written record of key aspects of the contract, either in one document, or by referring people to other documents that they can easily access.

Think of the job offer as having three elements:

- ✔ The offer letter – this can be quite informal, but also should include the conditions on which the job offer is being made

- ✔ The contract, or 'statement of employment particulars' which has a lot of the details about the terms and conditions

- ✔ An employee handbook, either printed or online, with policies and procedures the employee will have to follow

Making a conditional offer

Use the offer letter to specify the conditions on which you are offering the job, so that you don't have to honour the contract if the employee can't meet the conditions.

Use a phrase like 'this offer is conditional on your meeting the following conditions':

- ✔ Providing original documentary evidence of permission to work in the UK

- ✔ Satisfactory references (ideally two) from previous employers, or in the case of a young person or someone who has been unemployed for some time, character references from people who have known them for at least three years

- ✔ A written acceptance of the conditional offer by a certain date (usually two weeks after the date of the offer), after which the offer will be withdrawn

In addition to these basic conditions, your business may have others such as:

- ✔ Providing original documentary evidence of any qualifications or licenses you require the job holder to have – for example a clean driving license or forklift operator's license

- ✔ Satisfactory findings from any background checks you may require, for example to comply with Financial Conduct Authority regulations

- ✔ Evidence of meeting the basic or enhanced level of clearance from the Disclosure Barring Service

- ✔ A satisfactory medical report or examination

- ✔ Availability to start work no later than a certain date, if this is business critical

Be careful about how you use medical reports or examinations because if you refuse someone a job based on a medical condition you may be accused of disability discrimination.

Including all the must-haves

The Statement of Employment Particulars is often referred to as the contract, because it has all the terms you must specify in writing, within 2 months of an employee starting work with you; Table 14-4 outlines these terms. Some of the terms may be detailed elsewhere, but you must refer to them in this document.

Table 14-4   Terms and Conditions You Must Specify in Writing

Term	Content
Names of the parties	Full name of the employer and the employee
Effective date	The date the employment started, and whether any previous employment will count towards continuous service.
Place of work	Location of primary work and any requirement to travel to other places. Consider a mobility clause. See Chapter 12.
Pay	Rate of pay, and frequency and method of payment
Hours of work	Hours per week/working cycle and which are normal working days
Holiday	Holiday entitlement, including reference to public holidays. Detail of how holiday build up is calculated. Can refer to another document for full detail. See Chapter 6.
Notice period	Notice from you and from the employee, during probation period and after it. Must be at least statutory minimum of one week per year of service up to a maximum of 12 weeks.
Manager/ reporting to	Reporting relationship in the organisation
Sick pay	Rate of pay for sickness absence, rules about how to qualify, must include at least a reference to Statutory Sick Pay. Can refer to other document with full details. See Chapter 6
Collective Agreements	Refer to any agreements in place, or confirm there are none. See Chapter 15
Working outside the UK	Confirm there is no requirement, a requirement for up to a month, or a requirement for more than a month. Can refer to other document for full details. See Chapter 12.
Pension	Confirm at least basic details of pension plans, auto enrollment procedures, and opting out rules. Can refer to other document for full details. See Chapter 16.
Disciplinary and Grievance Procedures and Dismissal	At least the headlines of the procedure you will follow. Can refer to following statutory procedure, or to another document for full details of policies and procedures. See Chapter 6

Taking up references

There is a debate in the HR world about the value of references, as former employers have a legal obligation not to provide a misleading reference, or even one which might be inadvertently misleading. This means they often play it safe and stick to the facts of when someone was employed, and what job they did. Although it is useful to have the confirmation, it doesn't really help you to get a feel for how good your potential employee was at their previous job.

However, although people are very careful about what they will put in writing, you may be able to get them to open up a bit more in a phone conversation.

Start by giving the former employer some idea of what your business is like, and the job you are looking to fill.

Then ask questions such as:

> *'How should I manage this person to get the best out of them?'*

> *'How can I best support them to cope with a busy workload?'*

This often unleashes a torrent of advice, giving you some really good insights into how the candidate manages their time, or how much direction they need. Lots of people can't resist an opportunity to give free advice with the benefit of hindsight! Always be sure to ask how much time off work the candidate has had in the last 12 months and if they are generally punctual.

People are usually more honest on the phone than they would be in writing on their company headed paper. Finish with a general question like 'Any more tips?'

Checking that people have the right to work in the UK

People with a British or EEA passport can work in the UK without a visa. People from outside the EEA or Switzerland must have a work visa, which may have limitations on the type or maximum hours of work they are allowed to do. You must check all employees' right to work in the UK even if you know they have a British or EEA passport.

The following rules apply, and you could pay a fine if you don't follow them:

- ✔ You must see the original documents, either a passport, or documents from an approved list, while the person is with you.

- ✔ Take an unalterable copy of the documents, sign and date the copy and keep it on the employee's file for the whole time they are employed by you and for 2 years after they have left.

This is what you are checking:

- ✔ The dates for the worker's right to work in the UK haven't expired

- ✔ Photos are the same across all documents and look like the applicant

- ✔ Dates of birth are the same across all documents

- ✔ The person has permission to do the type of work you're offering (including any limit on the number of hours they can work)

- ✔ For students you see evidence of their study and vacation times

- ✔ If two documents give different names, the person has supporting documents showing why they're different, for example a marriage certificate or divorce decree

If you are not sure whether someone has the right to work in the UK, you can use this on line tool: `https://www.gov.uk/check-job-applicant-right-to-work`

Chapter 15

Managing People

*Y*ou can't control everything at work, and people will occasionally behave in ways you don't expect because of a personal problem or a personality clash with a colleague. However, taking some simple, practical steps can help to create a stable, supportive working environment, so that the flare ups are the exception rather than the rule.

Keeping Them Keen

When you recruit a new employee, you will probably go through a honeymoon period during which the employee is aiming to impress, and you are making allowances for their mistakes.

In a small business you can't afford to carry an ineffective employee for long, so you can use two key tools to get the employee up to speed as quickly as possible:

✔ Induction

✔ Probation

Introducing the company by induction

Induction is the term used to describe a structured introduction to the business for a new employee, sometimes called *orientation*.

Some of the information you provide during an induction will be very obvious to experienced people, and you won't need to dwell on it. However, you should cover the same content with all new employees, however briefly, to avoid misunderstandings later.

Some of the elements of an induction programme are required by law; for example, you need to tell everyone about:

✔ Fire evacuation and alarm testing procedures for the employee's workplace

✔ First aid provision and accident reporting

Other aspects of induction focus on your business, and where the employee fits in to it, for example:

✔ The history, culture and values of the business

✔ Your key customers or suppliers

✔ An introduction to the owners/senior people in the business

✔ An introduction to the other departments or teams and an explanation of how the employee's job fits in

✔ The policies and procedures for booking holiday, getting approval for overtime, reporting in sick

✔ Practical information like your opening hours, the location of the canteen, lockers and toilets, and where the employee can find stationery, equipment or supplies

The final element is the induction information specific to the individual employee, such as:

✔ A clear outline of the job and any deadlines, targets or standards you expect the person to meet

✔ The terms and conditions; pay, expenses, hours of work

✔ The dress code or rules about using protective clothing or equipment

If you don't give new employees any kind of induction, they will take longer to get up and running, make more mistakes, and be more likely to leave the business because they don't feel like they belong. But don't overdo it – see the subtly named sidebar 'Induction crisis' for the reasons why.

Induction crisis

The term _induction crisis_ is used to describe the stress a new starter experiences at work when they don't fit in. It's the reason why many employees voluntarily leave a job within the first six months. As social beings, we humans like to feel a sense of belonging, and some people value this even more than money or bonuses. You can avoid unnecessary employee turnover by giving everyone a good induction and supporting them through their first few months in the business, whilst simultaneously not overloading them with too much irrelevant information.

Using probation periods

Depending on how complicated their job is, and therefore how long you give a new employee to get up to speed, you will have a pretty good idea after one to three months whether the employee will be a success. Over the course of this time, use the _probation period_ to observe their performance, give them plenty of feedback and encourage them to ask questions.

 Always include a probation period in the employment contract. Three months is common for most jobs, but you may need to see them in action for up to six months, depending on the job. If the job involves slow burn activities like research, or building long term relationships, or setting up a completely new department for your business, you should probably set a six month probation period.

 Talk to new employees very regularly in their first eight weeks on the job. Ask them how things are going, and tell them what they have done well, and what they could do better. Ask if there is anything they need from you to do their job better. As always, keep notes!

If all goes well, you can keep this process as a very light touch one, and just have a brief meeting at the end of the probation period to let the employee know they have passed their probation, and confirm their permanent appointment.

 If the employee is not doing well, don't wait until the end of the probation period to tell them! Let the employee know what they need to do better, and set up regular reviews. Give them a chance to turn things around.

If an employee is fundamentally failing to perform during their probation period, follow a formal process, as follows:

1. Invite the employee to a probation review meeting.

2. Tell the employee how they are falling short of your expectations.

3. Ask the employee if there is anything stopping them from doing the job as you need it done.

4. Consider if you need to give them more training or guidance.

5. Warn the employee that if their performance doesn't improve they may not pass their probation.

6. Set a date for another review within the probation period, or if the probation period is nearly over, set the date for a final probation review meeting.

7. Follow up what you said in the meeting in writing, confirming your expectations and next steps.

8. Monitor the employee's performance, taking notes and collecting evidence if appropriate.

9. Hold a final probation review meeting. Give the employee feedback. Extend the probation period if there is some improvement but not enough.

10. Confirm the outcome in writing – tell the employee

    - Whether they have passed their probation, and confirm the appointment

    - Whether you have extended it, and the new end date

    - Whether they have failed, and the last date of their employment

Choosing Carrots or Sticks

In Chapter 16 you can read about the metaphorical carrots, or *incentives* you may offer to employees to encourage them to perform better. In Chapter 6 you can read about the disciplinary sanctions you could use as metaphorical sticks to punish people who break the rules or perform badly.

However, employees are not like the proverbial donkey who can be lured with a carrot or beaten with a stick to make them climb the mountain.

The *psychological contract* between an employee and their employer goes way beyond the pay and rations or the rule book. The psychological contract is a combination of unwritten mutual obligations and expectations between the employee and employer, which can be specific to individual employees, and can change over time.

The concept of the psychological contract was developed by Argyris and Schein in the 1960s and boils down to the perceived balance between the amount of work, loyalty and commitment an employee puts into their job, and the pay, conditions and general treatment they receive in return from their employer.

Because it's all about individual perception, you can't hope to always be in control of the psychological contract, but you can build trust and inspire loyalty, which are key features of the psychological contract, by following some simple principles.

- ✔ Be consistent in how you treat employees and in how you apply the rules
- ✔ Be open to having conversations with employees, and actively listening to what they have to say
- ✔ Be honest by telling employees how it is, even if the news is bad
- ✔ Admit when you don't know the answer, or you've made a mistake
- ✔ Deal with issues when they arise, rather than burying your head in the sand
- ✔ Recognise employees for going beyond the call of duty, even if it's as simple as saying thank you.
- ✔ Keep your promises, and don't make any promises that you can't keep
- ✔ Acknowledge employees' individual needs and preferences, even if you can't always meet them

Communicating with Your Employees

You can unleash amazing energy, focus and business performance by paying attention to communication in your business. As in any great relationship, two way communication is the glue in your relationship with your employees. Communication focuses on sharing information, and you know that your communication is great when people understand and respond.

Nature abhors a vacuum, so when one arises either air, water or gases will quickly and forcefully fill the space, sometimes causing volcanos to erupt or tsunamis to swell. In the same way, the people in your business abhor organisational silence, so in the absence of anything else from you, they will fill the silence with their own noise – some of which might not be very helpful.

Communicating top down

By regularly providing information to your employees you:

- ✔ Create a shared purpose – your vision and mission and shorter term plans for the business

- ✔ Create a shared expectation of what it is like to work in your business – the values, rules, policies and procedures that keep the business running smoothly

- ✔ Empower employees to make decisions and get on with their jobs

- ✔ Show that you are listening, by responding to employee feedback

- ✔ Build trust by being open about what is happening in the business

If you are in a very small business based at one workplace, give employees regular updates in a team meeting, or informal huddle without having too much structure, but once the business grows beyond about 10 employees, you will probably need to plan different ways to keep everyone informed.

Many leaders of growing businesses fall into the trap of sending out email updates, or relying solely on their managers to keep everyone informed, and losing the personal touch that probably attracted many of their early employees to join. Only one in ten employees in the Employee Outlook survey run every quarter by the Chartered Institute of Personnel and Development say that they feel fully informed about what is going on in their workplace!

Listening bottom up

By giving your employees the opportunity and the mechanisms to communicate upwards you are more likely to:

- ✔ Get new ideas for your products, services and ways of working

- ✔ Hear from the people in the front line what customers, suppliers and other stakeholders are saying about your business – the good and the bad

- ✔ Spot business or people issues while they are still small enough to handle

- ✔ Increase employees' satisfaction with their jobs and improve their performance

- ✔ Retain good employees because they feel that their opinions are valued

Employee engagement is a term used to describe the levels of motivation and commitment employees feel. The higher the level of engagement, the better employees perform.

According to many studies, two of the most important factors influencing employee engagement are whether employees feel they have a voice, and whether they believe that their opinions are valued.

If you're not even asking your employees for their ideas and opinions, you are missing a huge opportunity. Later in the chapter you can read about employee engagement surveys which are a formal tool you can use to get feedback from your employees (see the section, 'Employee surveys').

Day to day, you can encourage people to speak up in team meetings, use internal social media posts or even physical suggestion boxes, to share their ideas. You and your managers should have regular one to one meetings with team members, and encourage them to give feedback or make suggestions that they may not want to do in public.

 If you have a formal performance review process, you can allocate ten minutes at the end of the appraisal meeting to give the employee a chance to tell you what they think of you without prejudice!

Looking and listening sideways

By supporting employees to communicate effectively with each other, you can:

- ✔ Enable the business to react more quickly to problems and opportunities
- ✔ Increase employees' satisfaction and performance
- ✔ Reinforce the culture and values of the business through peer interaction
- ✔ Encourage employees to train each other and learn from each other
- ✔ Reinforce a sense of team working and shared purpose

If your business has grown to have more than one small team, you will need to proactively manage how the teams communicate across the business, as well as between themselves. For example, if you have a sales team and a delivery team, they rely on each other but they may not be very good at talking to each other, and they are likely to be very different kinds of people.

Regular cross-team meetings can be effective, if you stay on top of the agenda so that the content is always relevant. People try to avoid team meetings if they don't get anything out of them, so keep the meetings short, focused and informative, but relaxed enough so that people can speak up.

If you have the technology you can encourage employees to use a company intranet, or a cloud based site to post information, but even in small businesses, people forget to share, forget to check, and if you are not moderating it, the information soon becomes outdated and irrelevant.

If you have the space, give people a place to have coffee or lunch together, especially if your business involves a lot of work on computers or machines, or people doing manual work where they can't talk to each other while they are working.

Consulting Your Employees

At its simplest, consultation is about seeking employees' views and opinions. In the world of employment there are some situations where consultation is an informal 'nice to have' and others where it is formal and compulsory.

Whether you are consulting employees informally or formally, you should consult them before you have made a decision.

Taking employees' views into account doesn't mean you always have to follow them, but if you reject employees' suggestions you should give them sound financial or practical reasons.

Employees become disaffected if you have consulted them and ignored or disregarded their suggestions, more so than if you had never consulted them at all! Don't forget to tell them why you didn't take up their ideas.

Technically, any aspect of the workplace could be up for grabs for employee consultation, from the colour scheme in the canteen to a new structure for the business. However, there are rules about certain aspects of employment when you must consult employees.

Informing and consulting employees

The European Information and Consultation of Employees Regulations, often shortened to *ICE,* only apply to organisations with more than 50 employees.

The regulations mean that as a minimum, you must inform and consult your employees about the following matters:

- ✔ Inform them about the business's economic situation

- ✔ Inform and consult them about employment prospects

- ✔ Inform and consult them, with a view to reaching an agreement, on decisions likely to lead to substantial changes in their work or their employment contracts.

Read more about ICE on their website: `https://ico.org.uk`

You can use team meetings, notice boards, email updates, one to one meetings or any other means to keep employees informed, but whatever arrangement you put in place to keep people up to date, you must make sure the information will reach every employee.

For consultation purposes, you don't need to consult each individual, and you can use employee forums, or joint consultative committees, to consult with employee representatives.

Health and Safety

You must consult employees about health and safety matters, under the Health and Safety (Consultation with Employees) Regulations 1996. If employees are members of a union that you recognise for collective bargaining, you must consult them under the Safety Representatives and Safety Committees Regulations 1977.

If you don't recognise a union you can consult employees individually or through employee health and safety representatives. You don't need to set up a special group if you already have employee representatives in place.

You must consult employees 'in good time' about:

- ✔ The introduction of any measure which may substantially affect their health and safety at work, such as new equipment, new technology, the speed of a process line or shift-working arrangements

- ✔ The arrangements for appointing a competent person to advise on health and safety matters

- ✔ What kind of information they need to understand the risks they may face at work, how to reduce the risk and what they should do if they are exposed to a risk

- ✔ The planning and organising of health and safety training

Health and Safety representatives also have a role in representing employees to Health and Safety Inspectors.

When you consult employees you need to allow enough time for them to consider your proposals, and come back with ideas, suggestions or concerns.

The Health and Safety Executive provides information on their website here: http://www.hse.gov.uk/pubns/indg232.pdf

Transfer of Undertakings

The Transfer of Undertakings, Protection of Employment Regulations *TUPE* rules apply to organisations of all sizes and protect employees' rights when the organisation or service they work for transfers to a new employer.

Whether you are acquiring, merging or being acquired by another business, you have a legal obligation to inform and consult your employees at key points in the process.

You can read more about TUPE transfers in Chapter 12.

Redundancy

When you are considering making one or more employees' jobs redundant, you have a legal obligation to consult them. If you are considering 20 or more redundancies in a 90 day period, you have an obligation to consult employees collectively as well as individually.

Read more about the redundancy consultation process in Chapter 17.

Encouraging employee representation

Good business practice includes having a group of employee representatives in place, because it makes it easier for you to consult them about day to day matters such as health and safety, and how the business is performing, as well as to consult them in particular circumstances, such as when you are considering selling the business, acquiring another one, or making redundancies.

If you don't recognise a Trade Union, or you have a group of employees who are not represented by a union, you could set up a Joint Consultative Committee (JCC) or Joint Working Party (JWP).

Joint Consultative Committee

The purpose of a JCC is to create a forum, usually with nominated managers and elected employees, to discuss matters that affect people at work. It is not a negotiating body.

The JCC will work best if it has

- ✔ A formal constitution, specifying the number and type of members, frequency of meetings, election process, term of office and how it will report back to employees
- ✔ A good balance of representatives from various employee groups
- ✔ Structured meetings with agendas and effective chairing and note taking
- ✔ Clear guidance from you about how much paid time the members can take for meetings and to consult their constituents
- ✔ Good discipline and methods of reporting back to employees

Acas provide guidance about how to construct a JCC constitution here: `http://www.acas.org.uk/index.aspx?articleid=679`

Joint Working Party (JWP)

You might consider setting up a JWP if you have a particular challenge that would best be addressed by a group of employees and managers working together. A JWP will be most effective if you keep it small and focused, with a clear remit.

If you have a high turnover of employees, for example, a JWP could consider the factors, discuss options and make recommendations for how to address the issue, but it would not be empowered to negotiate new rates of pay on behalf of employees.

The advantage of using a JWP to solve problems is that you get the insight from different perspectives, so that the group's recommendations are more likely to be realistic and acceptable to both managers and employees.

If you do make changes based on the group's recommendations, you will find the implementation easier and more likely to succeed.

Employee action groups

Moving away from consultation and negotiation, and focusing more on action, you could set up project based groups to involve employees, with defined tasks and timelines, for example:

- ✔ Implementation of a new customer relationship management system
- ✔ Action planning in response to feedback in an employee survey

- Design and roll out of a new performance management process
- Improving internal communication
- Organising social activities and events

Collective redundancy consultation

If you don't have a representative group already in place, and you anticipate making more than 20 jobs redundant at one location in a 90 day period, you must set up an elected employee representative group, following these rules:

- Do everything you can to make sure the election is fair
- Set a total number of representatives, and if necessary a number from each part of the business or *class of job* so that there are sufficient numbers to represent all affected employees
- Before the election, decide a period of office for the representatives that is long enough for the consultation process to be completed properly
- Ensure that candidates for election are employees who will be affected, as of the date of the election
- Don't unreasonably exclude any affected employee from standing for election
- Make sure that all affected employees have the opportunity to vote for as many candidates as they wish, or if necessary, to vote for candidates who represent their class of job
- Run a fair election, allowing people to vote in secret. Count the votes accurately

If representatives step down during the consultation process, so that all or some employees no longer have appropriate representation, you must run another election to fill the gap.

If no employees wish to stand as representatives, you must provide the written information you would have provided to the representative group to each individual employee.

Content of collective redundancy consultation

You must provide written information to representatives about

- The reasons for redundancies
- The number and categories of employees involved
- The selection process and criteria you propose to use
- The calculation of redundancy payments

The three key areas on which you need to consult the employee representatives are

- ✔ Exploring ways of avoiding or reducing the number of redundancies
- ✔ Discussing the selection criteria to be used to make jobs redundant
- ✔ Discussing the redundancy payments and what support will be provided to redundant employees

Rights of employee representatives

You must give employee representatives reasonable paid time to consult their constituency members and attend consultation meetings. You must also enable the representatives to get access to the employees they are representing, so they can keep them informed, seek their opinions and answer their questions.

Make sure that you don't discriminate against employee representatives because of their role during the redundancy selection process as you run the risk of making the selection automatically unfair in law.

Recognising trade unions

If employees want to use a Trade Union to negotiate with you about their pay and working conditions, you must first recognise the Trade Union, through a recognition agreement.

If you refuse to voluntarily recognise a Trade Union which has requested the right to represent a group of some or all of your employees, known as *a bargaining unit,* the union can apply for statutory recognition, provided they have met the following criteria:

- ✔ The workplace must have at least 21 employees
- ✔ The Trade Union must have already applied to you for recognition
- ✔ The Trade Union must have at least 10 per cent of the workforce in membership and be likely to attract majority support in the event of a ballot
- ✔ If you have asked Acas to be involved in resolving the dispute, the union must have responded within 10 days

Acas, the Advisory, Conciliation and Arbitration Service, provides training and advice to employers about effective collective bargaining with Trade Unions: www.acas.org.uk

Collective bargaining

If you have a recognised Trade Union in your business, one of their primary purposes is to negotiate with you about the pay and working conditions of their members. Sometimes union representatives also negotiate on behalf of non-union members, if they belong to a particular group of employees, known as a *bargaining unit*.

Once you have recognised a Trade Union you need to agree with the union representative as to

- ✔ Who will represent the workers, or group of workers in negotiations
- ✔ Which workers are included in the bargaining unit
- ✔ How often meetings will take place
- ✔ Which issues, including which terms and conditions will be discussed
- ✔ How failures to agree will be resolved
- ✔ How discussions will work if more than one trade union is recognised

If you reach agreement about a matter, such as a pay rise, this is known as a collective agreement.

In your employment contracts, you must refer to any collective agreements which would affect an employee's terms and conditions, or specify that no collective agreements are in place.

You must give union representatives reasonable paid time off to undertake their duties, and you must ensure that you do not discriminate against them, or take disciplinary action against them for any matters relating to their union membership or duties. You can read more about this in Chapter 7.

Hearing the 'Employee Voice'

The concept of *employee voice* was first introduced to management thinking in the 1970s, and unsurprisingly to people old enough to remember what industrial relations were like in the 1970s, the term referred to employees suffering in silence and hoping that things would get better.

Now, employee voice is all about employees' ability to express their individual or collective views to managers or business owners and influence what happens next.

Whistleblowing

Whistleblowing, when a worker makes a disclosure in the public interest about a danger or illegal activity at work, is a form of employee voice, whether the employee uses internal processes to tell you what's going wrong, or goes outside the business to raise it with a regulator or the media.

The issues typically raised by whistleblowers include criminal offences, risks to health and safety, failure to comply with legal obligations, a miscarriage of justice or environmental damage.

Workers who make certain disclosures, called *protected disclosures*, could take you to an Employment Tribunal if you discriminate against them or victimise them for making a disclosure.

The government published a voluntary Whistleblowing Code of Practice in 2015, which recommends that all employers should have a Whistleblowing Policy and procedure, and provide training to employees and managers in how to raise and how to respond to whistleblowing disclosures.

The Public Concern at Work charity has produced a code of practice in partnership with the British Standards Institution: www.pcaw.org.uk/code

If you dismiss an employee who has made a public interest disclosure and they win a claim at an Employment Tribunal, there is no limit on the compensation you may have to pay, and the employee doesn't need to have two years' service to make an unfair dismissal claim to a Tribunal.

Employee surveys

Employee Engagement or *Employee Attitude* surveys are anonymous questionnaires you can use to take a temperature check of how switched on and happy your employees are feeling.

Use an employee survey to find out what employees think of your communication, how happy they are with their manager, and how likely they are to be working with you next year.

Communication, confidence in managers, and the likelihood of leaving the business within a year are three strong indicators of *Employee Engagement*. Lots of evidence shows a strong correlation between high levels of employee engagement and great business performance.

You can create your own survey very cost-effectively using a web based survey tool, some of which are free to use for small numbers of respondents. If you think your employees won't be completely open in a home made survey, you'll find various businesses who can host the survey and collate the results on your behalf, for a fee. You can also use social media to your advantage: check out the sidebar 'Hearing your employees via social media' for more ideas,

If you want to take part in nationally recognised awards such as *The Times* Top 100 Employers, or Investors in People, the government backed accreditation scheme, you can use an employee survey to find out how close you might be to the standard, and spot the gaps you need to fill.

A great employee engagement survey can

- ✔ Give employees an opportunity to tell you what they really think, especially if you give them some open questions with freestyle answers
- ✔ Give you ideas about how to motivate and reward your employees
- ✔ Give you an early signal if there are problems in certain teams
- ✔ Help you to spot which managers are doing a good job
- ✔ Flag areas where you might have employee turnover in the next year, so you can plan ahead
- ✔ Help you to identify training needs for employees or managers
- ✔ Give you some insights into what kinds of people like working for you
- ✔ Track your progress from year to year on key Employee Engagement indicators
- ✔ Give you a wake-up call if the employees tell you that your communication is rubbish!

Tell employees the survey results even if you don't like what you see. Be realistic about the things you can change, and honest about the things you can't or won't change. People will respect your honesty.

There's no point knowing what your employees think unless you plan to do something about it. The most effective way to act on employee surveys is to set up a mixed action group to look at the survey results, and come up with some ideas about how to make your workplace a better one.

Listen to what they have to say, and work with the group to identify the priorities, and agree on a budget. Some of the actions should sit with you, along with other managers or the business owners, but you can probably delegate some of the actions, and empower your managers to do things differently.

Hearing your employees via social media

The annual survey only gives you a snapshot at a point in time and you may take a while to getting around to taking any tangible actions. Outside work, many of your employees are actively engaged in using social media.

Internal social media and business collaboration tools such as Yammer, Chatter and Jive are increasingly popular, with their marketing materials promoting the idea of a fully connected and integrated group of employees, sharing, learning and collaborating. You could use social media tools such as these to share blogs, customer feedback, market trends or business updates with employees, but if you want them to be really effective, you should show employees that you are listening as well as broadcasting.

In the world of HR, we are inclined to write rule books to minimise the risks of employees cyber-bullying their colleagues, posting commercially sensitive information or abusing people's personal data.

If you've weighed up the benefits to your business of having engaged, informed and well connected employees against these and other risks, and you introduce an internal social media platform, it is probably worth sketching out a few guidelines for employees.

Include the guidelines in your induction for new employees, and have a briefing for your current employees, even if you don't go as far as writing a rule book.

Mediation

Mediation is where an impartial third party, the mediator, helps two or more people in dispute to attempt to reach an agreement. You can use it most effectively when an employee and colleague, or a manager and team member are in conflict, and neither is completely in the right or in the wrong.

Mediation works on the principle that both parties will agree on the outcome, so in that sense, it offers a form of employee voice. Unlike your grievance or disciplinary procedure, mediation doesn't start from the premise that one party has been wronged and the other is seeking redress. Mediation is voluntary, so if an employee doesn't want to take part they don't have to, and it is a less formal and more flexible way of resolving conflict than traditional disciplinary or grievance processes. It should still be confidential, and the agreement reached by the parties only has moral rather than legal status.

The main advantage of mediation is that it gives the parties an opportunity to repair a damaged relationship which could otherwise have a longer term negative impact on your business.

Various models of mediation may be used, but the outline process is always the same:

1. The mediator meets each party separately to hear their story and find out what they want out of the process.

2. The mediator sets up a joint meeting where each party puts their side of the story during a period of uninterrupted time. The mediator summarises the main areas of agreement and disagreement and draws up an agenda with the parties for the rest of the mediation.

3. The mediator helps the parties to explore the issues, encouraging open communication and helping them to focus on the future rather than the past.

4. The mediator helps the parties to work together to find a solution and to reach a practical agreement, which is then recorded.

5. The mediator closes the mediation and explains what each party has agreed to do, reiterating the confidentiality of the agreement.

6. If the parties don't reach agreement, nothing they have said during the mediation can be used by them in future proceedings.

You can use external mediators, or have training for yourself or other members of the team as mediators, to save costs and to instill a culture of positive conflict resolution in the business.

Chapter 16

Managing Pay, Benefits and Taxes

. . . .

In This Chapter

▶ Understanding how incentives can be designed and implemented

▶ Gaining insight into managing salaries

▶ Understanding the basics of job evaluation

▶ Ensuring that you stay within the equal pay legal requirements

▶ Reaping the rewards of providing benefits

▶ Offering pension provision

. . . .

Maintaining and increasing motivation should always be a key imperative for your business. The process of motivation within a team or an individual can be simply initiated by someone else recognising an unsatisfied need.

People can be motivated by rewards and incentives, but not every person is motivated in this way. Therefore your challenge is to establish how rewards might be used to underpin your business goals, whilst ensuring that everyone feels equally motivated through the use of appropriate goals and rewards.

In today's business world, linking targets with variable, performance-related reward has become a central and widely established leadership tool. This chapter looks in a little more detail at how you might use reward and specifically incentives and your approach to base pay in order to motivate and engage your employees. We also look at how you stay legally compliant when making pay decisions, as well as what types of benefits you might wish to provide.

Designing Incentive Schemes

Incentive design is not rocket science. Be clear about the aims of the incentive, keep the design simple and focus on effective implementation, and you'll have your employees' attention.

Agreeing on the basis and principles of the incentives schemes

Although none of the factors outlined in this section will surprise you, they are crucial to the success of the plan you intend to design and implement.

As you embark upon designing a new scheme in broad terms, ask the following questions to determine the *design principles:*

- ✔ Why does the your business need to reward through an incentive?
- ✔ What specific business performance are you looking to drive?

Once you have the answers to these questions you will have a pretty good set of design principles, which you can use to create a detailed design framework. The design framework provides the basic skeleton upon which to base the scheme and its operation.

Incentive design framework

At the next level of design you should concentrate on how the scheme will operate, who will participate, the targets and measures, and of course, the communication and payment details. In essence you need to establish the following:

- ✔ **What is the basic type of plan proposed?** Should you consider a commission scheme whereby you share a proportion of revenue or profit, or an annual bonus plan where you typically commit to deliver a fixed value of reward payment for delivery of a specific business outcome?

- ✔ **Who participates?** To help you understand which employees will participate in the plan and what governs participation, you could base it on the type of role undertaken (for example, sales roles), or an organisation level within your business (for example, senior management roles), or it could be at your discretion.

- ✔ **How will the plan be funded?** Have you engaged your accountant to determine where the money will come from to make payments to successful participants? If a commission plan is to be implemented, the financial implications are relatively easy to establish, as essentially you commit to share profit or revenue. If you propose to implement a traditional bonus plan then you need to work with your accountant to determine how you would finance the additional cost of the bonus plan.

The simplest approach to financing a bonus plan is to establish the maximum cost and to add it to your profit target. For example, if you target a profit of £100,000 and the cost of providing a bonus is £15,000 to your employees, then essentially your new profit target becomes £115,000.

✔ **What will the plan pay?** Do you have a 'target' incentive payment? Is this a percentage of salary or a fixed sum of money? How do the proposed payments compare to those of other companies who compete for your people?

Measures and targets

What business measures and targets will you use? Poor measurement criteria and unrealistic targets are the most common reasons for incentive plans to fail. If an incentive plan is perceived as being unfair or unrealistic, it defeats the purpose for which it was designed, and it is therefore important that you set realistic targets.

If rewarding a specific aspect of performance it must be measurable, and if it is measurable, can you place a target upon it?

Assessment and calculation

Once you have agreed on the basis of measurement, how will the results translate into payments? It's important that your employees understand how they will be assessed and what impact this will have on their benefits – otherwise how will they manage to strive for success?

Make the calculation transparent, so that participants can clearly see a link between results and payment: for example, if your employee achieves outcome 'a' they will receive a payment of 'x', and if they achieve outcome 'b' they will receive a payment of 'y'.

Keep assessment as simple as possible. For example, if you agree to share revenue through a commission plan, then agree what percentage of revenue is shared. If you plan to introduce a bonus plan, then agree that payments will be made when a specific target such as profit is achieved.

Communication

Don't forget to communicate the link between the incentive scheme and your overall business strategy and goals. Create a communication plan, outlining what you will tell participants, and when. This is a critical aspect of effective implementation.

When establishing a communication plan, the following principles should be applied:

- ✔ Think like your audience.
- ✔ Be clear on the "what" and show examples.
- ✔ Don't forget about the "why" behind changes.
- ✔ Authenticate the plans – "how" designed.
- ✔ Continually repeat the key messages – cascade approach.
- ✔ Don't reveal the new plan to the majority of participants until start of the plan.
- ✔ Provide an escalation path for understanding (local management).
- ✔ Hold managers accountable for delivery and engagement.
- ✔ Make sure to motivate the team.
- ✔ Undertake a review and study of communication performance and seek improvement during the communication cascade.

Rules and regulations

What are the broad rules of your incentive scheme? Be clear from the beginning about the general principles, and strike a balance between clarity and complexity.

Someone, sometime, will find a scenario that is not easily covered by the rules (for example, the part-time employee who only works 'term time', or the employee who has been on sick leave). Be prepared for this by ensuring that you are aware of all the employment circumstances that exist across your team. Most importantly, make sure that participation in the scheme is not a contractual right, and that all payments and continued participation is at your discretion.

Implementation

In many ways, the most important aspect of the delivery of a great incentive plan is the implementation. Before this stage, you have a very general overview of the design aspects to be considered when creating a scheme; however, how you implement your new scheme has a greater impact on its success then the design will ever have.

By far the most important consideration is to ensure that you get engagement from the participants! Often those that benefit from the scheme will understand what success looks like for both them and your customers. See the sidebar 'Evaluating the success of incentive schemes' for more ways of assessing how well you are dangling the carrot in front of the donkey.

If you have a finance team, ensure that they are involved. Don't let the scheme start and then be surprised when it is costing you more money than you expected.

Be clear to participants that the scheme and targets can change at your discretion. Successful companies increase targets gradually to ensure that their sales people are delivering more for the same financial outlay. In simple terms, if your sales people complain that they need to deliver a little more each year to receive the same reward then you will grow. But don't forget, don't make radical changes as all that will do is disengage your team, as they form a belief that the targets are unobtainable!

Evaluating the success of incentive schemes

The ultimate test of an incentive scheme is that your business grows financially and your team shares in the success of the growth. Continually re-think how you measure success. An effective incentive plan will underpin and encourage increased customer satisfaction and retention, in addition to promotion of new products and services.

If the sector in which your business operates is strongly regulated, be careful to ensure that you consider those regulations by which you are governed. For example, the FCA (Financial Conduct Authority) rules are driving financial services companies to reconsider their sales incentives schemes in the light of regulations designed to prevent mis-selling. Sales people should now be rewarded for identifying the right product for particular customers rather than for sales totals or, possibly inappropriate, cross-selling. These rules have of course been created to stop the mis-selling that was typified by the payment protection insurance scandal that has hit the sector. Consequently the FCA rules have hit the financial sector hardest, but any business selling finance as part of the product or service sale has to consider the implications.

Don't forget to analyse the data from incentive programmes from previous years. This is not a trivial task – blue chip multinationals have spent years fine-tuning incentive schemes to work well and within the rules. The easiest form of analysis is to look at the cost of the scheme relative to the additional revenue or profit achieved. If there isn't a clear positive correlation then your incentive scheme isn't working!

Lastly, if you find yourself in a position whereby your sales team is earning large incentive payments but your business performance doesn't correlate, it is most likely to be an issue with targeting rather than the scheme design itself! Don't rush to change a scheme: look at what you are targeting first.

Developing Approaches to Pay Management

Pay structures provide levels for managing the base pay arrangements of your employees. Many different approaches can be used, and in reality there isn't always an obvious answer with regard to what approach will best suit your business. You will be required to make a judgement on what is likely to work best for you and your business.

Understanding pay structures

The most widely used pay structures are known as *pay spines*. Typically these are found in the public sector, and the grade / role specific salary ranges are often found in the private sector.

Pay spines essentially create a structure that provides guaranteed increases to employees typically based upon service. They are by far the simplest form of pay structure as they require minimal line management judgement or support when implemented.

Pay spines consist of a series of incremental 'pay points' that extend from the lowest level of pay you are prepared to pay to the highest point for a specific role. Typically between the minimum and maximum will be a fixed number of points that tend to be 2.5 per cent apart.

The major issue with pay spines is that they reward increases to employees for just turning up without any reference to their individual contributions or performance. Pay spines can be costly for low employee turnover business as well, as by default everyone will drift towards the top of a pay range over a period of time.

Following introduction of the Age Discrimination legislation in 2006, service-related pay is only permitted for a maximum of 5 years after an appointment or promotion.

Salary ranges are often employed where extensive analysis has been undertaken to establish what a role is worth in the external market. Undertaking this analysis allows you to manage employee expectations with regard to how much they might be paid by use of a range of pay typically expressed as a minimum, target and maximum level of base pay.

The advantage of a pay structure based on salary ranges is that it will:

- ✔ Enable pay to be managed more flexibly (in other words, aligned to the competence, skills and performance of individual employees)

- ✔ Often move a business away from a time bound reward system whereby time served is rewarded rather than contribution to success

- ✔ If implemented with clear management guidelines it gives line managers accountability and autonomy to manage pay and reward appropriately

However, as an employer you should also understand that salary ranges are not a panacea, as a pay structure based on salary ranges will present different pressures on the business, namely:

- ✔ A risk that costs might spiral out of control as employee expectations are built on a belief that they should be rewarded towards the top of a given salary range

- ✔ A risk that equal pay claims will be made as broad-band pay ranges will potentially present base pay arrangements that are unique to each individual employee

Implementing a new pay structure

When deciding a new pay structure you must ensure that it meets the following criteria:

- ✔ Be appropriate to the culture and needs of your business and its employees

- ✔ Facilitate the management of salary relativities whilst maintaining equity, transparency, fairness and consistency

- ✔ Allow for pressures associated with market rate changes and skill shortages

- ✔ Recognise employee performance and attainment of relevant skills and competencies

- ✔ Enable control to be maintained in respect of application of policy and cost

Minding the National Minimum Wage

Most workers in the UK who are over school leaving age are entitled to be paid the National Minimum Wage. No national minimum wage existed before 1998, although there were a number of wage controls focused on specific industries such as agriculture.

The National Minimum Wage Act 1998 applies to workers, that is, anyone who has a contract to do work personally. Those working through employment agencies are also included. Home-workers are also included, and the Secretary of State can make an order for other inclusions. The Secretary of State can also make exclusions, as has been done for au pairs and family members in a family business. Share fishermen paid by a share of profits are excluded, as are unpaid volunteers and prisoners.

The National Minimum Wage is enforceable by HMRC or by an employee making a contractual claim through wrongful deduction of pay. In October 2013, rules were introduced to "name and shame" employers who fail to comply with the law.

You can find more details with regard to the "name & shame" legislation and process at: `https://www.gov.uk/government/news/national-minimum-wage-rogues-to-be-publicly-named-and-shamed-under-new-plans`

Every October the National Minimum Wage rate is reviewed and often increased. Details of existing minimum rates can be found at: `www.gov.uk/national-minimum-wage-rates`

Benchmarking pay

Data is available from specialist survey companies enabling you to establish the rate of pay for a specific job. These survey companies often invite similar businesses, usually by sector, to participate and share salary data with them. The surveys are undertaken on a confidential basis, and the participants' specific data is only shared with the survey company.

Finding the right data

The data is often presented back to participants by referring to a specific role type, which carries agreed responsibilities operating within a defined context such as budget or revenue value, for example, a sales manager with a regional responsibility and target revenue of £150,000.

There are many management consultancy firms, such as Hay Management (`http://www.haygroup.com/uk/services/index.aspx?id=2421`), Towers Watson (`https://www.towerswatson.com/en-GB`), and Mercer (`http://www.uk.mercer.com/services/talent/reward.html`) that are able to assist in establishing the right data for your organisation.

Avoiding benchmarking mistakes

The single biggest mistake businesses make about benchmarking is misinterpretation of the data.

The largest salary survey data providers can provide data that runs to thousands of lines. It is therefore incumbent upon the purchaser of the data to ensure that they match their role correctly to the data available.

A mismatch can lead to you believing that a role is worth more or less than it actually is. To avoid this mistake it is often best to work with a specialist reward management consultant who can help you with matching roles into salary surveys. To find a specialist simply use a search engine to establish what providers are local to you.

As an employer in the UK you have to adhere to the legal requirements to provide the National Minimum Wage to your employees. It doesn't matter how small an employer you are, you still have to pay the minimum wage, and the level of pay depends on a worker's age and whether or not they're an apprentice.

Paying equally

Discrimination arises when equals are treated unequally. Legislation has been in place since 1975 when the Equal Pay Act of 1970 was finally put into force. Subsequent legislation has updated and enforced the principles of equality.

Understanding the basis of equal pay

As an employer you must give men and women equal treatment in the terms and conditions of their employment contract if they are employed to do the following:

- ✔ Work that is the same or broadly similar ('like work')
- ✔ Work rated as equivalent under a job evaluation study
- ✔ Work found to be of equal value in terms of effort, skill or decision making.

Be aware that your employees can compare any terms in the contract of employment with the equivalent terms in a comparators contract. A comparator is an employee of the opposite sex working for the same employer, doing like work of equal value. Your employees are also entitled to know how their pay is made up. For example, if there is a bonus system, everyone should know how to earn bonuses and how they are calculated.

The Equality Act 2010 makes it unlawful to prevent employees from having discussions to establish if there are differences in pay. However, an employer can require their employees to keep pay rates confidential from people outside of the workplace.

Equal terms cover all aspects of pay and benefits, including:

- ✔ Basic pay
- ✔ Overtime rates
- ✔ Performance related benefits
- ✔ Hours of work
- ✔ Non monetary terms
- ✔ Annual leave entitlements.

An employee who thinks he is not receiving equal pay can write to you asking for information that will help him establish whether there is a pay difference and, if so, the reasons for the difference. If an employee cannot resolve the problem informally or through the formal grievance procedure, he may complain to an employment tribunal under the Equality Act 2010 while still working in the job or up to six months after leaving the employment to which the claim relates.

A new provision in the Equality Act 2010 (Section 139A) gives employment tribunals the power to order employers to carry out equal pay audits where they have been found to have breached equal pay law or to have discriminated because of sex in non-contractual pay, such as discretionary bonuses.

Running an equal pay audit

An *equal pay audit* involves comparing the pay of protected groups who are doing equal work in your business, investigating the causes of any pay gaps by gender, ethnicity, disability or working pattern and planning to close any gaps that cannot be justified on grounds other than one of those characteristics.

An equal pay audit is concerned with an important, but narrow, aspect of potential discrimination in employment – unequal pay for equal work. It does not directly address other aspects of inequality, such as the glass ceiling, but such aspects – which may well contribute to overall pay gaps between, for example, men and women – may be highlighted by the pay audit.

An equal pay audit is not simply a data collection exercise. It entails a commitment to put right any unjustified pay inequalities, and this means that the audit must have the involvement and support of managers with the authority to deliver the necessary changes. It is also important to involve workforce representatives to maximise the validity of the audit and success of subsequent action taken.

Most employers believe that they provide equal pay for equal work, irrespective of whether job holders are men, women, of minority ethnic origin, white, disabled, work part-time . . . and so on.

An equal pay audit is the most effective way of establishing whether your business is providing equal pay and rewarding employees fairly in practice, and is an effective demonstration of action to promote equal pay under the terms of the equality duties. It provides a risk assessment tool for pay structures.

The benefits of a equal pay audit

The benefits of an equal pay audit are:

- ✔ Compliance with the law and good practice
- ✔ To help you identify, explain and eliminate unjustifiable pay gaps
- ✔ To ensure that you have rational, fair, transparent pay arrangements
- ✔ To enable you to demonstrate to employees and to potential employees a commitment to fairness and equality
- ✔ To illustrate to those you do business with that paying equally is a part of your values.

Carrying out an equal pay audit

A full equal pay audit would include all employees in your business who are 'in the same employment' and would consider relative pay of each protected group.

For practical reasons you may find it is not possible for you to carry out such a comprehensive equal pay audit at once. Determine the scope taking account of practical considerations, such as availability of information, and do as much as you can.

You may decide to carry out the audit in stages, but you need to be aware that this increases the risk of an equal pay claim being made.

Acting on equal pay claims

Many employers genuinely believe that they are providing equal pay and they embark on a review with an expectation that no inequalities will emerge. This position is often found to be foolhardy! An equal pay audit is not simply a data collection exercise; it also entails a commitment to deal with issues if unjustified pay gaps are found.

What happens next following your equal pay audit depends entirely on whether you have found issues or gaps. If you do find potential inequality then you need to develop a plan of action.

If you find no justification for unequal pay then you should act to provide equal pay. It is important to ensure both that unequal pay is equalised and that pay policies causing pay gaps are changed as soon as practicable. Liability for equal pay starts from the point at which a claim is submitted (with up to 6 years' back pay).

Obviously, for some businesses the financial reality of making the required change could be considerable. You can look to address the issue by making salary adjustments immediately, or you could use your annual salary review process to ensure that those that are found to be unequally paid are given higher-than-average awards. Just be aware that whilst the identified gap remains, you are still liable to equal pay claims!

The amount of compensation a victim of discrimination can receive is uncapped, so the sky's the limit in terms of potential costs. This means it quite literally pays to make sure that as an employer you are aware of your obligations and are doing as much as you can to mitigate the chances of an employee filing a claim.

Establishing Whether All Jobs Are Equal: Job Evaluation

Job evaluation is a framework used to underpin and ensure equitable pay decisions, meaning that employees are not discriminated against. As you can read in the previous section of this chapter on equal pay, as an employer you have a liability to ensure that people in your business are not discriminated against.

Understanding job evaluation

The purpose of job evaluation is to:

- Provide a basis for design and on-going implementation of an equitable and defensible approach to pay (pay structure)
- Help you and the managers in your business understand and communicate the relativities between jobs

Putting job evaluation into action

People often think that job evaluation is a scientific or objective system. It isn't; job evaluation in its simplest terms is a purely judgemental process that allows you to evaluate the relative worth or size of a job against another.

Job evaluation is based upon the job and not the incumbent that may be undertaking it.

Many job evaluation frameworks exist and may be purchased and used by you. Organisations such as the Hay Group (http://www.haygroup.com/uk/services/index.aspx?id=2424) are able to provide a framework to enable you to understand how each job in your business contributes to your success and strategic goals.

Deciding What Benefits You Should Provide

Employee benefits are part of the remuneration package given to employees in addition to the cash elements such as salary or bonus. They provide a quantifiable value for the individual employee, either immediately (company car) or in the future (pension). They can also include insurance provision in the event of sickness or death of the employee.

Why have employee benefits?

Employee benefits are typically provided in order to increase the commitment and engagement of employees. In addition, in order to remain competitive in the external employment market, benefits often have to be provided.

Other intrinsic motivational reasons are often quoted as to why employers provide benefits, for example they meet an actual or perceived personal need of employees concerning security or financial assistance.

Types of benefits

Benefits can be subdivided into different categories to reflect the benefit to the employee and you as the employer. Table 16-1 covers the typical benefits provided and the rationale behind them.

Your legal requirements in respect of employee holiday provision is explained online here: www.gov.uk/holiday-entitlement-rights/entitlement. If you want to understand what other types of leave you legally need to provide to parents and carers, gain access to the ACAS website: www.acas.org.uk/index.aspx?articleid=1362

Table 16-1	Typical Benefits Offered by a Business	
Benefit type	**Business rationale / legal requirement**	**Benefit to employee**
Pension Schemes	Often regarded as the most important benefit provided by employers and therefore highly valued to employees.	Future income security (post retirement)
Insured risk based schemes, such as life assurance, private medical insurance, personal accident insurance.	Can often assist a business when specific issues arise. For example, private medical insurance plans can help key employees return to work more quickly and therefore the impact on your business is reduced.	Enhance an employee's personal security and therefore engagement.
Holiday provision (Annual leave)	Almost all workers are legally entitled to 5.6 weeks per year (known as statutory leave entitlement or annual leave). An employer can include bank holidays as part of statutory annual leave.	Entitlements such as holiday recognise the need for employees to manage work and domestic issues.
Other types of leave	Parents, and other people who combine work with caring for dependents, have some specific rights protected by law. These include various types of leave and the right to be considered for flexible working. These typically cover maternity, paternity, adoption and carers leave.	In addition to annual leave (holidays) and common types of leave, such as maternity, paternity or carers leave, there are other commitments for which workers might be entitled to take time off work
Job or status related benefits	Sometimes in order for an employee to undertake a role, they may need a specific benefit such as a company car. In addition, a benefit may also need to be given in order to attract and retain employees to your business.	For an employee to be successful at their role it is vital that they feel they have the tools for the trade. So provision of a company car could enable a travelling sales person or engineer to undertake their role. In addition benefits have been used to promote the status and therefore commitment of employees to your business.

Agreeing who gets what benefits

As a small business owner it is critical that you manage your cost base; therefore, providing unnecessary benefits to employees should be avoided.

However, as explained, there are some benefits that you must provide in order to be legally compliant with UK legislation. These include:

- ✔ Annual leave
- ✔ Maternity / paternity leave
- ✔ Pension (by 2016)

Any other benefits above and beyond those described are at your discretion. So how do you decide if you should provide additional benefits and to whom?

The simplest way to decide is to establish the cost of providing the benefits and then decide who should receive the benefit. Some benefits you might choose to give to every employee, others might be related to their job (for example, a company car for your sales person), and finally you might only give some benefits to the most senior or important employees.

Knowing the tax implications

All your employees who receive benefits are liable to pay tax on them. In most circumstances the tax is collected through the Pay As You Earn (PAYE) system.

The amount of tax paid is dependent upon what kind of benefits are provided and their value. Some benefits, such as childcare and canteen meals, are tax free.

If you provide a company vehicle and the employee has access to the car for private or family use, including commuting to a place of work, then it is liable for tax to be paid by the employee. The level of tax paid is dependent upon the value of the vehicle when purchased and the type of fuel it uses, diesel or petrol.

For other benefits the employee usually pays tax on the value of the benefit provided, for example if a loan is made by the company to purchase a season travel season ticket that costs in excess of £10,000. Your employees will also be liable to pay tax on the cost of providing the benefit, for example the premiums paid to provide private medical insurance.

Use your accountant and payroll provider to help you establish the tax implications of the benefits provided. Always be clear to employees that the benefits provided are subject to tax and allow them to opt out of the benefit if it has a detrimental impact on their net earnings.

Working into Our Old Age: Pension Schemes

The provision of pension to employees has always been a significant and valuable part of remuneration packages. The last 15 years has seen significant changes of legislation leading to the legal requirement for employers to provide pension arrangements in 2012.

At the same time, the state pension system in the UK has also changed to accommodate European anti-ageism laws but perhaps most importantly to recognise that as we all live longer, the cost of providing pension is increasing proportionately.

You can find out more about the recent British and European legislation here:

- ✔ http://www.eurofound.europa.eu/observatories/eurwork/articles/ecj-rulings-on-retirement-age-and-discrimination-law
- ✔ https://www.gov.uk/guidance/equality-act-2010-guidance

Understanding legal requirements

In October 2012, the UK government introduced new rules to encourage more people to save for retirement. This new process is called *auto-enrolment*. This means that from 2012 onwards, employers are obliged to offer a qualifying pension scheme to their employees.

The 2012 legislation says that all employees who are aged between 22 and state pension age and earn above a certain amount ($10,000 a year in 2014/15) are automatically enrolled into a pension scheme. If they work for a large employer, this happened back in October 2012. For those working for medium and small companies, all staff must be enrolled into a pension by 2016.

Employees can opt out and leave the scheme, but only after they have been automatically made a member.

Setting up a pension scheme

To comply with the auto enrolment legislation, your benefits broker will assist you to set up a legally compliant scheme.

A benefits broker is often a specialist insurance broker that is able to assist you when purchasing insured benefits, such as private medical insurance. A specialist pensions advisor will help you plan and implement pension arrangements for your company. You can find guidance with regard to selecting a pensions advisor from: http://www.pensionsadvisoryservice. org.uk/about-pensions/pensions-basics/top-tips-for-your-pension/choosing-an-ifa

The basic premise of auto enrolment is to ensure that employees and employers maintain a minimum level of contribution into an appropriate investment scheme to assist an employees with savings towards retirement.

The minimum amount an employer and employees have to contribute under auto enrolment will gradually increase between 2012 and 2018. It is a percentage of 'qualifying earnings' (between £5,772 and £41,865 in 2014/15):

✔ From 2012 to 2017, employees contribute 0.8% plus 0.2% tax relief, employers 1% (overall minimum is 2%)

✔ From 2017 to 2018, employees contribute 2.4% plus 0.6% tax relief, employers 2% (overall minimum is 5%)

✔ From 2018 onwards, employees contribute 4% plus 1% tax relief, employers 3% (overall minimum is 8%)

Many existing occupational schemes and business sponsored group personal pensions already qualify, but they will be extended to take in a greater proportion of the workforce.

If you wish to provide an enhanced pension benefit, you need to decide what type of pension scheme you wish to establish. There are two main types of workplace pension, and as an employer, you decide which type of scheme to offer:

✔ **Defined contribution pension schemes:** Sometimes known as *money purchase* schemes. The money is invested by a pension provider chosen by you as the employer, and the pension provider usually takes a small percentage of your pension pot as a management fee. The level of pension to be provided from these types of plans cannot be guaranteed and is unknown until shortly before retirement. The only risk the employer carries is associated with on-going contributions.

The amount of pension provided to employees when they retire usually depends on:

• How much has been paid in

• How long you've been paying in

• How well the investment has done

✔ **Defined benefit pension schemes:** Also known as *final salary* or *salary-related* pensions. They guarantee to give an employee a certain level of pension each year when they retire, based typically on earnings and service at retirement. These types of schemes have all but closed in the UK as the financial risk of providing a guaranteed pension has proved to be significant. It isn't unusual to see employer contribution rates of 25 per cent of base salary or above in order to meet the pension guarantee upon retirement.

Seeking guidance and advice

Pensions are a complicated benefit to provide. You should seek specialist advise when embarking on starting the pension scheme for your employees. Advice can be easily found, and you should start with seeking guidance from your insurance broker. If they are unable to give the guidance you need, they will know a specialist that can.

Alternatively, a great deal of initial guidance can be found from the regulators and other government sources. If you don't comply, the Pension Regulator can undertake enforcement action against you. They may take enforcement action through the issue of notices and penalties.

The Pensions Regulator can issue penalty notices to punish persistent and deliberate non-compliance:

✔ A fixed penalty notice will be issued if you don't comply with statutory notices, or if there's sufficient evidence of a breach of the law. This is fixed at £400 and payable within a specific period.

✔ If you fail to meet the demands of the statutory notice, the Regulator can also issue escalating penalty notices. This penalty has a prescribed daily rate of £50 to £10,000 depending on the number of staff you have.

✔ In addition the Regulator can issue a civil penalty for cases where you fail to pay contributions due into the agreed scheme. This is a financial penalty of up to £5,000 for individual Directors and up to £50,000 for businesses.

So failure to comply with this legislation will result in penalties and financial charges that could in some cases have significant financial consequences.

For auto enrolment there are a number of deadlines that must be met in order to comply with the employer's duties. This is a complex project for any employer, and we estimate that an employer starting with a clean sheet has 100+ actions to plan and undertake. Therefore, seek guidance at the earliest opportunity from a specialist workplace pensions advisor.

Chapter 17

Parting with People

*I*n Chapter 5 you can read in detail about the five fair reasons in law for dismissal and the process you should follow if you want to dismiss someone. In theory, if you carry out a thorough investigation, establish a reasonable belief that dismissal based on one of the five fair reasons is justified, and follow a fair process, the dismissal will be fair. In practice lots of potential pitfalls are thrown in your way and if you fall into one, it could cost you a lot of money and stress.

If you don't dismiss someone properly and fairly, they could make a claim to an Employment Tribunal for wrongful or unfair dismissal, and if you lose the case you may have to pay legal fees and compensation, or even reinstate the employee.

You may decide it's worth taking the risk, but you will save a lot of time, money and stress if you follow the rules.

This chapter focuses on the two trickiest aspects of capability – poor performance in the job, and incapacity due to illness.

Building a Case

You will not always see in your crystal ball that the outcome of a particular situation may be dismissal, but you can often spot the signs. Whenever any of the following crops up, start making notes!

✔ A manager or customer complains to you about an employee's performance

✔ You notice that an employee is taking a lot of time off sick or slacking off in their work

✔ Someone makes an allegation of misconduct against an employee

✔ You hear on the grapevine that an employee might be up to something

If you have to dismiss someone you should be able to show a reasonable belief that the dismissal is justified. Make notes after every conversation with the person or their manager about an issue that might ultimately lead to dismissal.

Check out Chapter 5 for more information about fair grounds for dismissal.

Just get rid of him!

One of the most common conversations a HR professional has with a line manager runs something like this:

Line Manager: 'Have you got a minute?'

HR person: 'Sure, what's up?'

Line Manager: 'It's Martin (or it could equally be Mary) – I've had it up to here, how can I get rid of him?'

HR person: 'What is the problem?'

Line Manager: 'He just doesn't get it. I don't think he's ever going to get it. I just had to apologise to another customer for his rubbish work. Can you just get rid of him?'

HR person: 'Have you spoken to Martin about the problem?'

Line Manager: 'He knows. He must know. We have had so many complaints from customers. He's always late, scruffy, just completely switched off. I've put up with it for long enough.'

HR Manager (discreetly checking the files and finding that Martin has worked there for nearly 3 years): 'So you haven't spoken to Martin about it?'

Line Manager: 'No, and before you say it, I haven't got time to go through some performance management poncey process that will take six months, and waste everybody's time.'

HR Manager (sighing): 'Right. Let's start with the facts.'

✔ Whichever role is yours in this scenario, always start with the facts.

Investigating poor performance

Countless reasons lead people to underperform at work, and you should try to understand the reasons for poor performance before taking any formal action. Chapter 5 discusses the correct procedure to follow.

Start by finding out when the poor performance began; this may help you to identify the cause of this behaviour.

Employees on probation

If the employee is relatively new and has never reached the required performance standard, check if they are still within their probation period.

If the employee is still within the probation period, follow the process outlined in Chapter 15. If the employee has not passed their probation, you should dismiss them, give them the reason in writing and pay them for their contractual notice.

If the poor performance started shortly after an employee passed their probation period a stern conversation sometimes does the trick to turn them around, particularly with less experienced employees who may think they can relax once they have passed their probation.

If the end date for an employee's probation period has passed without any formal review identifying any performance issues, they are deemed by default to have passed their probation period.

Longer serving employees

More experienced employees could have a drop off in performance for various reasons, such as:

- Ill health, disability or pregnancy
- Personal problems
- Personality clash with a colleague or manager
- Loss of confidence or lack of skill with new responsibilities

Investigating employee ill health

You may find during your investigation that an employee has an illness that affects their performance, either because they are absent from work, or because they are physically or mentally incapable of doing the work due to illness.

Incapacity due to ill health

You should establish, ideally with the employee, whether the impact of the illness is likely to be short or long term. For a short term illness, you should follow your normal sickness absence procedure, or discuss with the employee if any changes could be made in the short term to help them to do their job.

If the employee is withholding information about an illness, or if in your view they have an unrealistic perspective on how the illness is affecting their work, you may request a medical report from their doctor, or refer them to an occupational health advisor. Read about the Fit for Work referral scheme in the sidebar 'Occupational Health Advisors'.

If the illness relates to the employee's mental health, and their work is causing them stress, you should try to establish if it is the content of the work, the circumstances, work relationships or volume of work that is causing the stress. You may be able to make changes at work to remove some of the stress.

Read about requesting a medical report in Chapter 6.

Incapability due to a disability

If you discover during your investigations that an employee's poor performance is caused by a disability, you are legally obliged under the Equality Act 2010 to make reasonable adjustments to enable the person to reduce the disadvantage they suffer at work.

Occupational Health Advisors

A new government scheme rolled out in England and Wales in 2015 provides advice to employers and to employees who are absent from work for four weeks or more due to sickness.

The employee's GP can refer them to the *Fit for Work* service, unless there are clear and well defined reasons not to refer them. If the GP hasn't done it, you can refer the employee after an absence of at least 4 weeks.

A Case Manager will assess the employee's health and identify ways that you could support them to return to work, through a Return to Work Plan.

You can find out more about Fit for Work here: www.fitforwork.org/employer

You are not obliged to follow the advice in the Return to Work Plan but you can benefit from a tax exemption if you pay for treatment recommended in the Return to Work Plan or if you have one, your Occupational Health advisor, up to the value of £500 per employee (as of January 2015).

You can find out more here: www.hmrc.gov. uk/manuals/eimanual/EIM21774. htm

Under the Equality Act 2010, a *disability* is defined as

> *A physical or mental impairment that has a 'substantial' and 'long-term' negative effect on the person's ability to do normal daily activities.*

The *long term effect* is defined as longer than 12 months. Many aspects of an employee's work would be considered to be normal daily activities. Some illnesses qualify as a disability. For example, a person with a diagnosis of cancer, a HIV infection or multiple sclerosis meets the criteria defining disability.

If you don't know about a disability, or could not reasonably have known about it, you don't have to make the adjustments, but as soon as you become aware of a disability which is affecting the employee's ability to do their work, you must consider what adjustments you could make. The employee does not have to suggest them but it would make sense for you to ask them what adjustments would help them.

Although no exemption exists for small employers from the obligation to make reasonable adjustments for people with disabilities, one of the factors an Employment Tribunal will consider when assessing whether you have made reasonable adjustments will be your financial and other resources and how disruptive the required adjustments would be to your business activities. Other factors to consider are how practicable it is for you to make the adjustments and how effective the adjustments would be at overcoming the effect of the disability.

If you want to avoid an employee with a disability going to an Employment Tribunal at all, consider these three kinds of adjustments:

- ✔ The way things are done – for example allowing an employee with a mobility disability to park in a visitor car parking space to make access easier
- ✔ The removal of barriers in the physical environment – for example putting stickers on glass doors to help a visually impaired employee
- ✔ Providing additional equipment – for example providing a hearing induction loop system for a deaf employee

Read the government guidance on adjustments for disabilities here:

`www.gov.uk/reasonable-adjustments-for-disabled-workers`

If, following reasonable adjustments, the employee is still unable to perform to the required standard in the role, either because the adjustments were not effective, or because of other factors, such as long term absence, you may have to carry out further investigation before having a capability hearing, which may result in dismissal.

Holding informal conversations

If possible, start with an informal conversation with the person to identify the underlying reasons for their poor performance, and whether it is likely to be temporary or longer lasting.

Table 17-1 lists some of the common reasons employees may give, and suggests a potential way forward.

Table 17-1	Some Causes and Remedies for Poor Performance
Cause of poor performance	*Remedies you could use*
Lack of knowledge or skills	Training, coaching, support from a manager, time to practice and pick up skills, change of responsibilities, close supervision
Personal circumstances outside work	Paid or unpaid time off work, temporary arrangements with working hours, deadlines or responsibilities, access to counselling or other professional help
Personality clash with manager or colleague	Change of role, conversation with the people involved to agree a way forward, clear guidance about your expectations
Lack of confidence	More time, training, coaching from a manager or colleague, change of responsibilities
Lack of motivation	Clear guidance about your expectations and any rewards or sanctions you will use, close supervision
Physical factors – pregnancy, ill health, disability	Respond to individual employee needs, meeting at least the minimum statutory requirements

If you think that someone is performing badly because of a change at work like a new manager, a restructure or new job responsibilities, have a conversation with the employee to test out your theory.

Depending on the circumstances, you may be able to offer support, training or a temporary change in their responsibilities to help them through a difficult period.

If you discover that something outside work, like divorce, bereavement or a child care problem is affecting an employee's performance, you should have a conversation with them and flag your concern.

If you think the person is capable of doing the job, but is choosing not to, either because they are not motivated, or they have had a run in with a manager or colleague, you should tell them clearly that their performance is not acceptable and tell them what might happen if it doesn't improve. There may be a case for handling this kind of poor performance as misconduct rather than capability.

If an employee is pregnant, ill or has a disability, you have a legal responsibility as an employer for their wellbeing. You cannot dismiss someone just for being pregnant, or just because of a disability. On the contrary, you must take certain actions or make certain adjustments to enable them to do the job.

You may ultimately be able to dismiss someone who has an illness and even someone with a disability, for the reason of capability, but only if you have gone through a fair process first. However justified the reason, always be clear that the person's performance is a matter for concern. Express your expectation that their performance will pick up again, ideally within a certain time frame.

Keep notes of your conversations with employees about their performance. If the matter is sensitive you may want to write your notes straight after the conversation rather than scribbling notes while they are talking to you.

If the poor performance goes on for longer than you expected, and starts to cause serious issues in the business, you have already started building your case for taking action which might result in dismissal.

Progressing to formal investigations

If an employee's poor performance persists after your informal intervention, you should start a formal process.

In law, you must demonstrate that you made a 'reasonable enquiry' and that you had a 'reasonable belief' that someone is incapable of doing their job before you dismiss them.

During an investigation, you must collect tangible evidence that someone is not performing in their job, for example:

- ✔ Not hitting sales or piecework targets
- ✔ Not hitting a target number of telephone or sales calls
- ✔ Frequent or significant customer complaints
- ✔ A high rate of administrative errors
- ✔ Frequent absence from work
- ✔ A low rate of productivity
- ✔ A high rate of rejection of their work by quality assurance

If other people are doing similar work you may be able to draw comparisons, but make sure that you are not unfairly discriminating against the person you're investigating.

During the investigation phase you may have a meeting with the employee to establish or confirm the facts.

As long as the meeting is part of an investigation, you do not need to give the employee the right to be accompanied, but make sure that you don't allow the meeting to turn into a capability or disciplinary hearing, or you will be in breach of the statutory procedure.

Mitigating circumstances

You should also investigate whether there are any mitigating circumstances which might explain the employee's poor performance.

Part of building your case includes establishing a reasonable belief that dismissal is a proportionate sanction.

If you find out that an under-performing employee is the victim of a personal disaster outside work and you don't take it into account, you may not be able to show that dismissal was reasonable in the circumstances.

Formal performance review meetings

If you have investigated the possible reasons for an employee's poor performance, and any short term measures you have put in place have not been effective, you should formally advise the employee that their performance is not meeting the required standard, and tell them what might happen if their performance doesn't improve.

Follow the process outlined in Chapter 5 to formally review the employee's progress and performance before you hold a capability hearing.

The more evidence you can gather during the formal performance review process to build your case, the better.

Keep notes to show that you have

✔ Set reasonable targets

✔ Given reasonable support

✔ Allowed reasonable time for the employee to improve their performance.

There is no standard definition of 'reasonable' but just imagine yourself testifying at an Employment Tribunal and defending your actions.

Capability hearing

You should only call a capability hearing when you have reached the point where dismissal is a possible outcome, because you believe you have exhausted all the other possibilities.

If you dismiss an employee following a capability hearing, you must follow up in writing, pay the employee their statutory notice, and give them the right of appeal. Read about how to hold a capability hearing in Chapter 5.

When dismissal is a possible outcome, take extra care to follow the correct procedure about notifying the employee in writing, giving them the right to be accompanied, and behaving reasonably in everything that you do!

Misconduct

You can dismiss someone for misconduct, if they have either broken a big rule, or committed 'gross misconduct' or if they have committed a number of acts of less serious misconduct, and you have correctly followed a disciplinary procedure culminating in the sanction of dismissal.

You must follow the statutory procedure, or your own disciplinary procedure if you have one.

Read about the disciplinary procedure in Chapter 6. Follow the dismissal process outlined in Chapter 5 if you want to dismiss an employee for misconduct.

Contravention of a statutory obligation

You can dismiss an employee for breaking the law, or to avoid breaking the law as a business, but you must follow the correct procedure. Follow your own or the statutory disciplinary procedure.

You can read examples of breaches of statutory obligations and the dismissal procedure in Chapter 5.

Some other substantial reason (SOSR)

You can dismiss an employee for a reason that has a significant impact on your business, but doesn't necessarily fall into the other categories of fair reasons for dismissal.

As well as following your own or the statutory disciplinary procedure, you must be able to demonstrate that dismissal is a proportionate response and that you are only dismissing the employee as a last resort.

Read some examples of SOSR and the dismissal procedure in Chapter 5.

Managing Redundancy

As with other forms of dismissal, you should build your case for redundancy, whether it applies to a large number of employees or just to one. This is called the *business case*. The most obvious place to start building a case for redundancy is with the volume of work. The next building block is the finances.

If you are struggling to write a business case to justify a redundancy based on either reduced workload or tight finances, it is probably not a true redundancy.

Closing a business

If your whole business is closing down and you employ 20 or more people, you must follow the collective redundancy notification and consultation process. If you employ fewer than 20 people you should follow the procedures for smaller scale redundancies.

Even if the business is insolvent, you must pay the appropriate notice, outstanding holiday pay and redundancy pay to your employees.

If you are unable to make the payments, the government may pay from the National Insurance fund, if you meet certain criteria. To find out more about redundancies if your business is insolvent or closing, contact the Redundancy Payments Service Helpline on 0845 145 0004.

If you are planning to sell your business or you are merging with, or being taken over by another business, special rules protect your employees' rights: The Transfer of Undertakings, Protection of Employment or TUPE regulations. Read about them in Chapter 12.

Closing a workplace

If you are moving your whole business to a new location, or closing one site but moving the work to other sites, you may have a reason to make employees redundant.

However, there are a number of factors you should take into account when you are consulting employees about the relocation or closure of a workplace:

- ✔ If the locations are quite close together and it would be reasonable to expect employees to travel to the new location, and they would not incur significant additional expense or inconvenience, and their work will continue at the new location, their current roles may not be redundant

- ✔ If you have a mobility clause in the employment contract, which specifies that employees may be required to work at different locations, or move to an alternative primary place of work, you can ask them to move rather than making their jobs redundant

- ✔ Even if the jobs are not technically redundant for one of the reasons above, you may want to consider the impact on morale and productivity of other employees if people do not wish to relocate and you refuse to make redundancy payments

- ✔ A proposal to move an employee's place of work may appear to be reasonable and practicable, but you must consider the impact on particular individuals. For example, an employee with caring responsibilities or a disability might suffer a disadvantage in the move compared to other employees.

Removing a role

The most straightforward redundancy is where only one employee is doing a particular kind of work, and the requirement for that work ceases.

Regardless of the number of people involved, in every case of potential redundancy, you must

✔ Consult the employee, giving them the right to be accompanied at meetings

✔ Consider alternatives to redundancy

✔ Consider and offer any suitable alternative work with an appropriate trial period

✔ Give the employee the correct notice and payments

✔ Give an employee with more than two years' service paid time off to look for other work during their period of notice

✔ Give the employee the right of appeal.

If you have more than one employee at a single workplace doing *a particular kind of work,* and you have a reduced requirement for that work, you must follow a fair selection process to decide which employee's job will be made redundant.

If you have more than one employee doing the same or *similar work,* even if they have different job titles and grades, and you have a reduced requirement for that work, you must create a *selection pool* of the affected jobs and then follow a fair selection process to decide which job or jobs will be made redundant.

If you calculate that the reduction in workload or the extent of the cost cutting is likely to lead to 20 or more redundancies at one location, this is categorised as a *collective redundancy* programme, and you must follow some extra notification and consultation steps. If you think that you may make 20 to 99 jobs redundant at one place of work, or *establishment,* within a 90 day period, you must notify the Department for Business, Innovation and Skills at least 30 days before the first dismissal. For 100 or more potential redundancies you must let them know at least 45 days before the first dismissal. You must notify for each establishment and each 90 day period where 20 or more jobs are at risk.

To inform the Department of Business, Innovation and Skills of redundancies, use form HR1, found on their website: www.bis.gov.uk/assets/insolvency/docs/forms/redundancy-payments/hr1pdf

Consulting employees

Employees have the right to be consulted before being made redundant. Consultation should be *meaningful,* that is with the intention of genuinely considering the employees' representations and reaching agreement on an outcome.

Individual consultation

In the case of a single employee, the consultation process should consist of at least two *individual consultation* meetings.

First consultation meeting

Invite the employee to an individual consultation meeting, giving them reasonable notice and the right to be accompanied by a colleague or Trade Union representative.

At the first meeting, advise the employee formally that their job is at risk of redundancy, and explain the business case.

Depending on the circumstances, include the following in this meeting:

- ✔ Ask the employee if they have any suggestions about how a redundancy could be avoided.
- ✔ Tell the employee about any collective consultation discussions and any collective agreements affecting the redundancy situation.
- ✔ Explain any measures you have already considered, and why you believe they will not be effective in avoiding a redundancy situation.
- ✔ Tell the employee if they are in a selection pool, how many roles are at risk, and what selection criteria you will be using to decide which jobs are redundant. Explain how the selection process will work.
- ✔ Tell the employee about any *suitable alternative employment* which may be available in the business – see the definition later in this chapter. Explain the selection process you will use to offer people suitable alternative jobs.
- ✔ Tell the employee if there are no suitable alternative jobs.
- ✔ Explain the consultation process, and give them the date for the next consultation meeting and whether it will be a final consultation meeting. Ask the employee to consider any ideas they have to avoid redundancy before that next meeting.
- ✔ Explain the amount and timing of payments that you will make to the employee if you are unable to avoid redundancy.

Final consultation meeting

You may have more than two individual consultation meetings, but at the final consultation meeting you should confirm the outcome of the consultation, and follow up in writing.

You should leave at least a week between meetings to give the employee a reasonable length of time to consider their options. Give the employee the opportunity to talk about their ideas between the formal meetings if that is practical.

Explain the employee's right to appeal against a decision to make their job redundant. Ask them who to write to, and give them a reasonable time frame, usually five days, to make the appeal.

Collective consultation

If more than 20 employees are at risk of redundancy in a 90 day period at one establishment you must run a *collective consultation* process. The law defines a collective redundancy situation as

> *dismissal for a reason not related to the individual concerned or for a number of reasons all of which are not so related.*

You must consult in good time with a recognised Trade Union, or other elected employee representatives, and provide them with certain information, with the aim of avoiding or reducing the number of redundancies and mitigating the effect of redundancies. You can read about recognising Trade Unions and electing employee representatives in Chapter 15.

The Acas guidance on managing collective redundancies are extremely useful, and are available here: www.acas.org.uk/media/pdf/b/2/Handling-large-scale-collective-redundancies-advisory-booklet.pdf

Selecting employees for redundancy

If more than one employee's job is at risk of redundancy you must use objective criteria and a fair selection process to decide which employees will be dismissed due to redundancy.

Examples of the criteria used to decide which employees will be made redundant include:

- ✔ Attendance records (exclude absence for maternity or disability related illness)
- ✔ Disciplinary records (exclude expired warnings)
- ✔ Skills, competencies and qualifications
- ✔ Work experience
- ✔ Performance ratings
- ✔ Length of service (only in conjunction with other criteria to avoid indirect age discrimination)

If possible, have more than one person involved in making the selection decision. Use a rating scale, for example allocating employees with points from 1–5 against each of the selection criteria. If you are running a large scale redundancy programme you could set a minimum points threshold that employees must reach to get through to a second selection stage.

Avoiding redundancies

You must show that you have considered all possible alternatives to avoid making an employee redundant. This could include offering a suitable alternative job, or creating a job share or a part-time role.

You may try to negotiate a variation to employees' terms and conditions to reduce your costs in order to protect jobs. If the situation giving rise to the potential redundancy may be temporary, you could consider a period of short-time working or layoff:

✔ *Short-time working* is a temporary variation to the contract where an employee works shorter days or a shorter working week for less than their normal pay.

✔ *Layoff* is a temporary arrangement where an employer tells the employee they are not required for work and the employee is not paid.

If you want to use short-time working or layoff as a way to avoid redundancies, follow the guidance provided by Acas to avoid getting into hot water for not paying your employees! You'll find them here: `www.acas.org.uk/media/pdf/q/1/Lay-offs-and-short-time-working-accessible-version.pdf`

Suitable alternative jobs

If you offer the employee at risk of redundancy a *suitable alternative job*, that is a job that is similar to their own, or that you could reasonably expect they would be able to perform based on their skills and experience, that is of similar status and is paid at least at the same rate, you have fulfilled your obligation to mitigate the risk of redundancy.

If the employee refuses to take the job, you do not have to pay them redundancy pay because they have effectively resigned. You should give them a four week trial period in the new job, after which you or the employee may be able to demonstrate that the job is not a suitable alternative, and you would be obliged to pay them redundancy pay.

Redundancy pay

You must pay at least statutory redundancy pay to redundant employees with more than two years' service. See Chapter 5 for guidance and links to calculate statutory redundancy pay.

Avoiding an Employment Tribunal

Appearing as a defendant at an Employment Tribunal is expensive, time consuming and not good for your reputation.

The best way to avoid Employment Tribunals is to not give employees or potential employees a reason to make a claim against you, by behaving reasonably and following the correct procedures in all your employee relations matters. Even then, there's a risk in complex cases that you may lose at a Tribunal and incur legal fees and the cost of compensation payments.

Accepting that everyone makes mistakes, including predecessors whose decisions might come home to roost on your watch, and recognising that time is money, and you may not want to invest yours in preparing for an Employment Tribunal, the following are some pragmatic ways in which you can avoid an Employment Tribunal.

Exploring conciliation

If someone wants to make a claim for unfair dismissal against you to an Employment Tribunal, they must first notify Acas, the Advisory, Conciliation and Arbitration Service, using an Early Conciliation Notification Form.

Acas will offer to conciliate between them and you as their employer, with the aim of resolving the dispute without going to an Employment Tribunal.

The service is free to you and the employee, and the Acas Conciliator provides an objective perspective to both parties.

They will encourage you and the employee to resolve the matter using your own grievance or disciplinary process to reach a settlement or an agreement on a way forward. This is called Early Conciliation, and participation by both parties is voluntary.

You can read more about conciliation here:

www.acas.org.uk/media/pdf/o/g/Conciliation-Explained-Acas.pdf

The employee has three months from the date of dismissal to make a claim of unfair dismissal to an Employment Tribunal. They must have an Early Conciliation certificate from Acas to progress their claim, and once they notify Acas that they are planning to make a claim to a Trubunal, the clock stops on the Tribunal time limit, for up to one month, to give Acas time to manage the conciliation process.

If you or the employee are not willing to participate in Early Conciliation, or the conciliation is unsuccessful after a maximum period of one month, or longer if that is agreed, Acas will provide the Certificate to the employee to send to the Employment Tribunal.

Acas will continue to be available to conciliate and help you to reach a resolution, right up to the time when an Employment Tribunal makes a judgement.

An employee must pay a fee of between £160 and £250 to lodge the complaint, and then a Tribunal hearing fee of between £230 and £950 if it goes that far. That will probably put off most employees who don't feel they have a good chance of winning their case.

Reaching a settlement agreement

If you're unable to resolve a dispute between you and an employee and want to end the employment relationship, you could use a Settlement Agreement.

A *Settlement Agreement* is a legally binding confidential contract between you and the employee, in which you agree on the terms of how you will part company. Usually this involves the employer making a compensation payment, and sometimes offering other terms such as an agreed reference, in exchange for the employee waiving their right to make a claim against their employer at an Employment Tribunal.

The Settlement Agreement must include a reference to all the matters on which the employee is waiving their rights, so you should play it safe by including all the relevant employment and other legislation on which they might base a claim.

You can use an Acas template Settlement Agreement, and insert the particular terms you have negotiated:

To be legally binding, the employee must sign the Settlement Agreement only after having obtained advice from a qualified independent advisor. You must pay at least a contribution towards the employee's costs to obtain this advice. A typical clause in a Settlement Agreement will set a limit on the contribution the employer will pay directly to the advisor, on receipt of an invoice and signed certificate from the advisor confirming they are qualified to advise on such matters, they have advised the employee in question, and that they have in place the relevant professional indemnity insurance in relation to the advice given.

Insuring yourself against the risk

You can purchase a specific Employment Tribunal Indemnity insurance policy to insure you against the costs of legal fees and compensation payments to employees if you lose at an Employment Tribunal. However, the policies are usually linked to a help line service, and if you don't follow the advice you receive on the help line 'to the letter', the insurance is invalidated.

Search the internet using 'Employment Tribunal Indemnity' as key words and you will find a plethora of providers!

Part V
The Part of Tens

Head to www.dummies.com/extras/hrforsmallbusinessuk to check out ten tips for outsourcing your HR.

In this part . . .

- ✔ Discover ten HR jargon busters
- ✔ Follow ten tips to better manage poor performance
- ✔ Find out the ten best interview questions

Chapter 18

Ten HR Jargon Busters

In This Chapter

▶ Understanding the language you'll need in the world of HR

▶ Breaking down HR acronyms

HR lends itself to acronyms and abbreviations, so you can get started with this top ten and follow the pointers to find out more if you're interested.

Accrued Holiday

Employees are legally entitled to a minimum of 5.6 working weeks' paid holiday in every year, including bank holidays, which is usually eight in a year, unless the Queen has a special birthday or somebody royal gets married.

For someone who works a 5 day week, the 5.6 weeks of holiday comes to 28 days for the whole holiday year, which is 2.33 days per month.

The most common holiday year runs from January to December, but you might run a holiday year from 1st April to 31st March, or use other dates to fit with your financial year.

Accrued holiday is the term to describe the amount of holiday that an employee has built up, at any point in the holiday year.

So, if an employee started on 1st January, and they accrue 2.33 days per month, they will have built up 14 days by the end of June, half way through the year. You can read more about holidays in Chapter 6.

Acronyms Explained

HR – there's an acronym to get us started – is an ALHHH (*Acronym Lover's Heaven, Hater's Hell*). Here are some of the most commonly used ones . . . you'll probably want to memorise these ASAP.

ATS	Applicant Tracking System: Software, often available as a web based system, to track job applicants. You can store their details on a database, send automated messages, share candidate details with authorised users, and capture applications from multiple sources, like your website, job adverts, the job centre.
GOQ	Genuine Occupational Qualification: Under the Equality Act 2010 you may not discriminate against candidates for jobs based on a protected characteristic such as age, nationality, gender or race, unless there is a sound reason, or genuine occupational qualification. For example, a charity running a hostel for women who are victims of domestic abuse by men may show that they are justified in only employing women to work in the hostel.
SOSR	Some other substantial reason: This is a catch all phrase for a justifiable reason to dismiss an employee, which does not fall into one of the other four fair reasons for dismissal: redundancy, misconduct, capability or statutory/legal requirement. Examples include a conflict of interest, or an employee not disclosing required information.
OD	Organisation Design or Organisation Development: Some large companies employ specialists to do this work, which focusses on creating the best structure for a business, and helping people to work effectively together.
RTW	Right to Work (In the UK): All employees must have permission to work in the UK, and you must collect the evidence. You could be fined £10,000 by the UK Border Agency if they inspect your business and don't find the right records. Sometimes this acronym is used for Return to Work (after a period of sickness absence).
EWC	Expected Week of Confinement: This is an old fashioned term to indicate the week in which a pregnant woman is expected to give birth. It is used for working out the earliest and latest dates when an employee can request maternity leave. The maternity certificate, or MAT B1 form provided by the doctor or midwife, after the woman is at least 20 weeks pregnant, will tell you the EWC.
TUPE	The Transfer of Undertakings (Protection of Employment) Regulations: These protect employees' rights and outline employers' responsibilities, when businesses are bought, merged or sold, or contracts for services transfer from one provider to another.

Collective Agreement

This agreement, usually negotiated by a union, is about employment terms (most commonly rates of pay), which apply to all the employees in a defined *bargaining unit*. The bargaining unit could consist of union members, employees on a certain work site, or categories of employees. Read more in Chapter 15.

Employee Engagement

This describes the combination of motivation and commitment of employees to their work and their employer. It is often measured using employee engagement surveys, and research shows there is often a strong correlation between levels of employee engagement and productivity. A high level of employee engagement is the Holy Grail of HR, because it usually indicates strong leadership, clear goals, fair rewards, and positive working relationships. Read more in Chapter 15.

Flexible Benefits

They come in many forms, but the essence of flexible benefits is that the employer creates a budget or pot of money for each employee, and the employee chooses how they want to spend it. Flexible benefits options often include private medical insurance, health care cash plans, extra holiday, car or car allowance. They are most cost effective for large employers who have enough insured 'lives' to make it worthwhile for insurance and private medical health providers to do the administration. Read more in Chapter 16.

Job Evaluation

This is a method of comparing the relative size and impact of jobs in a business, and is usually used to find out the market rate for a certain job, to justify differences in pay, or to create scales for pay increases. The well established job evaluation systems like the Hay Points system have been around for long enough that there is a large bank of comparative data for jobs across sectors and industries. You usually have to pay for the data, and take part in a salary survey, so that your data becomes part of the whole picture. Read more in Chapter 16.

Mediation

In a work context, mediation is when a third party facilitates a resolution between two people who are in dispute. They could be a manager and team member, or two colleagues. Mediation is useful if a relationship has broken down but the unhappy parties don't want to raise a formal grievance, or don't have enough grounds to take disciplinary action. Good mediation takes skill and experience but can achieve excellent and long lasting results. Read more in Chapter 15.

Person Specification

This is a description of the skills, experience and knowledge that someone would need to have to do a job, and is most commonly drawn up at the same time as a job description. You can specify whether any of the criteria are essential or desirable, and if you have a good person specification, it is very easy to set interview questions or design selection tests when you are recruiting. Read more in Chapter 2.

Settlement Agreement

This used to be called a *Compromise Agreement*. It is a legally binding contract between an employer and an employee to settle their obligations to each other, upon termination of an employment contract. You would be wise to use one when you know you have taken a procedural short cut or terminated the contract for a reason that might not be fair. The employee signs away any rights to make claims against you, in exchange for a payment, and you must also pay for the employee to get legal advice on the agreement. Read more in Chapter 17.

Termination

This is the end of an employment or service contract, and can arise by either party giving notice, or by one party being in serious breach of the contract. If by your actions or omissions, you breach the terms of an employment contract, the employee could resign and claim constructive dismissal, which means that you terminated the contract by making it impossible for the employee to remain in the employment relationship. Read more in Chapter 5.

Chapter 19

(Nearly) Ten Tips for Managing Poor Performance

....

In This Chapter

▶ Making sure that your employees understand their contribution to the business

▶ Helping employees achieve their best possible performance

....

*A*s a leader or owner of your company, you must ensure that your employees get the big picture of their contributions to the overall performance of your company. Make sure your employees know what's expected of them in their duties, performance, and behaviour – and that helps you both to judge their contribution and feeling of value within the company.

Defining Underperformance

Underperformance or *poor performance* is a failure to perform the duties of the role or to perform them to the standard required by the business. Employers sometime confuse underperformance or poor performance with misconduct or poor conduct.

Here are the key distinctions:

Underperformance typically illustrated as:	Misconduct typically covers:	Gross misconduct
Unacceptable standard of work	Continued absence	Violence
Low productivity	Lateness or poor time keeping	Failure to undertake a reasonable management instruction
Poor output	Being rude to customers or colleagues	Theft
Failure to complete objectives		Alcohol or drug abuse whilst at work

Understanding the Causes of Poor Performance

Identify this before you consider whether to take an informal or formal approach to performance management. For example:

- Have you made your expectations clear?
- Has the employee had sufficient training to carry out the work requirement?
- Is the workload too high?

There may be other possible causes of problems such as:

- You hired the wrong person for the job.
- There may be personal outside influences restricting the person from performing the role.
- There is ineffective or lack of communication between the person and staff structure/people/colleagues/clients in order to perform the role effectively.

Once you have considered the above, you can set out a Plan for improvement.

Creating a Performance Improvement Plan (PIP)

A basic tenet with all performance management efforts is the notion that taking action early is better than waiting. The same holds true for the performance improvement plan. A PIP is more likely to be successful when the supervisor recognises there is a performance or behavioural issue that needs to be corrected. Early communication and early feedback (both positive and corrective) are good ways to prevent future performance problems. Investing time early is always time well spent, and the performance improvement plan can be an effective tool in preventing problems from getting worse or for intervening when performance and/or workplace behaviours have become counterproductive.

A *Performance Improvement Plan* is a formal process used to help employees improve performance or modify behaviour. The performance improvement plan, or PIP as it is sometimes called, identifies performance and/or behavioural issues that need to be corrected and creates a written plan of action to guide the improvement and/or corrective action.

Fundamentally, a PIP is a structured communication tool designed to facilitate constructive discussion between the employee and you. An effective PIP will:

- ✔ Specifically identify the performance to be improved or the behaviour to be corrected

- ✔ Provide clear expectations and metrics about the work to be performed or behaviour that must change

- ✔ Identify the support and resources available to help the employee make the required improvements

- ✔ Establish a plan for reviewing the employee's progress and providing feedback to the employee for the duration of the PIP

- ✔ Specify possible consequences if performance standards as identified in the PIP are not met

Providing Appropriate Time to Improve

Deciding what is an appropriate amount of time to improve will depend entirely on the performance issue being addressed. You will need to agree with the employee what is reasonable between you and ensure that it is documented appropriately.

Behavioural issues by default can take longer to improve on, whereas transactional performance objectives such as a sales target can sometimes be achieved more quickly.

Giving Feedback Along the Way

Provide feedback to the employee throughout the performance improvement process so that the employee is aware of his/her progress through the various phases of the Performance Improvement Plan.

Feedback should be consistent, timely, and ongoing feedback to the employee should be outlined in the Performance Improvement Plan documentation. Failure to provide regular feedback results in ineffective performance improvement and may extend the process.

Provide the employee with formal documented status or reviews of the employee's progress through the phases of the plan. The review should reflect cumulative information of the employee's status since the plan began. The frequency of a formal review may vary depending on the length of the Performance Improvement Plan.

Provide the employee with a signed copy of the formal review. The employee should sign the document to acknowledge receipt. Place a copy of the signed document in the employee's personnel file.

Dealing with Little or No Improvement

When an employee is not performing or meeting expectations, you have at your disposal several options to correct the behaviour. You can rely on oral and written warnings, or, in more serious cases, you can move to suspension, demotion or dismissal of the employee.

UK employment law recognises that small businesses may not be able to sustain an underperformer for a lengthy period of time.

Deciding If You Should Sanction or Dismiss

Deciding what action you should take for failure of the employee to turn performance around again depends upon the nature of the performance issue.

If the poor performance is ultimately leading to minor issues across your organisation, you might decide to undertake a sanction that might be a formal written warning that is placed upon the employees record. If the performance issues are somewhat more serious and are essentially leading to the employee being incapable of performing their job, you might want to dismiss them or move them to a role they can undertake.

Failure to improve performance within a set period would normally result in a final written warning. If an employee's performance is sufficiently serious, it may be appropriate to move directly to a final written warning. This might occur when the employee's actions have had, or are liable to have, a serious or harmful impact on the organisation.

A first or final written warning should set out the nature of the poor performance and the change in behaviour or improvement of performance required (with timescale). The employee should also be told how long the warning will remain current. The employee should be informed of the consequences of failure to improve performance, within the set period following a final warning. For instance, that it may result in dismissal or some other contractual penalty such as demotion or loss of seniority.

Dismissing an Employee for Poor Performance

Dismissal of an employee should be a last result with regard to dealing with an ongoing performance issue.

However, if there has been an ongoing failure of the employee to turn performance around then you may be left to undertake their dismissal in accordance with your own internal disciplinary policies and procedures.

If you proceed to the formal stage of a disciplinary and dismissal process, this should involve:

- Inviting the employee in writing to a formal disciplinary hearing, giving reasonable advance notice

- Allowing the employee an opportunity to be accompanied

- Clearly setting out the reason for the disciplinary hearing

- Allowing the employee to provide their feedback and any evidence before you make a decision on the level of sanction.

- Setting out that you wish to dismiss your employee at the end of the meeting and following up in writing

- Allowing the employee the right of appeal within 5 days of receiving the decision in writing

Refer to Chapter 5 if you wish to understand in detail how to dismiss an employee fairly.

Agreeing That Performance Has Improved

If performance has improved to a level that allows the employee to return to their day to day job then this should also be recognised and documented.

Ideally a formal record of achievement should be created and held with the employees record. In addition you should recognise the achievement by discussing the performance improvement plan outcome directly with the employee.

Chapter 20

Ten Great Interviewing Ideas

In This Chapter

▶ Finding out what the candidate is looking for

▶ Finding out if the candidate has what you need

In Chapter 2 we covered the mechanics of the recruitment process, and in Chapter 14 you can read about the legal aspects of recruitment. This chapter is about getting a feel for the candidate: understanding what makes them tick, and deciding if you want to work with them.

Experienced job searchers have most likely developed some standard answers to predictable interview questions, but if you phrase your questions in a slightly different way, you may elicit a more spontaneous answer.

Knowing what the candidate is looking for in a job

A well prepared candidate will have looked at your job advertisement, done some research into your company, and come up with a few reasons why they want to go for the job.

Instead of asking 'So, why do you want to come and work for us?' use a question like this:

> *What are your top three criteria for your next job?*

This question works for every job. Keep the form of the question simple for school kids coming on work experience, or people with limited language skills.

The question serves a few purposes:

- ✔ The candidate has a chance to warm up, with a meaningful but non-threatening question
- ✔ You get an early feel for how verbose the candidate is likely to be during the interview
- ✔ You can see if the candidate is really listening to your question – many candidates get side tracked and forget to list three criteria
- ✔ You get an insight into what makes the candidate tick
- ✔ You will get a sense of how well rehearsed the candidate is: if the three criteria they give you sound like they've been trotted out a few times before, you can dig deeper with follow up questions
- ✔ You may find out something very important like the candidate is only available to work in term time, or can't work on Fridays

Discovering what makes the candidate tick day to day

Past behaviour is the biggest predictor of future success. If you want to find the right person to fill your vacancy, turn it around and think about whether your job is the right one for the person sitting in front of you (assuming that you do your interviews sitting down).

So you need to find out what the candidate considers to be a great day, or a great week, or a great year at work.

To do so, ask a question similar to these two:

When you put your coat on at the end of a working day, and look back over the day, what does a great day look like?

As you leave work to go and relax, and think back over your day, what would you describe as the highlights of a great day?

The key here is to get the candidate in a frame of mind where they are really imagining the end of a great day.

- ✔ The candidate is more likely to let their interview best behaviour slip, and give you an honest answer.

✔ You get an insight into what the person enjoys doing at work: whether they need lots of people contact, or a complex problem to solve in a quiet room to make a great day at work. If your job doesn't offer that, the person won't like the job and they won't be successful.

✔ You are building rapport with the candidate which will help you to get more insights later in the interview.

✔ You are building a positive impression of your workplace, as somewhere that people can have great days at work.

Getting on with you as the manager

Assuming that you are interviewing someone who will report to you, it is important to find out if you are likely to click.

Following the principle that past behaviour is the best predictor of future behaviour, try to find out what kind of managers the person has worked with before. Therefore, ask a question such as:

Tell me about the boss (or line manager, or manager) who brought out the best in you.

Follow up with:

. . . and what about a manager who brought out the worst in you?

Ask supplementary questions along the lines of:

What did that manager do that particularly inspired you/annoyed you?

This question gives you:

✔ An insight into the candidate's awareness of their own responses to various management styles

✔ An idea of whether you could manage them in the way they like best

✔ An idea of whether the candidate is an independent thinker or someone who prefers to have a set of rules to follow

✔ Some insight into how they look at and describe other people, and their attitude to management; if they are very disparaging or dismissive, or judgmental of former managers, might they take the same view of you?

If the candidate has very limited work experience, having just left school or university, or been unemployed, you can ask a more general question like:

How would you like to be managed?

Getting on with the other people in the team

If you are building a team, bear in mind that personalities and working styles can be just as important as skills and experience, particularly in a small team.

Read Chapter 9 for some insights into what makes a great team; and in Chapter 13 you can read about shaping your team to do the business.

To find out if the candidate is likely to fit with the rest of the team, you can phrase these questions slightly differently, depending on who you've got on board already, and the nature of the job you are trying to fill.

Ask questions such as:

Tell me about a colleague with whom you have worked really well in the past.

When you are supervising a team, how would you describe your style?

Can you tell me about a time when there has been a conflict or disagreement in your team, and how you handled it?

What annoys you the most at work?

How do you handle it when you are working with a colleague you don't like?

One of the things that is really important to us here is integrity/telling it straight/communication/flexibility – can you give me an example of when you have demonstrated that in a previous role?

Knowing who inspires the candidate

Finding out who inspires a candidate can give you some insight into their values and attitudes, and to some extent, their level of self-awareness.

Ask a question similar to:

Tell me who has inspired you most in your life/in your work?

Follow up, if they haven't volunteered the information, with;

What is it about them that inspires you?

Testing the candidate's awareness of business relationships

Every business is different, but they all rely on relationships. You can structure questions to reflect the key relationships in your business, or the important relationships for a particular job. For example:

What are the three most important aspects of a good relationship with a supplier?

What is the key to good partnership working?

What do you think is the secret of great customer service?

Finding out whether someone is a team player

Many CVs start with a personal profile that includes the phrase 'I work well in a team but can also work independently'. Candidates want to show you they can tick any box you might have on your person specification.

To find out if someone is really a team player you need to test their idea of 'team':

What do you think makes a great team?

Follow up with a question like;

What do you bring to a team?

Imagine you are sitting in a weekly team meeting, round a table – what role do you play?

Asking questions like these give you:

✔ an idea of the candidate's attitude towards teams generally

✔ an insight into the candidate's perception of themselves in a team

✔ an idea of whether they will complement the personalities/team roles you already have in the team

✔ a sense of whether the candidate is parrotting what they think you want to hear, or really talking about themselves.

Probing the candidate's attitude to work

You may think that in a growing business, people should want to progress, should be flexible, and be hungry for more. You may believe that if an employee just wants to do the day job and go home, they're not right for your business.

But there's a place for the 'day job and go home' people in every organisation. Before you write them off, consider these factors;

✔ They may bring qualities that balance out the team, like steadiness, loyalty to the team and a commitment to quality. They are often known as the safe pair of hands. Every team needs one!

✔ They could have any number of compelling reasons for needing to leave on time that have nothing to do with laziness or lack of commitment – like having a life.

✔ In a small business, you can't give everyone career progression so it's good to have some less ambitious people

Ask questions such as:

Do you have the flexibility to work longer hours/in the evenings/at weekends/on Sundays when we need you?

Assessing the candidate's self-awareness

The candidate is busy trying to show you how well they meet all the criteria for the job.

People change jobs for all sorts of reasons, but it is quite common for people who are trying to progress their career to go for a job that has some stretch or something new.

Candidates expect a version of the question, 'What are your strengths and weaknesses?' so they will have prepared a platitude to answer it, like 'I am a bit of a perfectionist.'

Try to find out by asking slightly different questions along the lines of:

What are you hoping to learn in this job?

What parts of this job would take you outside your comfort zone?

If the candidate has worked in a large organisation, ask a question like:

Did you have an appraisal in your last job?

If they say yes, ask:

What did your manager suggest you needed to focus on learning this year?'
or
What did you do really well last year?

If they say no, ask:

If you were having an appraisal now, what do you think your manager would say you should be doing differently?

What things would your manager tell you to keep doing well?

Tapping into the candidate's potential

Whilst you are trying to fill the current vacancy, you should always have your eye on the longer term, and it is good to get an idea of how ambitious a candidate is, and to understand if they have other skills and experience you might be able to use in the business.

Tailor the questions to the career stage of the candidate, and your needs in the business.

Ask questions such as:

Where does this job fit in your career plan?

We're a small business – how quickly are you hoping to move up from this role?

We are a small business so we sometimes have opportunities for people to get involved in projects or other work – are there any other skills you can offer, that we haven't discussed in relation to this job?

How would you react if I said you need to do this job for at least a year / two years, before there would be a chance of promotion?

If you go off script when you are interviewing candidates, steer clear of any questions that could be considered as discriminatory. See Chapter 14 for more.

Chapter 21

Ten (Or So) Signs of Employees Who Are Ready for Promotion

*E*mployee promotion isn't only about a salary increase or a change in position name, a promotion means bigger responsibilities, sometimes managing people, and taking on more tasks than before. Not every employee is fit and ready for a promotion. In many cases, those who get promoted have a high level of employee job satisfaction, which pushes them to work harder than the rest.

Managers need to be sure that the person to be promoted is truly ready for a new challenge. Failure to select the best person to be promoted may be an obstacle for you and your company. As experts would say, choosing the perfect time to promote is critical.

This Part of Ten gives you my top guidelines to help you decide when an employee is ready for a promotion.

They Are Engaged in the Strategic Aims of the Organisation

So, is the employee you are thinking of promoting engaged in what you do and what you are trying to achieve? Do they buy into your short term business plans and constantly deliver their end of the bargain? If so they are showing the behavioural attributes of someone you would look to keep working for you and hence someone that you should wish to develop!

They Prove That They Can Manage Themselves – and Maybe Others?

One key indicator that an employee has really come into their own is when they require less and less of your time to manage them. They always seem to know what needs to be done and make sure it happens; they learn to spot opportunities and coordinate actions to seize them.

They Take Responsibility and Help Others

If your employee is concerned for their co-workers' success as much as their own on a group project, that's usually a very good sign you have a team player that wants others to succeed. Always look out for those that are selfless leaders who want the team to succeed together.

They Consistently Excel Above Others

This is perhaps the most important measure, specifically if you are employing people that you need to be technically gifted. When you naturally see them leading others in all their work and when they excel far above expectations in everything they are doing, it's probably time for a promotion. You don't want to lose them to someone else who's willing to give them that promotion when you're not!

They Show Ingenuity and Look for Solutions

A promotable employee is someone who not only manages existing tasks, but also takes initiative in creating or improving other tasks and processes for the benefit of the company. Employees who demonstrate these traits also tend to display ingenuity and critical thinking in the ways they perform on a daily basis, which should tell you that they are ready to take on more responsibilities and be promoted!

If the employee always seeks solutions rather than answers . . . then in reality this is another positive behavioural trait that indicates they are ready to take on more.

They Are Proactive

You should never want your employees to be on auto-pilot, but there is something to be said when a team member jumpstarts their workload without having to wait for you to instruct them further. If you find team members proactively asking questions to improve their output to the company, that's when you know they're ready.

They Seek Feedback and Use It

Not many people enjoy getting feedback, so if you have employees who constantly request it, take note.

By proactively asking you about the level of their current performance, how they can improve, and what they should be doing differently, they're showing initiative and the desire to grow within their roles.

And further, carefully observe what they do with the feedback you give. If you see that they put it into action and continue to improve with each project and task you assign, you can take it as an indication that they'll continue to strive for great things – especially in a higher role.

Their Work Ethic Speaks for Itself

It is unfair to expect all your team to stay late, skip lunch, or refuse to take breaks in order to be promoted. But when it comes to identifying team members who are ready to move up, there is often a big difference between those who do exactly what's expected and no more and those who are ready to go beyond the job.

You should pay attention to the employees who are willing to jump in wherever (and whenever) they're needed. This doesn't mean they always need to stay late, but it's nice to know that they won't leave you or their clients in the lurch.

They Own Their Development

Pay attention to how your employees find out new information. Do they specifically ask to be developed? Do they seek out resources in other areas (instead of just asking you to find it for them)? Maybe they just dive in and try their hand at something new, eventually refining their skills simply by being willing to *do* it.

They Share and Demonstrate the Values of Your Organisation

If you value integrity, and your team member experiences a quality problem in the manufacturing process, or they honestly inform your customer of the exact nature of the problem, they are essentially living the values of your company. The team member might also discuss his or her actions to eliminate the problem, and the anticipated delivery time the customer can expect. If integrity is not a fundamental value, the employee may make excuses and mislead the customer.

So in the end, if they show many of the attributes discussed in this chapter but don't deliver to the customer in the way that you feel is appropriate, you should be wary of promoting them! You will send a message that, ultimately, values don't matter in your company.

They Show Ownership

One sign is that your employee regularly shows a feeling of pride and ownership in his or her work. Employees who approach every task as if its success or failure is a direct reflection on them are on track to be the best ambassadors of your company.

They Want It and Ask for It!

In the end the smart employees will know when they are ready to work at the next level. If your employee has worked this out then eventually they will seek a conversation with you regarding their career prospects. You need to be careful if they ask and you reject out of hand their requests, because next time they seek a conversation it may well be a discussion regarding their desire to leave your company!

Notwithstanding this potential risk, the reality is that sometimes you can't accommodate everyone and sometimes it is best for everyone that you let them go to develop elsewhere. Perhaps they will develop and you'll get them back one day!

Index

• F •

• G •

• Q •

• R •

About the Authors

Marc Bishop is the Managing Director and partner of PlusHR Limited, an organisation that specialises in providing HR Management and administration services to small and medium sized companies.

From his leadership of PlusHR, Marc and his team have built a reputation of providing commercially pragmatic HR guidance advice whilst ensuring that their clients remain legally compliant.

Through his work at PlusHR and with leading Corporates such as Lloyds Group plc, Centrica plc, Reuters and British American Tobacco plc. Marc has also built up a reputation as a leading Reward and Performance Management specialist.

If you would like to talk to Marc about the HR needs in your organisation, then contact him at www.plushr.com or via email at: marc@plushr.com.

Sharon Crooks has worked in HR since graduating in 1987, for companies including Hilton International, Sony Music, and Diageo. She has a Masters Degree in HR and is a Chartered Member of the Institute of Personnel and Development.

She was an Associate and Director of PlusHR for a number of years and set up her own consultancy, Jade HR Solutions, in 2014.

As a consultant Sharon works with a wide range of clients including tech start-ups, media companies, charities and social enterprises, membership organisations, schools, shops, accountancy firms, doctors, manufacturing companies and service providers.

Managing the inevitable tension between organisational and individual needs is both the joy and the pain of working in HR. Sharon's passion is helping people in organisations to understand, motivate and manage the people around them so that the company or charity goals are achieved by a bunch of people who work hard and feel valued.

Sharon designs employee engagement and performance management tools, delivers training and helps business people and leaders to communicate better with their employees. When things go wrong, she advises on tricky employee relations issues, and comes up with practical ways to keep people switched on and focussed. When change is in the wind, Sharon advises on the steps people need to take to smooth the way, minimise the pain and navigate around the potential pitfalls.

sharon@jadehrsolutions.com

Dedication

From Marc: This book is dedicated to everyone that has supported me throughout my career and personal life. Specifically I would like to thank my wife Caroline, our two children Lillie and Alfie and my parents for giving me focus and pleasure beyond measure.

From Sharon: My contribution to this book is dedicated to Colin Blears, a true professional, for being wise and intuitive, pragmatic, warm, funny and loyal, a great listener and a man of principle. Thank you Colin for being a great role model throughout my career, and for your friendship.

Publisher's Acknowledgments

Executive Commissioning Editor: Annie Knight

Editorial Project Manager: Christina Guthrie

Development Editor: Daniel Mersey

Copy Editor: Simon Bell

Production Editor: Suresh Srinivasan

Cover Image: Tom Wang/Shutterstock

Take Dummies with you everywhere you go!

Whether you're excited about e-books, want more from the web, must have your mobile apps, or swept up in social media, Dummies makes everything easier.

FOR DUMMIES®

A Wiley Brand

BUSINESS

978-1-118-73077-5

978-1-118-44349-1

978-1-119-97527-4

MUSIC

978-1-119-94276-4

978-0-470-97799-6

978-0-470-49644-2

DIGITAL PHOTOGRAPHY

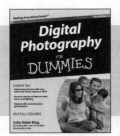

978-1-118-09203-3

978-0-470-76878-5

978-1-118-00472-2

Algebra I For Dummies
978-0-470-55964-2

Anatomy & Physiology For Dummies, 2nd Edition
978-0-470-92326-9

Asperger's Syndrome For Dummies
978-0-470-66087-4

Basic Maths For Dummies
978-1-119-97452-9

Body Language For Dummies, 2nd Edition
978-1-119-95351-7

Bookkeeping For Dummies, 3rd Edition
978-1-118-34689-1

British Sign Language For Dummies
978-0-470-69477-0

Cricket for Dummies, 2nd Edition
978-1-118-48032-8

Currency Trading For Dummies, 2nd Edition
978-1-118-01851-4

Cycling For Dummies
978-1-118-36435-2

Diabetes For Dummies, 3rd Edition
978-0-470-97711-8

eBay For Dummies, 3rd Edition
978-1-119-94122-4

Electronics For Dummies All-in-One For Dummies
978-1-118-58973-1

English Grammar For Dummies
978-0-470-05752-0

French For Dummies, 2nd Edition
978-1-118-00464-7

Guitar For Dummies, 3rd Edition
978-1-118-11554-1

IBS For Dummies
978-0-470-51737-6

Keeping Chickens For Dummies
978-1-119-99417-6

Knitting For Dummies, 3rd Edition
978-1-118-66151-2

FOR DUMMIES®

A Wiley Brand

SELF-HELP

978-0-470-66541-1

978-1-119-99264-6

978-0-470-66086-7

LANGUAGES

978-0-470-68815-1

978-1-119-97959-3

978-0-470-69477-0

HISTORY

978-0-470-68792-5

978-0-470-74783-4

978-0-470-97819-1

Laptops For Dummies 5th Edition
978-1-118-11533-6

Management For Dummies, 2nd Edition
978-0-470-97769-9

Nutrition For Dummies, 2nd Edition
978-0-470-97276-2

Office 2013 For Dummies
978-1-118-49715-9

Organic Gardening For Dummies
978-1-119-97706-3

Origami Kit For Dummies
978-0-470-75857-1

Overcoming Depression For Dummies
978-0-470-69430-5

Physics I For Dummies
978-0-470-90324-7

Project Management For Dummies
978-0-470-71119-4

Psychology Statistics For Dummies
978-1-119-95287-9

Renting Out Your Property For Dummies, 3rd Edition
978-1-119-97640-0

Rugby Union For Dummies, 3rd Edition
978-1-119-99092-5

Stargazing For Dummies
978-1-118-41156-8

Teaching English as a Foreign Language For Dummies
978-0-470-74576-2

Time Management For Dummies
978-0-470-77765-7

Training Your Brain For Dummies
978-0-470-97449-0

Voice and Speaking Skills For Dummies
978-1-119-94512-3

Wedding Planning For Dummies
978-1-118-69951-5

WordPress For Dummies, 5th Edition
978-1-118-38318-6

Think you can't learn it in a day? Think again!

The *In a Day* e-book series from *For Dummies* gives you quick and easy access to learn a new skill, brush up on a hobby, or enhance your personal or professional life — all in a day. Easy!

Available as PDF, eMobi and Kindle